CATHOLIC EMANCIPATION

1829 TO 1929

NIHIL OBSTAT

GEORGIUS D. SMITH, S.T.D.
Censor deputatus

IMPRIMATUR

EDM. CAN. SURMONT.
Vic. Gen.

Westmonasterii,
die 7º Januarii 1929

CATHOLIC EMANCIPATION

1829 TO 1929

ESSAYS BY VARIOUS WRITERS

WITH AN INTRODUCTION BY

HIS EMINENCE CARDINAL BOURNE

Essay Index Reprint Series

BOOKS FOR LIBRARIES PRESS, INC.

FREEPORT, NEW YORK

First published 1929
Reprinted 1966

CONTENTS

CONTENTS

vi

INTRODUCTION

WE enter to-day on the year that will see the centenary of Catholic Emancipation. Some months ago it was thought that this great event might be suitably commemorated by inviting prominent Catholic writers to set down some aspects of the progress which has taken place in the Catholic Church in England since the momentous date April 13, 1829. I welcomed this suggestion, because there are large numbers of Catholics who are almost wholly unacquainted with the many spheres of Catholic development during the last hundred years. There are many more who, while they realise that great progress has been made, have never considered it in its component details. Then there is the large public outside our own body to whom the words " Catholic Emancipation " convey no precise idea ; and who, while they recognise in a vague way that the Catholic Church in England is far more important than it was a hundred years ago, have no conception whatever of the far-reaching changes which have taken place. Such is the origin of this very interesting collection of essays. It is evidently neither exhaustive nor exclusive in its survey of the progress which it recounts. For instance, the essential and fundamental work of the Bishops, whether as Vicars Apostolic or united together in the Hierarchy, and the subordinate but no less essential and fundamental work of the Pastoral Clergy receive no mention : not because they are under-valued or disregarded, but because they are necessarily taken for granted, for without that essential and fundamental and all-pervading influence there would be no progress at all. Their work will doubtless receive its due measure of appreciation on many an occasion this year.

When we look at these essays as a whole, at once we find in them a most striking witness to the never failing vitality of the Catholic Church, as soon as it is given even a limited freedom of expression and expansion. Progress is shown in every department of human, spiritual and ecclesiastical life one after the other. We are led to trace summarily the harvest which was sown and is being reaped. With thankfulness to God we watch the growth and strengthening of the spiritual life and of that intimate personal union with God which is the object of all religion. We are shown how now in these years the age-long concern of the Church about education—primary, secondary, or of university character—has been receiving attention in proportion to the means and opportunities at our disposal. We are the witnesses of the upspringing of the new and definitely Catholic literature, a thing impossible when persecution was hampering all our energies, or confining them to strictly pressing needs. We see the slow establishing of a Catholic position in the world of scientific thought. And, again, in proportion to opportunity, we note the spread of interest in religious art, whether in music, architecture, or the decorative adjuncts to Divine Worship. The increase of Catholics in number, in education and in influence has gradually rendered possible for them fuller participation in public life. In this respect Catholics of every social position have shown themselves ready and able to stand on equal terms, side by side with their fellow-countrymen, in the upbuilding and upholding of public interests at home and throughout the Empire. Moreover, their names are to be found as active workers in every form of philanthropic effort. In a more restricted sphere we see the growth and spread of the religious life which, though not essential to the work of the Catholic Church in the same way as that of the Hierarchy and Pastoral Clergy, is yet invariably associated with it as a most valuable helper and support wherever the Catholic Church finds freedom. The old religious orders which had maintained themselves precariously in exile abroad have now flourishing houses at home, with churches and monasteries equalling or rivalling in many cases the greatest constructions of pre-Reformation days; and the almost innumerable societies of more modern foundation are to be found scattered over the country, carrying on a work of such extent and importance that even the best informed of Catholics are hardly fully conscious of them. Our laity, too, show themselves ready and able to fill nobly the places in public activity which the law no longer denies them. If we look at mere statistics, incomplete and consequently not fully reliable, yet not erring by exaggeration, there is an advance in every direction which none can call in question. Thus, whether we survey the past in company with the writers of most of these essays, or look forward to the new century that lies before us, there is on every side ground for hope and for well-rooted confidence in the future of the Church in England.

FRANCIS CARDINAL BOURNE,
Archbishop of Westminster.

January 1st, 1929.

JOY IN HARVEST

A Sequel to the Second Spring

BY MONSIGNOR WILLIAM BARRY, D.D.

I

JOY IN HARVEST

A Sequel to the Second Spring

When John Henry Newman preached his ever-memorable Sermon from the pulpit of St. Mary's College, Oscott, on July 13, 1852, he was addressing the restored English Hierarchy in Council assembled. " The past," he said with a deep feeling which thrilled his audience, " has returned, the dead lives. The English Church was, and the English Church was not, and the English Church is once again. This is the portent worthy of a cry. It is the coming in of a Second Spring."

Seventy-six years have gone by since Cardinal Wiseman with his suffragans heard this prophecy. How did it come to pass? And in what measure has it turned out true?

When the saintly Dr. Challoner took charge of that pitiful remnant who had been brought so low by the Revolution of 1688 and the Penal Laws unrelentingly applied, their numbers had fallen short of one hundred thousand, perhaps to half so much. They had no Hierarchy, no Colleges or Convents at home, and sought only the most entire seclusion. The supreme English poet of Challoner's early time was Pope, who refused to be a Protestant, but in his " Essay on Man " yielded more than he should have allowed by a great deal to Bolingbroke's free-thinking. In 1773, when Alban Butler died, the number who had conformed to the Establishment among families of position was great and seemed likely to increase. Yet Challoner did not lose hope. " There will be a new people," he said. Whence were

3

they to come from ? In Newman's discourse the story is not told. But we can trace it now in broad outline, and the centre round which it moves is Emancipation.

In England, then, a handful of titled leaders, with perhaps five hundred families of distinction and their dependents, counted as "the Catholics," for whom relief was humbly sought after 1776, when the American Congress had invited them to settle in the United States, under a promise of religious freedom. The oppressed had found a deliverer. All, however, that Challoner and his colleagues ventured to ask was " a free toleration of religion in private " ; and Edmund Burke drew up for them an exceedingly humble address to the Throne, which was graciously accepted. But when the Catholic Relief Bill was brought in (May 1778) a " Protestant Association " provoked disorder in Edinburgh, and on June 2, 1780, the Gordon Riots began a week of anarchy in London, the like of which it never went through before or since. And yet in 1850-51, on occasion of the New Hierarchy, which was repelled as a " Papal Aggression," the whole country went into a paroxysm of rage— Queen, Parliament, Bishops and Clergy, all stirring up the people without regard to what outrages might ensue. But on this provocation no Gordon Riots followed, and the law forbidding our Bishops to take English titles proved to be a dead letter.

We should, therefore, date Emancipation from 1776, when in the graphic phrase of Flood " America shouted to liberty," and its echo was heard on both sides of the Atlantic ; but loudest in Ireland, where the need was greatest. After the Battle of the Boyne, for quite a hundred years, Catholics—deprived of their natural leaders by the " flight of the wild geese "—sank into a stupor which resembled enchantment. There is, indeed, an illustrious Irish eighteenth century, but all its outstanding figures are Protestant—Swift, Berkeley, Goldsmith, Grattan, Burke, Sheridan. Yet from this downtrodden inarticulate folk a leader was to spring up, "such as is not given once in a generation" to an oppressed people longing for a saviour. The Celts have constantly obeyed champions who were not of their blood. Parnell was a striking instance, as Napoleon from Corsica dominated France. But O'Connell was a Celt, a Catholic, in no single quality English; neither did he at any crisis of a long career take England into account. He felt abhorrence for the Jacobin whom he had seen close at hand in France. He felt as devotedly loyal to the House of Brunswick as did Sir Walter Scott; and in both men of such exceptional gifts we feel surprise at their enthusiasm for a character like George IV. But while even the principles of America did not shape or guide O'Connell, he moved forward in his simplicity to a stage beyond 1789 and even 1893. Instead of revolution he preached and practised agitation. He insisted on the peaceful and persevering effort, as it were in open Parliament, of a nation determined to secure its rights. How to conduct such a movement with success no man has ever shown more triumphantly than O'Connell. And so he won Emancipation without shedding a single drop of blood.

By means of his Associations, in spite of Government efforts to put them down, O'Connell gathered Irish Catholics as if in a genuine Parliament, year after year. He used violent language, but kept beyond the range of prosecution. And when by the Clare Election of 1828 he, a Catholic, was returned for the House of Commons, it became apparent to Sir Robert Peel that the system of Penal Laws had been smitten with a fatal blow. Next year Emancipation was granted, not magnanimously, but in a Bill cumbered with restrictions and still treating our Religious Orders as if they were criminal associations. However, O'Connell had won the day, and henceforth he was called with justice the Liberator.

What share had English Catholics in this Revolution which was to play so momentous a part during the next ninety years at Westminster, affecting the course of legislation most intimately? They had petitioned for it annually, as well as given support to measures of Relief brought in, although without success, by men like Grattan, Canning and Burdett. Nevertheless, that Emancipation had been delayed for twenty years—since 1808— by the question of what is known as the Veto ; and here we must acknowledge that an English Bishop, scholar and controversialist, John Milner, takes the foremost rank, side by side with O'Connell, nor yet unworthily.

In the " Second Spring " we hear of Milner, who was Bishop of the Midlands, and resided at Old Oscott. The preacher called him " the champion of God's ark in an evil time," he graciously imagines him rapt in vision, and beholding the procession of the new Hierarchy as it wends its way along the college cloisters—clergy, monks, bishops—with " a prince of the Church, in the royal dye of empire and of martyrdom, a pledge to us from Rome of Rome's unwearied love," closing the scene.

But Newman, who perhaps went so far as to term Milner the " English Athanasius," did not enlarge upon the achievement which we owe to this rugged champion of our cause, without which Emancipation would have been merely a fresh disguise of slavery. What did the word " Veto " imply? It meant the claim put forward by England's Prime Minister to disallow the appointment of any Catholic Bishop unless he were agreeable to the Crown, in plain terms to the party in power. Still worse would have been the Exequatur—a Royal licence without which no Papal document was to be published in these Kingdoms. But on such terms, as more than one statesman hinted, the concurrent endowment of several Churches, including the Roman Catholic, might become law. From this point of view, Emancipation would leave the recognised principles of Church and State intact.

So thought many among English Catholics; so Milner did at first. He foresaw indeed and loudly affirmed that Catholic Ireland would win political and therefore religious freedom; but when he consulted the Irish Bishops in 1807 he found them willing to grant a Veto, while men like Archbishop Troy would probably have welcomed an Establishment analogous to that which the Holy See tolerated in Lutheran Prussia. The tragedy and glory of Milner's life moved round this earlier adhesion to what would have been a fatal policy, followed by his conversion and repentance when he found it out, and his life-long heroic struggle against its consequences.

For the Irish people would not hear of a liberation so devised; they clung to their Bishops' freedom as the last shred of independence, which, in fact, it was. Ireland had kept up the Hierarchy derived from Rome when English Catholics by a deplorable misfortune lost it. And now at their people's voice the Bishops rejected State endowments, declined to grant any Veto whatsoever, would give no security beyond the oath of allegiance, and threw themselves, as they had always done, on the generosity of the faithful.

Milner had misread his own character, which was made for resistance, not for compromise. He now withdrew from the position he had first adopted, became the resolute opponent of all bargaining with Government, and by years of protest in London defeated every measure that would imperil our freedom. O'Connell shared Milner's convictions, which Burke had long ago

7

anticipated; the Irish Bishops recognised in this great English prelate the "unwearied champion" of their common faith. Acting as their agent in London, while the English Catholic Board and those excellent men the Vicars Apostolic were attempting to revive an anachronism, Milner came like Benjamin Franklin from a new world, to teach the old what was meant by freedom.

He did not live to see Catholic Emancipation carried. But largely by his heroic stand O'Connell was able to demand it without conditions or sacrifice of democratic principles. Oaths against "Popery" and guarantees imposed by mere politicians had lost their significance. "A Bishop," said Milner, "is either loyal or not loyal," to which Charles James Fox might have added his own doctrine, "Action, not principles, is the concern of Government." We have thus reached a working formula, in the light of which Emancipation becomes much more than a simple expedient and men of diverse opinions may dwell together, if not in unity, yet in peace.

During the twenty years which came between Emancipation and the Hierarchy in 1850 Ireland still occupied or controlled the stage. Consider the Tithe War of 1832, which my own parents well remembered. It was part of a Liberal movement, in which ten of the Irish Protestant bishops were suppressed, the Cathedral system in England gave way, and the Establishment was declared to be in danger. At Oxford in 1833 Keble foretold a "National Apostasy," and Newman began the Tracts by appeal to Catholic Tradition, the Fathers, and Apostolic Succession. Behold where this had brought him on July 13, 1852! He was preaching as a convert and an Oratorian before Cardinal Wiseman, to whom he had given up his sword.

But how scanty were the numbers of English Catholics in 1829! Whence might that "new people"

8

come, so confidently anticipated by Challoner? They did come, in their thousands, driven by repeated famines from the land they loved so well, under a mysterious Providence which was scattering them far and wide, not only in Great Britain, but in America and Australia, where they have since built up churches, schools, convents, and given zealous clergy and bishops to new worlds. If Catholics in England, Scotland and Wales are now eight times as many as in 1840, that is mainly due to the influx of Irish emigrants. Carlyle observed it soon, not without disquietude. He would rather have beheld the native Britons increase and multiply at home than be dispersed over new Continents. But still it remains true, as Bishop Ward observes, that "this Irish addition to Catholic numbers was the most important event in our Church annals during the nineteenth century."

For it found only a remnant, and made of them a people. The Irish multitudes flocked into Liverpool and Lancashire, they invaded the Midlands, streamed into London, sought the centres of industry—these village-folk who had seldom left home before. They required priests, churches, schools. Almost all wage-earners, they contributed enough out of their poverty to support the clergy who took up this heroic task. And to the day passing over us that union of pastors and flocks continues unbroken. It has made of the Catholic Church, so long hidden away and wellnigh to extinction, a visible power of which Westminster Cathedral fronting the Abbey is a symbol to London and the British Empire.

Thus we have been led from the Second Spring to joy in Harvest. It was, indeed, as Newman foretold, "an English spring, of bright promise and budding hopes, yet withal of keen blasts, and cold showers, and sudden storms."

The preacher was a true prophet. As we have been

taught, " a threefold cord is not quickly broken " ; but
to bind it at first requires no little skill. How should
the old English Catholics, the Oxford converts, and
the emigrants from Ireland, be united out of Church ?
Happily, at the start a man of genius, Nicholas Cardinal
Wiseman, was vouchsafed to them, and while health
lasted he guided them with success. The pastoral,
innocently dated " from the Flaminian Gate " might
have been a blunder, and it excited Protestant England to
fury against this " Papal Aggression." But Wiseman
rose to the demand, was candid and convincing, and long
before he passed away had won the hearts of Englishmen.

Neither did the Catholic Restoration suffer so much
as might have been feared, in the long run, from within
its own borders. Newman and Faber, becoming
Oratorians of St. Philip Neri, brought a Roman fervour
into the good old " Garden of the Soul," which made
it blossom like the rose. Both of these, let us remark,
were of French descent ; so were Manning, Dalgairns,
Mathurin, and not a few other converts. And Cardinal
Gasquet's name indicates that he is not entirely English.

F. W. Faber, a singularly attractive character, who
died before his time, set up the Oratory in London,
published books of religious wisdom that became
popular immediately, and has left a collection of Hymns
which are sung wherever the English language prevails.
" The Dream of Gerontius," by Newman, is a masterpiece
which Elgar has set to music. W. G. Ward, editor of
the *Dublin Review*, was a deep metaphysician, who completely annihilated the sophisms of Mill and Spencer,
while his son, Bishop Bernard, judicially narrated the
history I have thus far summed up, and Wilfrid became
a leading man of letters, editor of the *Dublin Review*, and
Newman's biographer.

But our old-time Catholics, whose admirable representative was W. B. Ullathorne, held their own, as they do to this day. That sailor-bishop, by birth a Yorkshireman, by choice a Benedictine, had made himself a name in Australia, where he encountered, and did not a little to mitigate, the horrors of the convict-system. The English Vicars Apostolic deputed him to represent their views in Rome. He carried through the arduous negotiations for the Hierarchy, and became first Bishop of Birmingham, a See which this remarkable sailor and monk, and his chosen successor, Dr. Edward Ilsley, occupied from 1850 until 1922—a period of seventy years. Bishop Ullathorne's deeply meditated works on the religious virtues came to be accepted as classics and for examinations by the University of Oxford.

The first public school set up by English Catholics in this country despite the Penal Laws was at Sedgley Park, near Dudley, in Staffordshire. On its centenary in 1863 (at which I was present as a student) Bishop Ullathorne magnified its founder, the Venerable Challoner, in most expressive terms. Himself destined to carry on that tradition, he, though a simple monk of St. Benedict, founded the Australian Hierarchy, and was the chief agent in restoring its own Bishops to England. He became the guide or spiritual director of the Dominican nuns, who hold a distinguished rank in that revival (going far beyond expectation) of the nursing and teaching Sisters, without whom our elementary schools could never have been saved all over England. This has been perhaps our greatest achievement, for it helped to preserve religious education even in schools belonging to the Anglican Church.

A far different, yet scarcely greater prelate, was Wiseman, who shed tears of joy while listening to Newman on the Second Spring. Irish by descent, Spanish by birth, Roman by training, after an early education at Ushaw, he held a unique dignity among scholars and Church statesmen. Unhappily his health gave way during the next few years, but not until he had won the esteem and affection of the English public, while his journey through Ireland was a triumph. Thus it came to pass, in the language of Abbot Butler, that "the old stock of English and Irish Catholicism, fire-tried in the long years of persecution and penal laws, has proved itself the strongest, and has maintained itself in its essential characteristics." Other beneficent influences call for our gratitude ; but this witness, I think, is true.

Wiseman, who was quite free from envy, promoted good wherever he saw it. His hopeful temperament suited the demands of a Revival, brought out a spirit of enterprise in many directions, and enlarged the shrunken Catholic inheritance. He invited to London the Religious Orders, old and modern, from Italy. He encouraged Newman to undertake a revised English version of Holy Scripture, which unhappily fell through ; he delivered lectures on Shakespeare, wrote the charming and unsurpassed "Fabiola," was received with special honours in Rome at the great gathering of Bishops in 1863, and held his own in the Sacred College as if a European ambassador. He recognised and promoted Manning, who was to succeed him, thus making sure that his memorable work should not "pause for death."

And it never has done so. Each of the six English Cardinals bears a record which will endure of great and distinctive ideas realised, with a prospect of more. Wiseman was a pioneer. He made St. Philip known to Newman, and St. Charles to Manning. He took note of Herbert Vaughan. These two succeeded him, and were very unlike. Manning, an Oxford convert, though not

12

of Newman's following, might have died rich and first of England's peerage, in Lambeth Palace, as Archbishop of Canterbury. He chose to die at Westminster, poor and ascetic, in frayed garments ; therefore, while living, he was the rescuer of London's Catholic children from the otherwise " submerged tenth," the advocate of Temperance on Christian motives, the arbitrator in the Dock Strike, when he won for Labour, as I said then, its " Battle of Valmy " and the era of an Industrial Reformation according to Pope Leo's doctrine of a " living wage " was inaugurated. That Magna Charta, which defined the duties and rights of economic justice, owed its inception to Manning and Gibbons, although Leo XIII needed no counsellor beyond his own sense of pity for the toiling millions. But in that truly epoch-making work the English and American Cardinals had their full share.

One point in Manning's policy is now regarded as a mistake. He would not allow Catholics to frequent the National Universities ; and so for thirty years we were shut out from Oxford and Cambridge, when religious disabilities no longer existed. The motive was laudable ; but experience during another thirty years is a proof that our scholars need not fear peril to their religion under due care. " This," says Abbot Butler, " is exactly what has been done, and in a measure far beyond earlier dreams." Wiseman's " grand vision of Catholics entering into all the paths of public life " is in course of fulfilment. Our monks and nuns attend University lectures and take degrees. The Religious Orders have their " houses of study " at both Universities and Benedictines, Dominicans, Franciscans, Jesuits, form a succession at Oxford, so that St. Giles's Street has been wittily called " the Roman Road." Thus, to the satisfaction of all concerned, our University question has been solved.

Manning, conspicuous in London, appeared still more prominent in Rome under Pius IX, though not yet a Cardinal. He was a convinced advocate of the Temporal Power, and foresaw truly that its disappearance would mean the breaking up of the old order of things. But his renown abroad reached its culminating point at the Vatican Council. He may almost be termed the commander-in-chief of the majority who voted for the Decree of July 18, 1870, by which the Pope's inerrancy *ex cathedra* was acknowledged. He came back to refute in 1874 his old friend Gladstone's pamphlet against " Vaticanism." And in 1879 he was the bearer to Rome of Newman's letter in which the recluse of Edgbaston accepted the Cardinal's hat.

All this was unprecedented. That two convert clergymen from the Church of England should be admitted to the Sacred College, and the nation not ill-pleased—what a change compared with 1850 ! At last Englishmen saw that the former disputes, owing to which Tudor sovereigns broke away from St. Peter's Chair, had become obsolete. Catholics demanded nothing but the common rights of subjects or citizens. And in the Lower House of Parliament where, thanks to Ireland, they could muster some eighty members, their votes went in favour of all that made for justice and humanity. The so-called Church of Ireland, concerning which Macaulay said there was not its like in Christendom, was disestablished and partly disendowed by Gladstone, who had once maintained that it must be kept up, even if Irish Catholics would never accept its teaching. The scarcely less unjust and oppressive Land Laws were then taken in hand. But a quarter of a century slipped away before " landlord wrong " yielded to the wisdom of enabling men to purchase on reasonable terms the land by which, not without steady toil, they lived. All

14

these things were part of a Catholic Restoration, and our "joy in harvest" recalls them with deep thanksgiving.

Cardinal Newman, at so great an age, was not burdened with official duties. He continued to live as hitherto in his Oratorian cell, reissuing the thirty-seven volumes which had now become religious classics, and acknowledged as a supreme wielder of the English style. His poem, "The Dream of Gerontius," is a national possession. In 1877 Trinity College, "the one and only seat of my affections at Oxford," as he described it, had made him an honorary fellow, and he returned thither more than once. His last public act was to receive a deputation from the Catholic Truth Society, then holding their conference at Birmingham in July 1890, when he expressed a deep interest in what they were doing for the Faith. On August 11 he died after two days' illness; and his funeral was a tribute such as England had scarcely paid even to Wiseman.

I have written, in my widely-circulated sketch of this incomparable genius, how he showed that "the question of Rome is the question of Christianity"; and that if we admit a revelation in the Bible we must come down by sure steps to Rome and the Papacy as inheriting what the Bible contains. "To demonstrate this," I said, "was to make an end of the Reformation, so far as it claimed authority from Scripture, or kindred with Christ and His Apostles." Therefore, "when Newman arrived at this conclusion, and followed it up by submitting to Rome, he undid, intellectually speaking, the mischief of the last three centuries." He was not simply the voice of reaction terrified at scepticism. For his "Development" completes the static truth of Bellarmine and Bossuet. It anticipates the laws of evolution years before Darwin had caught a glimpse of them. Such as this, we may say with grateful hearts, was Newman's legacy to England and Christendom.

His contemporary, rival, critic, admirer, H. E. Manning, followed him into the unseen on January 14, 1892. When Leo XIII heard of the event he said "a great light of the Church has gone out." It was true. Royal honours attended the obsequies; better still, "behind Bishops and Peers marched solid lines of working men." They had recognised the friend of Labour, who never proved false to it. In that day the power which I have celebrated as "the Glory of Toil" did homage to its Catholic champion; and Manning's accord with Edmund Burke, in the estimate of true social values, would be henceforth a prelude to the long-desired Emancipation of our people from economic slavery.

Another, whom we may style at once Cardinal Vaughan, comes to the front. He was the eldest son of a numerous family, Welsh and Spanish by descent, all devoted to faith and good works. Early in life he had jotted down, " mon métier est d'arriver "—" it is my business to succeed." To that programme he kept through life. Singularly handsome, unaffected, never weary of work or travel, he had joined Manning's Oblates of St. Charles and begun at Mill Hill a missionary enterprise on behalf of which he traversed Spain and went, it may be said, all over South America. During the Vatican Council he edited the *Tablet*, becoming to the London journals " our mitred contemporary," for he was now Bishop of Salford. It has been said by Mr. Snead-Cox that the qualities which endeared him to friends were " the romance of his character, its tenderness, its strange humility, its utter unworldliness, and its high spirituality." For classical studies he had no time and little inclination. His training was on the old Catholic lines, but as an Oblate of St. Charles he learned fresh ideas from Manning. While Bishop of Salford, he, in conjunction with Dr. Clifford of Clifton obtained from the Holy See in 1881 that historical decision (Romanos Pontifices) which by its wisdom and equity cleared up the difference between Bishops and Regulars.

Another great beginning, of which Dr. Vaughan and James Britten share the honours, was the "Catholic Truth Society." This now celebrated name and the policy it carries out with ever-widening success we owe to Britten, a convert from Anglicanism, unwearied in well-doing and a master in organisation. But it was eagerly taken up by the Bishop; and its modest efforts at starting have led on to last year's issue of over one million publications from headquarters, opposite Westminster Cathedral.

Herbert Vaughan's time as leader of the Church in England was not lengthy—from April 1892, until June 1903. But in those eleven years he did many notable things, and one which gives him fame in the centuries— he began that Cathedral at Westminster on a site purchased by Cardinal Manning, which was opened, we may say, to receive its dead founder. The Byzantine conception, a stroke of genius, came from the architect, Bentley. Neither Gothic nor classic might have dared to challenge the Abbey or St. Paul's. But our Cathedral, with its never-ceasing Liturgy, its inherited Church music, its crowded official celebrations, and its Eucharistic Congress, will now bear comparison with any other religious centre outside Rome and Lourdes.

Cardinal Vaughan was of one mind with his predecessor in barring out Catholics from Oxford and Cambridge. But all Manning's devices for a substitute only provoked fresh disaster; and the laity, at once loyal but severely tried, expressed their views in an address presented by the Duke of Norfolk. It had the happiest effect, as already intimated. The Cardinal was only unrelenting where he deemed the Faith in danger; and here safeguards were at hand. When the advance of Modernism from crisis to crisis alarmed authority, instances like those of Mivart and Tyrrell were distressing, but English Catholics left the movement to go its own way, and were not interested. Neither was the Archbishop, whose energies went to the creation of orphanages, rescue Homes, and other counter-checks of sin and suffering. His last years, known to us by undesigned but most edifying disclosures, reveal (let me say it under submission) the lineaments with which we are familiar in the Second Nocturn of a Confessor and Bishop. What more can be added?

I enjoyed the privilege of meeting at Canterbury, on occasion of the centenary in 1897 of St. Augustine's arrival there thirteen hundred years previously, two men who were chosen to play most illustrious parts in the near future. One was to be Cardinal Mercier, the other Cardinal Bourne.

Francis Bourne is the son of an English convert and an Irish Catholic mother. He was brought up at St. Edmund's College, studied for the priesthood at St. Sulpice, and was consecrated Bishop on May-day 1896. Seven years later, in 1903, he succeeded to Westminster. Like both his forerunners he had to uphold the religious independence of our schools against secularist attacks and measures in Parliament. That resistance owed no little of its triumph to Archbishop Whiteside, backed up by Catholic Lancashire. Another influence for good was due to the historical researches and winning personality of F. Aidan Gasquet, O.S.B., who demolished the slanderous Protestant legend about monastic corruption too long current in popular textbooks. Dom Gasquet, called to Rome by Leo XIII, has become during successive reigns a trusted consultor of the Holy See. In 1911 made Cardinal, he is now in charge of the revision of St. Jerome's Vulgate and also Librarian of the Vatican. While ruling over Downside he erected the magnificent Abbey which will stand comparison with our grandest architectural efforts in the last eighty years.

No prelate of the twentieth century has wrought more at home, or travelled on public missions in East and West so widely, or uttered a word in season concerning faith and social progress more appositely than Cardinal Bourne—to give him the title which Pius X bestowed on him in 1911. The world-war was at the doors, and presentiments fixed its very date. We saw, however, the Eucharistic Congress in London, and some agitation stirred up against it by Puritan prejudice, but our people's faith and fervour were not lost on England.

One feature of the last thirty-five years was the settled policy of Republican Governments in France to put down our Holy Religion. Although disestablished, the Church enjoyed little freedom. Our monastic Orders were suppressed, their possessions confiscated, their members driven out to starve or die, and this in the name of liberty. Where could they turn for refuge? Exiles of every defeated cause pay England this compliment; they cross the Channel. As at the Revolution, so during the Third Republic we gave shelter to monks and nuns without stipulations or limit. And in reward we have gained many blessings. One most remarkable consequence deserves mention here which few of us anticipated—the growth of convents in England and Wales beyond calculation. In 1850 how many were there? I cannot ascertain. The law strictly forbade them to exist, and I doubt if they reached threescore.

Now, the last Catholic Directory enumerates, if I reckon aright, eight hundred and sixty-five. These dedicated Sisters teach in school and college, nurse in and out of hospital, manage Homes of Rescue for fallen and un-fallen, write books of spiritual wisdom, live and die among the poor of Christ whom they serve. And French atheists on their death-beds send for the nuns to nurse them who have persisted in keeping their vows at home, though proscribed by law.

Another large Catholic movement was that of Temperance, for ever associated with Father Mathew, who " gave the pledge to millions in O'Connell's days." When Cardinal Manning reigned, he took up the crusade with such vehemence that some were offended, but he might well answer, " Is there not a cause ? " Cardinal Vaughan held with him in principle. But a successor to the mission of Fr. Mathew had been already found in Lancashire. This was a secular priest who became known and loved in the English-speaking world as " Father Nugent." An unwearied apostle of the for-saken and afflicted (born 1822, died 1905) "philanthropist, temperance advocate, and social reformer," he set up the "League of the Cross" in 1872 as a crusade against the abuse of drink and the misery caused by it. " This he considered his greatest work," even more than his " Refuge for Homeless Boys," which rescued thousands, and the launching of the *Catholic Times*. In 1893 I had the honour of representing the League as his delegate at the Chicago Exposition. The City of Liverpool gave him public honours while living, and on December 8, 1906, erected near St. George's Hall a bronze statue to the " Apostle of Temperance " and " Father of the Poor."

James Nugent had the " Social Problem," as it now vexed the eyes and pierced feeling hearts, full in view.

Manning inspired the decisive Encyclical of Leo XIII, which we have termed the Magna Charta of Labour. But a movement inaugurated by Karl Marx, essentially secularist, was bent on establishing the Absolute State, and this our Church, our Religion, never could or would acquiesce in. Accordingly, Cardinal Bourne not only reiterated the Leonine teaching, but by a bold and happy stroke advertised it in all the leading newspapers of England. We had taken our stand.

But Cardinal Manning foresaw that the " dynastic era " was passing away, democracy coming in. By peace or by war? Lammas Day, August 1, 1914, gave the heart-shaking reply. War called upon us to do our duty. Catholics went to all the fronts and their priests tended on wounded and dying. At home we gave our heartiest welcome to some hundred thousand Belgians. Cardinal Bourne was entrusted with a mission by supreme authority to the Near East, and travelled from Egypt into the State of Serbia, being welcomed everywhere as the Holy Father's representative. When the War ended the Catholic Church had been revealed to thousands of English soldiers. They saw the crucifix hanging un-broken amid storms of cannon-shot. And the seamless robe of Christ was unrent by schism. Many thousands of Catholics fought on both sides, but they did not quarrel about creeds. In the Thirty Years' War (1620–1648) religion was at least a pretext. But from 1914–1918 autocracy, the absolute divine right of kings, did all it could by land, sea and air to annihilate demo-cracy. Manning foresaw and said that it could not be done. The Church was to flourish amid free peoples.

Here would be the place to sum up our fortunes and policy with regard to the Tractarian Movement when it developed into Ritualism. We should also glance at the Pre-Raphaelites, who made a return to Cimabué, Giotto, and the other early, or primitive religious artists, forever associated with Assisi, Padua, the central Italian shrines. Of all that is herein significant the literary spokesman was John Ruskin, who renounced his early prejudices, did honour to St. Francis and has had a large following. But the relation of Catholics to art and letters since 1850, which gives ample motives for satisfaction, will be described in another essay. I conclude my own by pointing out the foundation on which the whole of our Catholic revival rests.

It is, of course, a trained, devout, and zealous Clergy, under rule and guidance by the Hierarchy. Without this, Emancipation would have been of little avail. But now, thank God, canonical Seminaries like St. Edmund's, Oscott, Upholland, Wonersh, and others, conformably to the decrees of Trent, bring up candidates for Holy Orders fully prepared. A College like the venerable Ushaw keeps its grand tradition, and Sedgley Park grows young again at St. Wilfrid's. We have not given up a single elementary school, and our great foreign Colleges thrive in Rome and elsewhere. Finally, though we no longer have the Irish Members at Westminster, Catholic Ireland (not, alas, all of it) has become a " Free State." In the battle of ideas Ireland, which stands for home, liberty, and religious faith, has taken the winning side. Something not unlike Repeal has followed upon Emancipation, and Daniel O'Connell's triumph is assured.

THE CATHOLIC CHURCH AND THE SPIRITUAL LIFE

BY THE MOST REV. ARCHBISHOP GOODIER, S.J.

II

THE CATHOLIC CHURCH AND THE
SPIRITUAL LIFE

From the nature of things it cannot be easy to estimate
the spiritual life of any period, or its influence on the
individuals who have composed it ; much more difficult
must it be when that period is virtually our own. For
the spiritual life is essentially a hidden thing ; it belongs
to the inner soul of each man and woman who has lived
it ; its influence must needs, therefore, be hidden,
however much, here and there, significant signs may
appear. " The kingdom of heaven is likened to leaven."
Moreover, when we do recognise the signs, we have no
gauge by means of which to measure the life beneath ;
all we can do, in most cases, is to say that such and such
a thing could never have come about without an intense
life of the spirit behind it. Lastly, to a very great extent,
the spiritual life is unconscious of itself. The more it
knows itself the less, usually, is it spiritual, the more
unconscious and spontaneous the more true ; and this
particularly in regard to its effects. The saint seldom
knows either his own sanctity, or the benefit his sanctity
has been to others ; often enough they are not recognised
till years after. What is true of the saint is no less true
of others who may not be strictly saints ; it is true of a
whole community.

Still there are many indications which can scarcely
be mistaken. When a saint is dead, and men are able to
survey his life's work as a whole, the perspective is more
accurate, cause and effect are more clearly connected, it
is seen that what have been called good and evil may have

quite other definitions. So it is with periods. " Diligen-
tibus Deum, omnia cooperantur in bonum." History
and biography have no deeper lesson than this ; the fact
that so many sufferings and misfortunes have been
blessings in disguise, not only to those who come after,
but even to those who have suffered, and who have seen
in their suffering only failure. This certainly is the lesson
taught to us, and to all who have eyes to see, by the story
of the Catholic Church in England during the last four
hundred years. Others have sown, and have watered
the ground with their life's blood ; we are reaping, and
posterity, please God, will reap yet more.

When we come down to more recent times and study
the spiritual conditions of a hundred years ago, the first
thing that must strike us is the utter apathy and lack of
interest in almost everything religious which had settled
down upon England previous to that date. The witness
of all writers is unanimous ; they acknowledge the fact
and look for its causes. The atheistic philosophers of
the century preceding had done their work ; reactions
had set in after the Wesleyan and other revivals ; the
Church by law established had found herself too com-
fortable, and had settled down to a life of ease and
idleness. The French wars were over, and security had
brought laxer living ; the industrial age had begun, and
had absorbed all other interests, with its new visions of
wealth and so-called progress. The universities had
waned ; religion in them was at a discount. These and
many more are reasons adduced for the irreligion of the
time, but that it existed all are agreed. It was not an age
of opposition ; it was one of utter lack of interest. Men
did not care about religion, one way or another.

Indeed, this may be taken without doubt as the
source of the three great religious movements of the
time. John Wesley was stirred to act, chiefly, perhaps,

because he saw the moral results of this apathy; let religion die, so he believed, and corruption must follow. The leaders of the Oxford movement saw further still. To them it became clear that if religion was to live it must rest on something more than mere emotion and exhortation; it must be dogmatic, it must have something definite to believe, or in the end it would be nothing. Alongside of these, from the opposite camp, the very lack of interest in things religious made tolerance of religion, of whatever kind, almost a matter of course. Of this we have evidence enough in the first supporters of Catholic Emancipation in England. An example we have in Sydney Smith, who pleaded eloquently and constantly that Catholics should be free, almost entirely on this very ground; and though on this ground alone we might never have succeeded, still that this argument should be regularly used is proof enough of the mentality of the time.

There were thus, at the time of Emancipation, and for some fifteen years after it, two distinct forces at work to mould the spirit and mind of England. The one was indifferent, tending to no religious creed, endeavouring to build up a moral code on an avowed pagan basis; the other was religious and dogmatic which, the more it emphasised its own first principles, found itself becoming more and more Catholic. By both sides the tenets of the Protestant Reformation were felt to be a hindrance; by both the truth of English history was again being illustrated, that with all its outer success the Protestant Reformation has never been happy, has always been restless in this country. From the first it has been an exotic forced upon the land; and though the Englishman's law-abiding spirit has allowed it to be imposed upon him, nevertheless the same spirit has always made him eager to get rid of it. He has altered its shape, its teaching, its very name; to-day he scarcely knows what it means. Our Government keeps it, not because it is Protestant, for it is not; it keeps it, on its own avowal, merely because it happens to be the law of the land.

The more, then, England aimed at becoming definitely religious, apart from being more moral, the more definitely Catholic became its aspirations. This was no isolated movement; the same was going on elsewhere, and events in other countries inevitably had their repercussions here. Already in Germany the list was long of names that were known throughout Europe of men who had submitted themselves and their talents to the service of the Catholic Church. There they had no Oxford Movement; the German mind was too logical for that; the leaders who might have made one surrendered without reserve. Still more marked was the revival in France. The madness of the Revolution was over; Napoleon was gone; the philosophers had had their day; the country which, in spite of all, had remained Catholic in name responded to the call of men who put before it Catholic truth in its bare simplicity. France was not entirely saved; but the renewal of its religious life is evidenced by the rise and spread of its religious orders, which have influenced France and many other countries to this day.

But most impressive of all was the awakening that had taken place in Rome itself. Englishmen went there in plenty and came away with their perspective altered. They had seen the Papacy reduced by Napoleon, as it was said, to nothing, a withered antiquity at best; they went to Rome and found it, not only alive, but more alive than any other power on the continent of Europe. They had been used to hear of it as reactionary; they found it a centre of learning, round which the learning of other countries gathered. Its religious influence was spoken of as degenerate, at most a mere display; they could not witness the Roman ceremonial, or listen to Roman disputations, or gain admission into Roman schools and libraries, without realising that its religious power was still a thing of youth, and was reaching out to all the world.

It was under such conditions, and with such influences at work about them, that our forefathers of a hundred years ago at last crept out of their catacombs. Among the many things of the past which we in our time find it difficult to visualise, few are more difficult than the spiritual mind of Catholics in England of only a century gone. The winter, indeed, was past, but the spring had not yet begun; and they stood "between two worlds, one dead, the other struggling to be born." Time had been when their ancestors, with all their bloodshedding and loss of estate, had yet hoped on with confidence that there would come a change; this hope, among the rank and file at least, had long since perished. They did not even think about it any more. There was left, and had now for a long time been left, nothing but a stolid acquiescence in their fate, as the ostracised class who might not serve their country however much they would, whose only lot was to stay at home, and live their own lives apart, and be faithful to their prayers, waiting for another life to bring them the reward of their endurance.

Yet this patient endurance, little though they knew it themselves, still less those who lived about them, bore its own fruit even here. While, as we have said, religion and the effects of religion had sunk to its lowest ebb in England, hidden away a new life was stirring which needed only its opportunity to appear. While above the ground churches were neglected, and prayer had become virtually none, here, in isolated places, round an old manor or among the poorest dwellings, chapels or barns or public-houses were found where masses were regularly said, and when they were said they were attended by large congregations. To these same congregations exhortations were given, to the life of faith, to the frequentation of the sacraments ; for their benefit books were circulated, of prayer, of meditation, of instruction, but of little else. In the home, a fact scantily recorded, and what records there are threaten soon to perish, Catholic life was fervent. Family prayers were daily said, in forms handed down from their fathers, round the cottage table, at the mother's knee, before the cheap statue in the bedroom. Whatever the atmosphere in which the toilers had to live and work outside, the atmosphere within the home circle was intensely Catholic, and the silent years had made it only the more intense. Many of us who are old enough, and have had the good fortune to be partakers of the inheritance, will remember the country squires who would recite their office day by day, or the poor who would never willingly omit their daily Universal Prayer or weekly Jesus Psalter, dwelling especially on the petition : " Jesus send me here my purgatory."

Such was the standard of spiritual practice in those days. But while this was going on within the spirit began to move upon the waters. First, from the continent the exiles of centuries already had come home ; and they brought with them a faith, a devotion, a power of resistance, seasoned not weakened by three centuries of persecution and injustice. The colleges and convents abroad during all these generations had been steadily fed by the youth of England from the families, high and low, that had held firm ; in their turn they had sent back their children to fight the good fight, often to the shedding of their blood. Now, by the Providence of God, they found their way back to their own country. They brought with them new strength, and encouragement and energising faith. All through the years, in spite of their exile, they had remained intensely English; when they came home, in spite of their disabilities, there were none in England more English than they.

After these, immediately in their wake, another stream soon began to flow. The Revolution in France and the many troubled years that followed drove many of its best sons and daughters to other lands, and of these England received a copious share. They came, priests and laymen; as foreigners they were given allowances which somehow could not be given to Englishmen. It is one of the paradoxes of the average English mind, that while it seems to assume that other peoples may, and perhaps should be, Catholic, somehow the Englishman must not. These came; they were found to be noble men and women, in many ways superior to those who received them. It was noticed that they were Catholics, and that before everything else; it began to be said that they were what they were because they were Catholics, and that on that account they possessed something which Englishmen in general had not. When that was said the first breath of spring had begun to blow.

Yet another force from without contributed to the awakening, and gave it momentum in a particular direction; the influence from Ireland. We do not speak of O'Connell and his stalwarts, who fought the fight on the political platform, for that does not concern us here. We speak rather of three other courses of the stream, on account of which Catholicism in England owes to Ireland a debt of undying gratitude. For though Emancipation concerned all the British Isles, Ireland no less than England, still in Ireland persecution had not, as in England, trampled out the faith; throughout the darkest days, and when the awakening came, Ireland was able to proclaim her faith and her devotion with no uncertain voice. To a great extent, at first, her scholars were our spokesmen, her guides were ours, and were the guides of many outside the fold. We need only mention Russell of Maynooth, the trusted friend of Newman long before he entered the Church; Wiseman, in great measure, owed his faith to Ireland. When the great immigration came, then, too, the more expansive faith of Ireland came over and enlightened ours. Through the Irish immigrants alone to this day, and through their practice of the faith, many parts of England owe all that they know of Catholic life.

But the influence has not stopped there. Not only in politics, not only in the field of scholarship, not only by immigration has Ireland materially affected the spiritual life of England. From the beginning and still to this day, Catholic England has looked to Catholic Ireland for much practical help. Religious, priests, bishops—without Irish assistance what would England have done for these last hundred years? What would she do without them now? The Irish Sisters of Charity, the Sisters of the Presentation, the Irish Sisters of Mercy, who have come over in communities and made here their homes; the individual men and women without number who have left their own country that they may help us, the families now long settled in the land till they have become one with the Catholic body here, all these have inevitably given to our spiritual life something of their own special colour. And this, perhaps, most in ways that the historian least notices. We may smile at the Irish Biddy selling her cabbages at the corner of the market-place; but the telling of her beads as she has sat behind her stall, and the patience she has shown in her poverty, are not the least influence that has told for good in the regeneration of England.

These, then, were some of the ingredients that went to the making of our spiritual life in the last hundred years. However hidden, these ingredients were strong and vigorous; a fact which soon became evident to non-Catholics more than to Catholics themselves. Contact with Europe, as we have already seen, which since the fall of Napoleon had been increasing every day; a broader understanding of scholarship, which compelled our scholars to look for their learning elsewhere; a desire to revive a spirit of religion that was wellnigh dead; these brought it home to many that the Catholic Church was still the power in Europe, and that, therefore, their despised brethren in England could be by no means so contemptible. When they emerged from their hiding they were more honoured than they knew, more observed than they knew, by the more thoughtful of their countrymen. In no other sense can we read the literature of the last hundred years and to-day, whether it be in our favour or bitterly against us.

But they did not know; to a very great extent they do not know it to-day. Writers on Catholic Emancipation speak successively of the bewilderment of Catholics when they were first set free. They were like men blinded by the light when they have come out of darkness. They could not believe in their good fortune; if they believed in it they did not know how to use it; much less, at first, could they believe in or trust those whom centuries had taught them to look upon as their hereditary persecutors. They had grown used to living among themselves; they had developed a solid spirituality, stereotyped by time; they could not at once adapt themselves to their new surroundings. In their hidden places they had accepted and practised devotions

33

sanctioned by long usage ; they looked with suspicion on new things, even on things sometimes from the heart of Rome itself. They could neither see nor hear. They were content, nay preferred, to practise their religion as they had been used, hidden, unobtrusive, certainly with no wish to proselytise, or inflict themselves on others ; nevertheless with a firmness and fervour of faith that could not but win admiration, and even reverence, from those who saw.

Not only could they neither see nor hear ; they were also inarticulate. A few defenders of the faith there were, some worthy, others less deserving ; these, from then till now, from the nature of our circumstances, have tended to predominate among our Catholic writers. But a mere defender of the faith seldom expresses its soul. Tertullian may speak for the Church of the martyrs, but for the martyrs themselves we need an Ignatius of Antioch ; and the soul of the Catholic Church in England, for many years after Emancipation, was unable to speak for itself. It had been too long used to keep silence ; it was unlearned, an infant not knowing how to speak ; its members, for the most part, belonged to those sections of society which of all are least able to express themselves, the lower middle class and the poor. Nor even to this day have we wholly overcome this trouble ; to a very great extent we are inarticulate still.

But if Catholic England could not speak for itself, first there was sent to it one who was able to give it a tongue. Steeped in the spirit of the Church abroad, our first Cardinal spoke, not only in defence but also as a living voice among his English brethren. Next, thanks without a doubt to a striving after Catholic ideals, there was brought about a movement which drew into the Church many of the best in the land ; and through these again, inarticulate Catholic England began to speak.

They came to it ; they learnt from it. At first they drew their Catholicism from elsewhere ; but soon they grew to know the strong, living faith at their own door, and loved it as a thing with an individuality of its own. Wiseman, Newman, Faber, Coleridge, Fullerton, Drane —this in the spiritual life of England is the chief significance of these names. They spoke for those who could not speak for themselves ; they interpreted to them their own spiritual lives ; they showed to their fellow Catholics how much they were one, in body and in soul, with the whole universal Church.

But if they could not speak they could act ; and very soon, with the liberty given them, the need for action was asserted. The Church had become again a living thing ; then it must produce fruits of its own. The great Catholic institutions, as we have seen, had come over, and recruits began to flow in with a regularity and increase that spoke volumes for the homes from which they came ; to Ushaw, to Old Hall, to Stonyhurst, to Ampleforth and Downside, to Augustinian Canonesses and Benedictine nuns. French and Belgian orders followed and they, too, flourished, till their homes became entirely English. But even with these the spirit of Catholic England and Ireland was not satisfied. It formed its own provinces, soon it founded its own orders. Who shall say what England, and Ireland, and the colonies, and America owe to such great names as Margaret Hallahan, Mary Aikenhead, Cornelia Conelly, Magdalen Taylor ? In religious vocations alone, multiplied as they have been under most trying circumstances, coming alike from the highest and lowest, to the priesthood and to convents, we have the amplest proof of the strong spiritual life that animated the whole community.

In a striking way this was enabled to bear fruit.

Twenty years after Emancipation the Crimean War broke out. A brave woman took it on herself to form a band of women who would tend the sick and wounded on the battlefield. Some followed her lead, but they were all too few. She looked for more; nowhere was her appeal more welcomed and answered than from among our Sisters of Mercy. Had she or our Government asked for more they would have been forthcoming. The nurse upon the battlefield has now become a public institution; let us not forget that her very existence is due in no small measure to the nuns who came to the help of Florence Nightingale. Without their assistance, she tells us very plainly, she could not have carried on. Already in them the Catholic community was paying back to England a hundredfold for what she had granted to it.

One happy result of this must here be mentioned; a little thing it might appear, but one which has been the source of untold good, especially in the poorer quarters of our great cities. The nun from this time began to be a welcome figure in our streets, and to be honoured, not by Catholics only, but by all. Nowhere, we would say, is the Sister of Charity more respected than she is in our country to-day, nowhere more assisted, or given free access wherever she may choose to go. She is protected by all, she is helped by all; in return she gives her assistance to whoever may be in need. What this has meant, not for the sisters, not for us, but for the uplift of our downtrodden masses, especially in an age of industrial crisis, who shall say? One thing we may justly claim. As the century has gone on, and the opportunity to help our suffering fellow-countrymen has grown, Catholic institutions, and Catholic communities to serve them, have increased out of all proportion, either to our numbers or our wealth. Had not the spiritual life of our people been strong, this could never have been done ; it has supplied where wealth has been wanting.

Alongside of these have grown and are ever growing our schools and churches. In another place it will be shown what Catholics have done for the religious education, not only of their own, but of the whole community ; here it is enough to remind ourselves of the spiritual force behind, which alone has made possible the continuous sacrifice, and will make victory certain in the end. Perhaps in no other way has the strong faith of our people more impressed itself on the mind of our fellow-countrymen. To those who could pay so dearly for their faith, men have argued, that faith must be very dear ; and a faith that can become so dear must in itself be something very real. In this way has the example of our Catholic laity won its respect, and therefore its influence, on others. For we have loved education no less than they, but we have loved our faith more ; and the price we have steadily paid out of our poverty, that while keeping the one we might not lose the other, has won the respect even of those who have been opposed to us. It has done more ; in a generation in which irreligion threatened to absorb all our schools, almost alone Catholics have fought for the Christianity of England and have saved it. In this again they have repaid their country for what she has restored to them, full measure, flowing over.

Of our churches, and the life that is in them, and that has flowed out from them, what shall we say ? The book is open for everyone to read, and many read it ; many more, please God, will read it in the near future. It is a long cry, though barely seventy years, from Newman's picture of non-Catholic ignorance and the state of things to-day. Ignorant as many still are, they know that the faith of Catholics is a very real thing ; and more and more they have come to respect it, to welcome its display among them, to feel and know that a procession of the Blessed Sacrament is an honour and a blessing to the streets through which it moves. More than that; those who are not ignorant have gone further. Mistaking the external for the internal, the matter for the spirit, they have sought to capture the soul of Catholicism by imitation. If imitation is the greatest praise, then indeed have the Catholics of England been greatly honoured in the last hundred years.

The Age of Wiseman was an age when foundations were laid; we have seen how God fostered the work, once it had begun. The Age of Manning was an age of adaptation; when Catholicism, imagined to be in some sense foreign, was found to be English after all. This, with its application in particular among the poor, is the significance of the age of our second Cardinal Archbishop. But with his going it may be said that the new era of true life began; this is the significance of Cardinal Vaughan. He was no convert; he saw the Church wholly from within. He was of the old aristocracy that had held the faith through all the troubled times; as such he represented that silent but firm core of Catholicism of which we have already spoken. His education was not of our universities, but such as belonged to Catholics themselves. Yet in him one seems to recognise a vision transcending that of either of his predecessors, reaching out beyond England, beyond the British Empire, to all the world, a vision truly Catholic.

Already in his early life, in spite of the fact that at home missionary priests were sorely needed, by his foundation of a society of foreign missionaries he had brought the Catholicism of England in line with Catholicism abroad. But naturally it is in England, within his own province, that we see his spiritual genius best portrayed. One with his own people, more literally than either of his predecessors, he shared with them, and reflected more accurately, their lives and their short-comings. Like them he was slow to speak, but in action he did much. His addresses and pastorals catch the mind of English Catholics and give it back ; simple, unadorned, if you will unlearned, but devotional, practical, believing in prayer, not only as a proof and fosterer of faith, but as a power in the world. Like them he had ambitions, all of that kind which spoke of a living fire, risen at last from the long-glowing embers. The intense increase of schools, for the poor, for every class ; the bold opening of the door to our universities ; the building of Westminster Cathedral ; the encourage-ment of every society or organisation which would make his people more conscious of themselves ; these are some of the signs by which we may learn both him and the Catholic spirit of his time. The outward signs : for since his death we have come to know, in addition, the inner sanctity which inspired him. And what we know to have been true of him, we know to have been true of many more heroes of his generation.

It was before this, but in his time it became more systematic, that the movement for the checking of the leakage among our poor and working classes began. The new life had been too much for many ; they had lost their way and wandered. Many from Ireland, in the struggle for bare existence, had found faith less easy in the bewildering atmosphere of England and had failed. For such as these, far more than for those outside, the missionary spirit now set in, and missions and retreats became an intrinsic element in the spiritual life of Catholic England. After the schools, for to them and to their army of teachers we would give the first place, it is to these incessant missions and retreats that we would ascribe the saving of the faith of thousands, in a time of more subtle crisis than may at first appear. They have saved many, they have won back many that were lost; had all been saved, it would be hard to estimate what might have been the influence of the Catholic Church on England to-day. England, not the Church only, has been the loser.

It may be well here to ask ourselves what, if any, are the characteristics which the Catholicity of England, either in itself or in distinction from that of other countries. In the first place, as we have seen, it has an ancestry which has peculiarly marked it with blood, and a history which has left it even yet to a great extent silent. It has not sought, hitherto, to be noised abroad; for most of the century it has asked only to be left alone, enjoying the same liberty and rights as others. But this has produced a more intense interior spirit, however hidden. For centuries our Catholics had to rely upon themselves and their own private loyalty to prayer; this has had lasting effect, notably among our working classes, and these are by far the strongest element in the Catholic Church in England to-day. It has taught them, too, to value the mass and the sacraments, to secure which their forefathers paid so great a price. We may doubt whether in any country in the world these are more esteemed than here; whether anywhere in the world Sunday mass is attended more regularly, or more willingly, than here.

Upon this very solid basis much has been built up. First, a wider field in the practice of devotion, at first looked upon with fear and suspicion, has now been accepted. Though still the English character, as Newman long ago pointed out, has little sympathy with many forms of devotion which prevail abroad, yet it has found place for many which have the more formal sanction of the Church.   The Sacred Heart, Our Lady, many of the modern saints, the Souls in Purgatory, these are devotions specially dear to our people ; while the marked growth in recent years of processions and similar displays, both in our churches and in our streets, the ever-swelling pilgrimages to Lourdes, to Rome, to the Holy Land, and to less known shrines at home, would seem to be full of significance, internal as well as external. It is not many years since such manifestations were received with scant respect by those outside the fold. To-day, almost everywhere, the Catholic procession is honoured by almost all, interpreted aright as a proof of living faith in at least one community, for which the rest are thankful and of which they are proud.

Still even these are not the English Catholic's chief characteristic.   For that we must revert to much that has been already seen ; it is the intensity of his faith. Deep down, silent, but undoubted, there it is.   " Faith of our fathers, holy faith," has not been ringing in his ears for centuries for nothing ; no other hymn to-day more wins his response.   As we have said, he is not demonstrative ; he is not always easily aroused to be ambitious for religion's sake.   He is slow to win others to his way of thinking ; he is content, in his surroundings, to live and let live.   It is many centuries now since one of his nation has been raised to the honours of the altar ; the fact does not disturb him in the least.   He is satisfied that it has produced saints in abundance ; but when the thought is suggested of introducing the cause of any one of them, he promptly tends to be on the defensive. Somehow he looks upon these things as non-essential, possibly dangerous.   He fears that to strain after them may lead to untruth, and sham virtue, and vainglory. Even miracles, perhaps, he holds of less account than do his brethren elsewhere.   He seldom looks for them, he does not expect them; his *beati* did not work many miracles, but they endured many tortures, and they shed much blood, and he is of their kin.

But behind and beneath this unemotional exterior is a fixed, almost a stolid faith; an intense faith in God and in His Christ, which is utterly unaffected by the rationalising blindness around him; a faith in the Mother of God to whom, as did his fathers long ago, he continues to offer his country as her " Dowry "; a proud faith in that universal Church of which he knows himself, by everyday experience and obedience, to be a member; a loyal faith in the Holy Father, which is for ever seeking opportunities to manifest itself; a faith that is ever willing to make sacrifices, that schools may be built, that churches may be beautified, that priests may be trained, that convents may be supported, that foreign missionaries may be equipped, that the poor may be fed, that the downtrodden may be rescued. Taken as a whole, the Catholics of England are poor; yet, taken as a whole, we may justly claim that no Catholics in the world have, of their own accord, made more sacrifices for their faith than they. They have their reward, and they are contented with it, that by the goodness of God the faith that is in them and in their children is strong, and living, and splendid.

We have ventured to make this digression because it seems to us that we may thus best express the significance of Catholic life in the last quarter of a century. Though the battle of the Church in England has not ceased— indeed, in some way it must always go on—still during these last twenty-five years there has steadily grown a certain sense of strength, and security, and confidence. We no longer fear; in truth, we are rather feared. We are sure, we know, others do not know and doubt; and to cover their doubting they " agree with their rivals betimes " lest they fall. And with this confidence, this certainty, we have ventured forth to action in ways of which our fathers never dreamt. When he witnessed, in 1908, the Eucharistic Congress in London, Newman in heaven must indeed have thanked God. For that Congress meant much, not only for Catholics, but also for England. It meant an impulse to frequent Communion just at the time when it was needed. It meant the last blow to that shameful bigotry which had been stereotyped in the Royal Oath. It meant a reawakening throughout non-Catholic England to the truth of the Blessed Sacrament, with a longing to regain that which its ancestors trampled under foot.

Another sign of these last years has been the growth of vocations, especially to the contemplative life. Among men it has been less marked ; the vineyard of the Lord still demands every labourer it can muster. Indeed, the demand to-day is greater than ever it has been before, for the fields were never whiter for the harvest. Still, even among men the stream flows, and there are signs that soon it will flow stronger. But among women the growth has been such as to astonish even the most sanguine. In another place will be seen statistics giving the increase of our contemplative convents ; here it is enough for us to speak of them as signs, of the living faith which alone can produce such ample fruit, of the lasting fidelity which fosters it, of the sanctuaries of prayer spread about the land, bringing down the blessing of God on every man and woman in it. And, thank God ! it is not only we Catholics who recognise this fact. It is recognised and welcomed by hundreds and thousands of non-Catholics ; perhaps it is recognised by all who have any faith in prayer.

We come to our own time, the period of the Great War and after. What the war brought home to many has often been told; the work of our chaplains, the valour of our men, especially the Irish regiments, in facing death; the spirit of religion that prevailed in the devastated areas of France; these have left an indelible mark upon the rank and file of our countrymen. Men came back with their conceptions altered; since that time they have not been ashamed to listen to those who would tell them more of the one Church Universal. And our youth has risen to supply the need. The Catholic Evidence Guild, the Catholic Social Guild, the Catholic Action Society, the missions to non-Catholics, are evidence of this in abundance.

But these last are evidences of something more. They tell of that within which gives us great hope for the future. Early in this essay we spoke of the inarticulate condition of our fathers; now we would say, of our own generation, that at last it has learnt to speak. Not in every way, it is true; there are still many things of which English Catholics are scarcely yet able to speak or write, and which must be sought abroad. But the voice, nevertheless, has been heard, in our streets, in lecture rooms, on bookstalls. The vision of the Church has been seen. And both alike tell of a soul and a life which are sturdy; which have weathered many storms and will weather many more; and which will bear fruit in season, for the good and uplift of their country, and for the greater glory of God.

THE CATHOLIC CHURCH AND EDUCATION

BY SIR JOHN GILBERT, K.B.E., K.C.S.G.

III

THE CATHOLIC CHURCH AND EDUCATION

In any comprehensive survey of the remarkable development of the Church in England and Wales during the past hundred years (1829–1929), it will be found that no section of Catholic activity has made more significant and fruitful progress than that of education. Certainly no phase of Catholic endeavour has contributed more largely, both directly and indirectly, to the extension of Catholic influence generally than the persistent efforts of the Catholic body, especially during the second half of the century, for the retention of their schools within the national system of education. Not only has the erection of many a new church resulted from the prior establishment of a school, not infrequently in most adverse circumstances, but in every large parish the school has served as a centre of religious and social work in the district. The serious financial disability under which Catholic schools have suffered, subsequent to the passing of the Education Act, 1870, in particular, although the position was substantially ameliorated by Lord Balfour's Act of 1902, has united all sections of the Catholic community in the defence of their schools, and in the long-drawn-out struggle for obtaining adequate assistance from public funds for their support. Moreover, nothing has assisted more materially in securing for Catholics a recognised position amongst their non-Catholic fellow-countrymen than their courageous efforts to safeguard their schools, at times against odds apparently overwhelming, when unfriendly efforts at legislation have threatened their existence. A retrospect

47

of the past hundred years would have undoubtedly been far less consoling and inspiring if Catholics had remained educationally inactive during that period, and from 1870 onwards had passively allowed their schools to be transferred to local education authorities and their children to attend undenominational public schools.

As a hundred years ago no national system of education existed in this country, it is difficult to contrast the position of Catholic schools then with the highly-developed Catholic educational system of to-day. In 1829 Catholics had no access to English university education, as entrance to Oxford and Cambridge was subject to religious tests. Training colleges for teachers had not been instituted. For the higher education of boys and girls, Catholics possessed, as a result in most cases of the revolutionary troubles in France towards the end of the eighteenth century, the small beginnings of some of their largest public schools of to-day and a few convent boarding schools. The work of primary education rested almost entirely in the hands of charitable associations, Anglican and Nonconformist, which organised schools for the children of the poor, with the fundamental object of providing religious education for them. Similar Catholic charitable associations had been founded in London and different parts of the country within the previous half-century, which, by 1829, had succeeded in establishing some sixty to seventy Catholic primary schools.

What a contrast does the position of Catholic education present in this country in 1929 ! Catholics have not only unfettered access to, but many halls of residence at Oxford and Cambridge, whilst at the younger universities, from London to Reading, large organised groups of Catholic students may be found. The development of higher education has been equally remarkable. The schools in existence in 1829 have extended considerably the scope and character of their work, and some hundreds of additional boarding and day secondary schools, established by the initiative of religious communities of men and women, or under the direction of the secular clergy, have grown up, especially in the large towns, in all parts of England and Wales, convent schools in particular. The small handful of Catholic primary schools in 1829 can be compared to-day with nearly 1,200 Catholic public elementary schools, many with two or three departments, with accommodation for nearly 425,000 children, all recognised by the Board of Education, and maintained by public funds under the Education Act, 1921. Indeed, beyond this, the Catholic body in 1929 can claim the possession of considerably more privately-maintained elementary schools than its predecessors a century ago were able to organise with so much sacrifice and persistency.

Throughout the past hundred years Catholic schools have usually been at a serious disadvantage with regard to aid from public funds compared with other schools. At the time of the passing of the Emancipation Act, primary schools depended entirely for their support on fees and voluntary funds or endowments resulting from the same source. Four years later the Government voted the first grant from public funds towards the erection of primary school buildings, amounting to £20,000, a ludicrous sum contrasted with the present annual vote of about £40,000,000 for public educational purposes by the Board of Education under the Education Act, 1921. For many years the benefits of this building grant were restricted to schools organised either by the Anglican National Society or by the Nonconformist British and Foreign School Society, Catholic schools having no share therein. The grant, of course, proved inadequate, but by 1838, 714 National schools and 181 British and Foreign schools had been assisted. Although in that year Parliament refused to establish a special Government department for education, in 1839 Queen Victoria appointed a Committee of the Privy Council to administer both building and maintenance grants, from which time dated some form of official inspection of the schools benefiting. The first training college for teachers was opened in 1841, whilst the pupil-teacher system and the " Queen's Scholarship " examination, which conferred upon successful candidates free entrance to the first named, were initiated in 1846.

Catholics did not secure a share in the Government grant until the end of 1847, and their success was due mainly to the efforts of the Hon. Charles Langdale, who was chairman of an education committee formed in 1845 by the Catholic Institute for the purpose of agitating for a share in Government grant, which by this time amounted to £100,000 annually, for Catholic schools. A long correspondence with members of the Government, undertaken by Langdale in 1846, followed by a deputation, and afterwards by protest meetings, when a grant was voted to Wesleyan schools apart from the ordinary grant to British schools, led in 1847 to the supersession of the Catholic Institute, and the formation by the Vicars-Apostolic of the Catholic Poor School Committee—the predecessor of the Catholic Education Council—as an organisation for Catholics, parallel with the National Society and the British and Foreign Society, with the Hon. Charles Langdale as its chairman, a post which he retained until his death in 1868. Langdale's conciliatory methods received ample justification in December 1847, when the Committee of Council on Education passed a minute authorising grants to Catholic schools, and Parliament the following year increased the total grant to £125,000 to make provision for this development.

During the twenty-two years between the date of Langdale's first success and the introduction of Mr. Forster's Education Bill into Parliament in 1870, many developments in Catholic elementary schools in England and Wales took place. In 1850, St. Mary's Training College for men teachers, in the first instance for religious, was founded at Brook Green, Hammersmith, a substantial addition for lay teachers being made five years later. In 1856, the Sisters of Notre Dame, from Namur, founded their training college for mistresses at Mount Pleasant, Liverpool. Whilst according to a table published in that year the Government grant to primary schools in 1855 amounted to £369,602, of which Catholic schools received only £13,272, and, up to December 1854, Church of England schools had obtained in Government building grants no less than £415,000, whereas Catholic schools had only secured £3,131, the report of the Catholic Poor School Committee for 1871 recorded that Government grants made to Catholic schools from 1847 to 1870 amounted to £487,799.

The agitation throughout the country, responsible for the introduction of the Education Act, 1870, into Parliament, caused considerable anxiety amongst denominationalists. So far the education of the poorer classes had been entrusted to the oversight of religious organisations on the principle that religious education and secular education could not be separated. If additional school places were required, the supporters of the denominational schools suggested that further State help should be granted to the religious bodies which for many years past had accomplished so much useful educational work mainly on a voluntary basis. The economists, too, feared that the introduction of a new type of school, under the care of popularly elected bodies, supported largely by public funds, would tend to diminish assistance from voluntary sources. That supporters of Catholic schools shared in this anxiety is evident from the annual report of the Catholic Poor School Committee for 1868. Although Catholics came into participation in the Parliamentary grant ten years later than Anglicans and Dissenters, in the last accounts previous to the 1868 report they could point to 507 day schools with 67,143 children present at inspection, and 138 evening schools with 9,686 pupils at inspection, with a staff of 618 schoolmasters and mistresses and 631 pupil teachers. For the year ended August 31, 1867, the income of Catholic schools in England and Wales was £55,842, of which £21,591 came from Government grant. The financial disability of Catholic schools was urged, for whilst in Anglican schools the income worked out at £1 6s. 9d. per scholar, and in Dissenting schools £1 6s. 9½d., in Catholic schools it was only £1 0s. 2½d.

The question of impending legislation again figured in the report of the Catholic Poor School Committee for 1869. After explaining that no school received a maintenance grant unless it provided sixty per cent. of the entire cost of maintenance, and no school a building grant unless seventy-five per cent of the total cost of the project was forthcoming, the report suggested that the fact that the denominational system had not reached the whole population did not mean that the system had failed, but that the conditions imposed by the Privy Council were unsatisfactory. If the Privy Council had promised the balance necessary between fees and the total cost, as proposed for the new type of public schools, the denominational system would have had a fair test. The figures with regard to Catholic child population in

Great Britain were also examined. 100,000 children were already in Catholic grant-aided schools, and assuming that the total Catholic population in Great Britain was 1,200,000, it was estimated that 178,000 Catholic children should be under instruction.

The introduction of Mr. Forster's Bill the following year provoked considerable activity on the part of the Catholic Poor School Committee, which formed a special committee to examine its sections in detail and to report to the Hierarchy. Representations on points affecting Catholic interests were made to the Government, a memorandum on the subject being sent to the Prime Minister by Lord Howard of Glossop, who had been elected chairman of the Catholic Poor School Committee on the death of the Hon. Charles Langdale. The great concern of the Catholic body was not only the preservation of their existing schools, but the provision for the large number of Catholic children outside these schools, who, if Catholics remained inactive, would be compelled to attend the new public schools, in which definite religious instruction could not be given.

As all the Bishops were in Rome for the Vatican Council, consultation with them had to be carried on by letter. The Catholic Poor School Committee report for 1870 contains a joint letter of instruction from the Eternal City, signed by all the Bishops, suggesting certain amendments in Mr. Forster's Bill. Its assured passage through Parliament prompted immediate action with regard to provision of additional Catholic school places. A crisis fund was started at a meeting at Norfolk House, under the presidency of the Duke of Norfolk, which soon amounted to nearly £50,000, the Duke himself and the Marquess of Bute each contributing £10,000. This fund, aided by persistent local effort, led to a remarkable expansion in the provision of Catholic school places in

various parts of the country, as the following figures
will show :

Date.	No. of Catholic Schools.	Accommodation.	Present at Inspection.
1870	350	101,556	83,017
1874	567	150,000 (?)	119,582
1879	737	242,403	159,576
1884	828	284,514	200,158
1890	946	341,953	223,645

To have more than doubled Catholic school accommodation in less than ten years was a great achievement.

As many had anticipated, the Board schools, set up by
the Education Act, 1870, soon became competitors of the
voluntary schools. In 1870 the average annual cost of
educating a child in grant-aided schools was £1 5s. 5d.
Although this amount had increased by about one-third
in the previous ten years, it was confidently assumed that
the cost per child would not eventually exceed £1 10s.
per year, which could be met in the case of the Board
schools by a rate not exceeding 3d. in the £. Expenditure on the public schools, however, increased at a
standard not expected, gravely to the disadvantage of
the denominational schools. By 1882, in voluntary
schools the maintenance per child in average attendance
had increased from £1 5s. 5d. per year to £1 14s. 6¾d.
Of this sum the Government grant provided 15s. 9d. and
voluntary contributions 6s. 10¼d. In Board schools the
cost was £2 1s. 6½d., 16s. 2d. coming from Government
grant and 17s. from the rates. Thus the supporters of
voluntary schools, whilst paying their rates for Board
schools, had in addition to find large sums from voluntary
contributions for the support of their own schools,
which, with much less money at their disposal, were
expected to reach the same educational standard as the
rate-aided Board schools. Catholic schools could not

have continued the unequal struggle if it had not been for the self-sacrificing work of Catholic teachers, religious and lay, who gave their services generously to the work of Catholic education for salaries which compared very unfavourably with those paid to teachers in Board schools. Despite the inducements offered by the latter, hundreds of Catholic lay teachers remained throughout the whole of their careers in Catholic schools.

Notwithstanding the strong efforts made by the supporters of voluntary schools to meet the deficiencies in school accommodation in the years immediately following the application of the Act of 1870, the great financial strain placed upon those responsible for the maintenance of these schools soon began to tell in the case of individual schools. Nonconformists, finding the undenominational religious instruction provided in many Board schools at public expense to their satisfaction, began to transfer their voluntary schools to School Boards. In many districts, too, passive Anglicans followed the Nonconformist example, with the result that by 1884, despite the increase of the total amount of voluntary school accommodation, nearly 1,000 schools, about two-thirds of which had been Church of England, were transferred to public authorities. It is a singular tribute to the self-sacrifice and devotion of the Catholic body that not one of these transferred schools was a Catholic school.

The financial strain, too, was greater in the case of Catholic than of other voluntary schools. According to official figures published by the Board of Education for 1884, the proportion of free admissions was greatest in Catholic schools : in Board schools 4·16, in Church of England schools 2·64, in Catholic schools 13·11, in Wesleyan schools ·84. Similarly, Catholic schools had the lowest receipt per pupil in school pence.

The conditions of the Government grant, which fixed a limit of 17s. 6d., unless the income from fees and voluntary contributions exceeded that amount, affected Catholic schools more adversely, owing to the poverty of the Catholic body. Every form of increased expenditure by Board schools, therefore, inflicted a double hardship upon the supporters of Catholic schools. Catholics had both to pay the larger rate for the support of Board schools and at the same time increase their voluntary subscriptions to enable their own schools to compete with the educational developments of the former. To emphasise the injustice, on every new Catholic school, provided at the cost of great self-sacrifice, they actually had to pay education rate for the support of the Board schools. How well Catholics endeavoured to face the situation may be gathered from the fact that voluntary contributions for their schools increased from £25,000 in 1870 to £66,000 in 1884.

Catholics did not remain inactive under this ever-increasing injustice, for, in addition to frequent meetings of protest in London and other parts of the country, repeated representations were made by the Bishops and the Catholic Poor School Committee to the Government for the time being. In 1884 a movement known as the Voluntary Schools Association, the object of which was to agitate for the removal of the financial inequalities of the voluntary schools, was initiated in Salford by Bishop (afterwards Cardinal) Vaughan. This organisation, which soon spread to other parts of the country, asked for an immediate increase of the Government grant by twenty-five per cent. and for the removal of four specific grievances : (1) the 17s. 6d. limit of the Government grant unless the total income per child from other sources exceeded that amount ; (2) the necessity for Catholic parents to apply to Boards of

Guardians for remission of school fees if attending Catholic schools, whereas School Boards could remit the fees of children attending Board schools ; (3) the rating of voluntary school buildings for the support of Board schools ; (4) the refusal to recognise Catholic schools as necessary if vacant Board school accommodation existed. A preliminary concession to the continued protests of the supporters of voluntary schools was the appointment of a Royal Commission in 1886 to enquire into the working of the Education Act, 1870, with Sir Richard Cross as chairman and Cardinal Manning amongst its members. The Commission, after sitting for two years, issued as usual a majority and a minority report, the latter being signed by eight out of twenty-three commissioners. The majority report was favourable to the voluntary schools, recognising the unfair financial conditions under which they worked and recommending that they should receive rate aid for the secular instruction given in them. The Government, however, took no immediate action on the report.

The first substantial relief to Catholic schools came, strange to say, from the Act of 1891, which secured free education for the elementary schools. Introduced by a Conservative Government, the scheme for free education safeguarded the fundamental position of voluntary schools. Catholic schools actually derived greater financial advantage from the proposals than other denominational schools, on account of the exiguous character of their former income from school fees. The Act provided an annual grant of 10s. per child between the ages of three and fifteen years, if no fees were charged. As the average annual amount of fees per child in Catholic schools was 9s. 5d., a slight advantage accrued to these schools on the number of children then in attendance. Indirectly the Act greatly benefited them,

as it led to a substantial increase in the average attendance, as parents were no longer obliged to go through
the long process involved in making application for a
remission of fees. Whatever relief was gained, however, was soon counterbalanced by increasing demands
for raising the educational standards in the schools, and
consequently Catholic agitation for a redress of the
financial inequalities continued.

The Conservative triumph at the polls in 1894 filled
the supporters of Catholic schools with hopes of securing
a reasonable settlement of their difficulties. In November
of the following year Cardinal Vaughan, who had succeeded Cardinal Manning as Archbishop of Westminster
in 1892, and the Duke of Norfolk, who had been elected
chairman of the Catholic Poor School Committee in
1885, presented a memorial to Lord Salisbury, the Prime
Minister, strongly deprecating the necessity for voluntary
contributions in support of Catholic schools, and asking
that denominational schools should receive the same
support from public funds as Board schools. A few
weeks later, however, to the great surprise of Catholics,
an influential Anglican deputation to the Prime Minister
declared that the Church of England had no desire to be
relieved of its obligations to make voluntary contributions, and expressed its willingness to accept a condition
of a fixed proportion of voluntary contributions in any
settlement effected. A joint pastoral by the Catholic
Hierarchy in response to the Anglican proposal
strongly reaffirmed the plea that the Catholic body could
not continue indefinitely the double burden of finding
voluntary contributions for their own schools and paying
heavy rates for the support of Board schools. This
serious division in the ranks of denominationalists, no
doubt, explained the inadequate character both of the
abortive Education Bill, 1896, and of the Education

Act, 1897, which Catholics accepted merely as an interim arrangement. This Act gave an additional grant of 5s. per child in the voluntary schools, which was pooled and distributed according to the necessities of the schools concerned by diocesan voluntary schools associations statutorily set up by its provisions, abolished the 17s. 6d. limit, and exempted voluntary school buildings from rating. These three substantial benefits, whilst ameliorating some of their difficulties, still left the denominational schools at a grave disadvantage compared with the publicly-maintained Board schools.

As a result of the General Election in 1900, after an unsuccessful attempt at legislation in 1901, the following year the Prime Minister, Mr. Arthur Balfour, introduced his famous Education Bill, which proposed to give denominational schools for the first time a share in the rates raised for public education purposes. In its final form the Bill, which was mainly attributed at the time to Sir Robert Morant, the Permanent Secretary to the Board of Education, not only promised substantial relief to the harassed denominational schools, but endeavoured, successfully, to bring under the oversight of one authority all sections of educational work, elementary, secondary, higher and technical, greatly to the advantage of each. With regard to denominational elementary schools, it laid down certain definite principles. The local education authorities constituted under the Bill were given control of secular education and of all expenditure thereon from public funds, both taxes and rates, the responsibility for religious instruction being retained by the managing body of each school, the right of nominating one-third of the members of which was accorded to the local authority. Upon the last named was placed the duty of maintaining from public funds every denominational school within its area declared to be necessary by the Board of Education, whilst the obligation of providing the site and building and keeping same in structural repair remained with the managers. As to the appointment of teachers, whilst the local authority fixed the number and qualifications of the staff of each school, the managers appointed the teachers, but the former could veto an appointment on educational grounds, subject to an appeal to the Board of Education. The local authority could also in a similar way direct the dismissal of a teacher on educational grounds : the managers could only dismiss a teacher by their own authority on grounds connected with the giving of religious instruction. The Bill also contained arrangements for applications to the Board of Education for the recognition of new denominational schools.

Catholics, of course, welcomed the new Bill, although it removed the control of secular instruction, save for the appointment of the teacher, and the ordinary management of the schools from Catholic hands, accepting it as a compromise upon the best terms then obtainable. London, owing to the complexity of its local government, was excluded from the 1902 Bill and dealt with in a separate measure the following year. The Bill, which was introduced in March 1902, met with bitter opposition. As it involved the abolition of School Boards, whose powers were to be merged in County Councils, Town Councils, and Urban District Councils, considerable local opposition was also engendered. Extreme Nonconformists even raised the cry of " Rome on the Rates," an example of the unfair character of their opposition. In the protracted debates in the House of Commons, Catholics owed much to the Parliamentary experience and skill of the members of the Irish Parliamentary Party in stating the Catholic position, and in safeguarding the interests of Catholic schools. After several months the Government carried their Bill in the House of Commons, but only by means of the " guillotine." When it had secured the approval of the House of Lords and was placed upon the Statute Book, Nonconformists again organised a scheme of opposition to its application, by initiating a League of Passive Resistance, whose members refused to pay that portion of their education rate which they estimated would be applied towards the upkeep of denominational schools. A summons for payment, followed by a distraint on the resister's goods, occurred quarter after quarter for many years after. The protests, however, proved generally ineffective, as the man-in-the-street did not appreciate how those, who prior to 1902 had paid taxes towards the support of denominational schools, could, after 1902, have conscientious scruples against paying rates for the same purpose.

The 1902 Act came into force the following year: the 1903 Act, the London Act, in 1904. Their application, of course, proved an immense relief to the Catholic body. From the appointed days under these Acts, the local education authorities became responsible for the maintenance of all Catholic public elementary schools. Difficulties, however, immediately arose. Local authorities with majorities opposed to the new Act, in many cases, began to harass denominational, or non-provided, schools by administration. To make matters worse, before the Board of Education could deal with many of the appeals against the unfair action of local authorities, the dissolution of Parliament in 1905 resulted in a sweeping victory for the Liberal Party, which meant that afterwards in many parts of the country Catholic schools had to face a hostile education authority co-operating with an exacting Board of Education.

A typical example of the courageous and self-sacrificing manner in which the Catholic body met the determined attack of the opponents of their schools by administration can be found in London, which at that period was governed by an unfriendly education authority. From 1904 onwards London Catholics must have expended about £200,000 in satisfying the demands of the local authority and the Board in connection with their school buildings. Many schools were rebuilt, a large number were remodelled, all were substantially improved. From 1904 to 1909 the present Cardinal Archbishop of Westminster created a record in laying the foundation stones of new school buildings. Fortunately for London Catholics, the unfriendly majority on the London County Council suffered a severe defeat at the Council triennial election in 1907, and the new Municipal Reform majority, which has remained in power ever since, initiated a regime of friendly co-operation with the denominational schools, mitigating the former harsh decisions of the Council and the Board as far as practicable, and setting an example to the rest of the country in a generous administration of the Act.

A far greater danger than local administration, however, soon threatened Catholic schools. Urged on by their Nonconformist supporters, the majority in the House of Commons in 1906 determined to revise the Education Act, 1902. The new Prime Minister, Sir Henry Campbell-Bannerman, who appointed Mr. Augustine Birrell Minister of Education, announced that in the first session of the new Parliament a Bill would be introduced to amend the Balfour Act.

Under its provisions, as later appeared, the dual system was to be abolished : all rate-aided schools were to be transferred to the local education authorities : undenominational religious instruction was to be obligatory in all schools : in transferred schools, religious teaching of a definite denominational nature could be arranged on two mornings a week at the expense of the denomination : in urban districts for schools of a denominational character " extended religious facilities " could be given on every day in the week, provided four-fifths of the parents demanded it, and under this arrangement teachers could volunteer for the religious instruction with the permission of the local authority. The last named proposal was intended as a concession for transferred Catholic schools.

The introduction of the Bill stirred the Catholic body in this country in a really remarkable manner in defence of their schools. In response to an appeal of the Hierarchy, from one end of the country to the other, enthusiastic demonstrations of protest were held, with the reiterated demand for Catholic children of " Catholic religious teaching by Catholic teachers in Catholic schools under Catholic control." Lancashire, as usual, led the way with monster meetings in Liverpool, Manchester, Preston, and other towns : Yorkshire and the Midlands followed with demonstrations in Leeds, Halifax, Birmingham, Nottingham, Leicester, and other large centres of population : London co-operated with meetings north, south, east, and west—the writer remembers addressing an open air demonstration, 15,000 strong, on Clapham Common on a Sunday afternoon. The climax to these wonderful gatherings was reached in the huge meeting in the Albert Hall, under the presidency of Archbishop Bourne, on the first Saturday evening in May 1906, on the eve of the debate on the second reading of the Bill in the House of Commons, a demonstration which created an extraordinary impression in London and the country on account of its whole-hearted enthusiasm, determination and unity of purpose, despite all political and racial differences. Inside, the vast hall was thronged with an audience of 10,000 persons, whilst outside an overflow meeting, estimated as numbering between 30,000 and 40,000 stalwarts from all parts of London and district, who could not secure admission, assembled.

Notwithstanding all protests, the Bill passed the House of Commons without any amendments which rendered its provisions more acceptable to the supporters of denominational schools. Undismayed by this result, Catholics immediately proceeded to carry their opposition to the Upper House, a representative deputation, headed by Archbishop Bourne, waiting upon the Marquess of Lansdowne, the leader of the Conservative Peers. When the Second Reading and Committee stage were again reached, the House of Lords altered the Bill fundamentally. By skilfully-drawn amendments provision was made for denominational teaching in every type of school, and for the existence of State-aided schools free from the control of local authorities. The erection of new denominational schools in areas with a deficiency of school accommodation was also authorised. In accordance with general expectation, the House of Commons refused to accept these amendments, and a joint committee of the two Houses appointed to consider the impasse failed to find a solution. In face of the widespread opposition which the Bill had aroused, the Government, much to the chagrin of their Nonconformist supporters, merely dropped the measure. Catholics undoubtedly contributed materially by their efforts to this remarkable victory, for their organised protests in every part of the country strengthened the opposition of the denominationalists generally. They were greatly indebted to the members of the Irish Parliamentary Party and to the Catholic Peers, headed by the late Duke of Norfolk.

The Government made two further attempts to amend the 1902 Act, both of which did not pass beyond the House of Commons. In 1908 Mr. Reginald McKenna, who had succeeded Mr. Birrell at the Board of Education, introduced a Bill embodying the principle of contracting out, whilst later in the same year the third Minister of Education in the Government, Mr. Walter Runciman, was also responsible for a further Bill. Nonconformists, however, derived some satisfaction from Mr. McKenna's regime at the Board, by his revision of the Board of Education's grant regulations both for training colleges and for secondary schools, which made it impossible for any new institution in either category to be placed upon the Government grant list, unless in effect it became undenominational in character. A deputation, led by Archbishop Bourne, to the Prime Minister in 1908, with regard to amended regulations for existing training colleges, aimed at securing admission for students without regard to creed, stated quite frankly that Catholic colleges would ignore the alterations. These secondary school regulations, which greatly impeded the development of Catholic secondary schools, were modified for England to Catholic satisfaction by Mr. H. A. L. Fisher in 1919, whilst the present President of the Board of Education, Lord Eustace Percy, two years ago extended the modification to Wales and similarly altered the regulations for training colleges for both countries.

Since that time, both before and after the Great War, many fruitless efforts have been made, apart from Catholics, to arrive at a settlement with regard to the education question. Failure to discover an agreed solution does not mean that meanwhile Catholic elementary schools have been free from difficulties. Since the "compromise" of 1902, the character of school buildings has greatly improved, and educational developments, not then anticipated, have taken place, all involving considerable additional expenditure on the part of the managers of non-provided schools. As a result of the Great War, too, the financial standards existing when the 1902 Act was placed upon the Statute Book have been completely altered, the cost of building having more than doubled. Meanwhile a large number of Catholic school buildings, accepted as suitable for their purpose twenty-five years ago, have become out of date and require substantial alterations and improvements to bring them into line with modern school buildings, which, under existing legislation, will have to be carried out by the managers at the greatly enhanced post-War prices, making an intolerable financial burden for the supporters of these schools. Moreover, the provision of large housing estates by local authorities under recent Housing Acts, making substantial grants-in-aid from taxes and rates in order to assist the housing shortage and slum clearances, has necessitated the establishment of many new Catholic schools, again at post-War prices. Catholics are courageously facing these new problems, having provided many central schools and many new ordinary elementary schools, and having remodelled successfully many condemned school buildings, but at a prohibitive cost, which it is both unjust and unreasonable that they should be called upon to bear from their own resources. They are therefore again agitating for a removal of their financial grievances with regard to their elementary schools, claiming equality of treatment with Council schools.

Despite even greater difficulties than those experienced with primary schools, the Catholic body can point to substantial development in their provision for secondary education during the past hundred years.

Their progress in this respect is more notable as Catholic public attention and interest have necessarily been almost entirely riveted upon the provision and preservation of elementary schools. For the first seventy years, in the absence of direct assistance from public funds, Catholics had to depend almost entirely for their secondary schools upon the religious communities of men and women. All the colleges and schools in existence at the time of the passing of the Catholic Emancipation Act have materially extended their scope and character, increasing their accommodation and providing school buildings, with senior and preparatory departments, in many cases comparable with the great non-Catholic public schools in the country. Stonyhurst, Ushaw, Downside, St. Edmund's, Ware, Ampleforth, St. Wilfrid's, Cotton, the Oratory School, Caversham, Mount St. Mary's, Chesterfield, Ratcliffe, and many others, more recent additions for boys, and convent schools for girls of every grade, have given the Catholic upper and middle classes a wide choice of boarding schools for their children.

The whole position of secondary education in this country, however, was revolutionised by the Education Act, 1902. Prior to the establishment of the Board of Education by the Act of 1899, Catholic secondary schools could not secure assistance from public funds, except indirectly. The Science and Art Department, South Kensington, which was merged in the Board of Education by the 1899 Act, made grants to schools in respect of science classes held therein. As a secondary school provided science classes, it was possible for it to obtain grants in this way. Similarly, under the Technical Education Act, 1889, County Councils were empowered to give grants to schools for courses in general education in preparation for technical education, and were entrusted with the disbursement of the "whiskey" money, the results of a tax on spirits allocated for educational purposes. Some Catholic schools received small grants and allowances for scholarship holders under this category. Direct grants from the Board of Education began in 1901, whilst the 1902 Act committed the oversight of secondary education within their areas to county councils and county boroughs, empowering both to spend money on the provision of secondary schools, and to aid voluntary secondary schools already in existence. As these authorities also control elementary education, it was possible for them by means of scholarship schemes to build a ladder from the elementary schools by way of the secondary schools to the university.

As soon as the 1902 Act came into force, it resulted, especially in the large towns, in the establishment of many municipal day secondary schools, both for boys and girls, financed, apart from fees, entirely by public funds, taxes and rates. At first local education authorities for higher education used sparingly the *power* of aiding voluntary secondary schools conferred by the Act. Catholics, therefore, found themselves at a disadvantage in establishing day secondary schools, as they received only the Board of Education grant and fees towards their support, whereas the municipal secondary schools had in addition large subsidies from the rates. To make matters worse, during Mr. Reginald McKenna's tenure of the office of President of the Board of Education, as has already been mentioned, the Board's secondary school grant regulations were amended in a manner which proved a great obstacle to the development of Catholic secondary schools until they were modified some ten years later.

Since 1902, a large number of Catholic day secondary schools, both for boys and girls, have been opened, mainly in the large towns, by the initiative of the secular clergy or religious communities such as the Society of Jesus, the Salesian Fathers, the Marist Fathers, the Brothers of the Christian Schools, the Xaverian Brothers, the Irish Christian Brothers, the Sisters of Notre Dame, the Faithful Companions of Jesus, the Society of the Sacred Heart, the Ursulines, Sisters of Mercy, Sisters of the Sainte Union and others. Nearly one hundred such schools are recognised as efficient by the Board of Education, two-thirds of which are upon its grant list and one-half receive a certain amount of aid from local authorities. Unfortunately, in the Education Act, 1902, these authorities were given a *power* not a *duty* of making such grants, the reason for this distinction being that twenty-seven years ago many endowed schools did not require much assistance from the rates. Few authorities have so far used the power generously. London, Birmingham, Bradford, Middlesex, and Cardiff have adopted the deficiency grant system, the most equitable arrangement for these schools : others make a capitation grant, generally comparing unfavourably with the cost per pupil to the rates in municipal schools in the same area : a third section vote a lump sum grant, similar in character : and many make no grant at all. In recent years, frequent representations on this inequality of treatment have been made both to the Board of Education and to the authorities concerned.

Despite the difficulties under which many of these schools labour, they generally reach a satisfactory standard compared with the municipal schools, for not only do they figure well on university lists in the General School or similar examinations, but many retain satisfactory numbers of pupils for advanced courses for the intermediate degree examinations. In addition to schools recognised by the Board and local authorities, many other efficient Catholic secondary schools exist. The following figures, taken from the returns of the Diocesan Religious Inspectors in the *Catholic Directory*, give the total number of secondary schools by dioceses:

Diocese.	Catholic Secondary Schools.	Pupils.
Westminster	73	8,473
Birmingham	47	4,016
Brentwood	16	3,094
Cardiff	12	1,166
Clifton	16	1,454
Hexham and Newcastle	15	1,705
Lancaster	12	1,021
Leeds	11	2,307
Liverpool	19	5,568
Menevia	12	377
Middlesbrough	12	700
Northampton	27	1,728
Nottingham	13	1,163
Plymouth	19	617
Portsmouth	35	2,568
Salford	25	4,854
Shrewsbury	14	1,363
Southwark	108	12,291
	486	54,465

For the past twenty years, a potent influence in the development of Catholic secondary schools has been the Conferences of Catholic Colleges and of Convent Secondary Schools, the former founded in 1896, the second later, by the late Canon Driscoll, the first headmaster of the Cardinal Vaughan School. These conferences meet annually at different colleges or schools for the consideration of papers on educational subjects, followed by discussion. They have led to common action in the interests of Catholic secondary education, and to the organised teaching of Catholic apologetics in the schools. Under the scheme for the constitution of the Catholic Education Council, the Conference of Catholic Colleges elects twelve members as representatives of secondary schools.

To the religious communities, again to those of women in particular, Catholics are indebted for a large number of special schools for defective children of various types : physically defective, mentally defective, epileptic, blind, deaf and dumb, tubercular, some of which are models of their kind. Similarly they possess a good supply of residential poor law schools, industrial schools, and reformatory schools. More recently, keeping pace with modern medical developments, the school hospital supplying skilled orthopædic treatment for crippled children has been established, two good examples of which may be found at Eastcote and Clacton-on-Sea.

The continued development of Catholic elementary and special schools would have been impossible but for the existence of Catholic training colleges. St. Mary's Training College for men teachers, established at Hammersmith by the Catholic Poor School Committee in 1850 and enlarged upon two occasions, with a final accommodation for 120 students, the only source of supply for Catholic men teachers in this country, was four years ago transferred, as a result of the sale of the old College site and buildings, to Strawberry Hill, Twickenham, originally the home of Horace Walpole and recently the property of the late Lord Mickleham, with thirty acres of ground attached. A substantial addition has been made to the buildings, which now have recognised accommodation for 150 students, with no less than 70 private students in addition from two religious communities, Northern Ireland and Malta. For many years in charge of the secular clergy, the College is now directed by the Vincentian Fathers, owing much in recent years to the ability of its present

Principal, the Rev. J. J. Doyle, D.D., M.A. Mount Pleasant Training College, Liverpool, founded by the Sisters of Notre Dame of Namur in 1856, with accommodation for 20, has developed into one of the most efficient training colleges for women in the country, with extensive buildings and practising school on the same site and direct connection with the University of Liverpool near by. Its marked progress will always be associated with the name of Sister Mary St. Philip, for many years its principal. It has now on its rolls 178 students, of whom 13 last year took a four years' course. Provision for training women teachers has developed much more rapidly than in the case of men teachers, for equally well-equipped colleges have been established for many years by the Society of the Sacred Heart at St. Charles' Square, Kensington (formerly at Wandsworth), for 122 students, and at Newcastle-on-Tyne for 120 students : by the Faithful Companions of Jesus at Sedgley Park, Salford, for 131 students : by the Sisters of Mercy at Hull for 112 students : by the Sisters of the Sainte Union at Southampton for 126 students : and more recently by the Sisters of Charity of St. Paul at Selly Park, Birmingham, for 50 students. All these training colleges are upon the Board of Education's grant list. In addition, the Holy Child Sisters have a small training college for Catholic secondary school teachers in Cavendish Square, London, W., which, so far, has not received assistance from public funds. The above facts show the deep debt of gratitude which the Catholic body owes to the religious communities for the continued existence and development of their elementary schools.

For university education, Catholic colleges had to depend mainly in the earlier part of the century upon the University of London, then only an examining body.

For many years, Ushaw, Stonyhurst, Downside, and other leading Catholic colleges figured prominently upon its honours lists at the intermediate and degree examinations. Even after religious tests were removed at Oxford and Cambridge, the Hierarchy maintained for many years a prohibition against Catholic students going into residence at these universities. As a result of a widely-signed petition by Catholic laity to the Holy See in 1894, with the support of Cardinal Vaughan, Rome, the following year, authorised the withdrawal of the prohibition, subject to certain arrangements being made to facilitate opportunity for Catholic practice for the Catholic undergraduates and to the Catholic authorities being satisfied that adequate Catholic religious instruction was received by students before entrance. In order to fulfil these conditions, a Catholic Universities Board was constituted by the Hierarchy, charged with the oversight of the necessary arrangements, which included the appointment of a Catholic chaplain for the Catholic undergraduates at each University, and the provision of a private chapel for their use in each case, in which, during term time, conferences on subjects of Catholic interest are held by well-known Catholic preachers. At each university, too, Catholic societies have been formed, which from time to time arrange lectures by Catholics, both clergy and laity, followed by discussion. The secular clergy and the religious orders, who for many years previously prepared their students for the external degrees of the University of London, now avail themselves to a great extent of the advantages offered by the older universities, at which they have founded houses of residence, some officially recognised by the university authorities.

The great extension in secondary education and scholarship schemes, following the application of the

Education Act, 1902, has also led to considerable development in the younger universities. The organisation of the internal side of London University in 1900, and the establishment of universities at various centres in the provinces, have brought university education more readily within the reach of Catholics who ordinarily would not have been able to undertake the expense of a degree course at Oxford or Cambridge. At each of the younger universities, largely owing to the advocacy in recent years of the Rev. C. C. Martindale, S.J., a Catholic University Society has been formed for the purpose of uniting Catholic students, with a local priest serving as chaplain, all of which are associated by means of a Federation of Catholic University Societies, which publishes a quarterly magazine, holds an annual conference, and sends delegates to the International Federation of such societies, the Pax Romana. The latter last year actually held its annual conference at Cambridge, under the presidency of Professor Edward Bullough, honoured by the presence of a Prince of the Church, the Cardinal Archbishop of Westminster, and attended by nearly three hundred delegates from various parts of Europe, a significant note of development in the year preceding the centenary. The wide-spread character of the Catholic University Society movement in this country may be gathered from the existence of local organisations at Aberystwith, Bangor, Birmingham, Bristol, Cambridge, Durham, Leeds, Liverpool, London, Manchester, Nottingham, Oxford, Reading, Sheffield and Southampton.

No retrospect of Catholic educational progress during the past hundred years would be complete without some reference to the work of the Catholic Poor School Committee and its successor since 1904, the Catholic Education Council, reconstructed to cope with the new situation created by the Education Act, 1902. This organisation, both in its earlier and later forms, has been an advisory body to the Hierarchy on all matters relating to elementary schools and training colleges, and, later, secondary schools as well. It has always been recognised by the Committee of the Privy Council, and by the Board of Education, as the agent of Catholic managers and governors in any difficulties arising in the administration of the Education Acts as affecting Catholic schools. Supported by an annual collection in all churches by direction of the Bishops, it makes grants to Catholic training colleges, towards the cost of religious inspection, towards struggling private primary schools not receiving assistance from public funds, and towards travelling expenses of children in scattered districts to the nearest Catholic school. It also acts as a bureau of information and advice for Catholic managers. These services, as can be imagined, have been at times invaluable to the Catholic body. Founded in 1847, and reconstituted in 1904, its principal officers have been :—*Chairmen* : Hon. Charles Langdale, 1847–68 ; Lord Howard of Glossop, 1868–77; the Marquess of Ripon, 1877–85 ; the Duke of Norfolk, 1885–1917; Mr. W. Fitzherbert Brockholes, 1917–20 ; Sir John Gilbert, 1920–7 ; and Mr. F. N. Blundell, M.P., since 1927. *Secretaries* : Mr. S. Nasmyth Stokes, 1847–53 ; Mr. T. W. Allies, 1853–90 ; Mr. W. M. Hunnybun, 1890–1905 ; Sir Francis Anderton, 1905–27 ; Sir John Gilbert since 1927. By common consent, one name outstands. For nearly fifty years the late Duke of Norfolk was the leader in all Catholic lay effort on behalf of Catholic schools, a tower of strength in every way, the value of whose assistance to progress achieved it would be difficult to overstate.

REFERENCES

Reports of Catholic Poor School Committee and Catholic Education Council.

Board of Education Reports.

Catholic Directories.

Catholic Encyclopædia, Schools in England, Rev. M. Maher, S.J.

Sequel to Catholic Emancipation, Bishop Ward.

Life of Cardinal Vaughan, J. G. Snead-Cox.

History of Elementary Education, C. Birchenough.

Secondary Education in XIXth Century, R. L. Archer.

NOTE

The above retrospect deals only with education directly or indirectly connected with the national system of education.

J. G.

THE CATHOLIC CHURCH AND LITERATURE

BY ALGERNON CECIL

IV

THE CATHOLIC CHURCH AND LITERATURE

ANY discussion of the relations between the Church and Literature falls, obviously and conveniently enough, under one of two headings. There is to be considered the attitude of the Church to the Literature that is peculiarly her own—to the Divine Library (Bibliotheca Divina) as St. Jerome named it—and to all manner of commentaries upon it; and there is also to be considered the attitude of the Church towards the great pagan literature that she found and towards the great secular literature, often of mixed origin and mixed tendency, that has come into being during her age-long attempt to restore all things in Christ. Such a discussion, ranging over the events of nearly two milleniums and conditioned by a thousand considerations of period and place, can only be fruitful if we are content to treat it on the largest lines, to recognise that the mission of the Church is not only to the wise but also to the unwise, and that, apart from *ex cathedra* definitions of faith and morals, she claims no more for the decisions of her ministers than is implied in that rendering of honour to whom honour is due, of which St. Paul spoke and which St. Peter would have us extend, presumably according to the measure of a man's office and knowledge, to all men whatsoever. Mistakes in regard to literature and learning, of which the world has never forgotten one, have doubtless been made by Church authorities; and, whatever may fairly be urged in favour of the Roman Inquisitors on the ground of insufficient evidence at the time,[1] or possibly, as it may appear now, of the metaphysical implications of Einstein's theory of relativity,[2] there is still reason to regret the condemnation of Galileo. But, when all has been said, there remains a great commonsense to be appreciated in the bearing of the Church authorities towards the problems of thought and the expression of them ; and because a great commonsense, therefore a great humanity. We can see this at once as regards the Scriptures, if we are willing to concede that the continuous purpose of the Church was to give them protection against rash or paradoxical or political usage ; and we can see it again as regards secular literature, if we are ready to admit that the perpetual purification of Christian civilisation from alien and antagonistic influences was legitimately the Church's concern. There has been no real difference of principle in these matters between the attitude of the Church towards the household of faith and the attitude of the Englishman in his most religious post-Reformation phases towards his family. Each discovers a solicitude to maintain the divinity that hedges in the Bible ; and in each there is to be found a like desire to put a ban upon books that inculcate spiritual error. We may detect exaggeration in such a theory of verbal inspiration as Protestantism once proclaimed, and find entertainment in the mutability of standards, which could evoke from Miss Broughton the remark that she had begun as Zola and ended as Miss Yonge, but these, if we will, crude efforts to give the Bible a unique position and to keep fiction free from taint should be proof enough that the more discreet attempt of the Catholic Church to safeguard the honour of Scripture and the purity of faith and ethics is in the same line of conduct with much that is instinctive in those who like her least.

[1] *Cf.* Huxley, *Life and Letters*, ii, p. 113.
[2] See Nordmann, *Einstein and the Universe*, p. 26.

To these general considerations may fairly be added another which, if it were more usually apprehended, must tend towards the removal of whole mountains of prejudice. The notion that the Church is essentially obscurantist could hardly survive if her philosophy were generally familiar. No theory of knowledge has, in fact, ever presented a nobler conception of the intellect, or attached greater weight to the claims of evidence than hers. According to Catholic epistemology, the intellect lies open to the light of truth, " sees," as we say, " straight," and does not of itself lapse into error. If error occurs, we must recognise that, as the scholastics argued, it comes accidentally (*per accidens*)—is, in fact, the result of some intrusion of the will, of some delusive association of ideas, of some indolent neglect to apply the tests of reason to each separate step in an argument, or, perhaps, of what we can only describe by analogy as a blind spot in the eye of the mind. The intellect, as God made it and meant it, is within its limitations utterly trustworthy—a sound organ, well-conceived; and the evidence admitted at this bar of judgment should furnish, according to its measure and cogency, the sure criterion of truth.

Obscurantism, then, if we mean by it any depreciation of reason or disregard of evidence, is no feature of the mind of the Church; and, in every case where it is alleged, we might do wisely to make certain at the outset that we do not accuse those of darkening counsel whose real purpose is to insist upon a fullness of demonstration that leaves no place of entry for paradox or prejudice.

. . . . .

The Church, it has been somewhere said, came into the world with a book in her hand, but that book not the Bible. The fact, if its significance had been appreciated in this country, should have saved much disastrous controversy and all the vain endeavour to set up the divine literature as a rival authority to the divine community. The Hebrew Scriptures were indeed there from the first, although with their canon still indeterminate; but the Church had yet to create a literature specifically her own and to recognise where the wind of divine inspiration, bending the frail reeds of Humanity to its purpose, had drawn from them heavenly music. There was an identity of origin and a difference of character between the new literature and the old; and the difference, as well as the identity, had consequences worth observing. The Old Testament is plainly the history of a nation; the New the biography of a Person. But this is not all. In the history of the Chosen People, with its constant exhibition by precept and example of the conditions upon which alone a society may hope to maintain itself in health, the whole nature of Man—of man in his unregenerate, fallen state—is analysed and displayed. To this end an almost, or quite exhaustive number of literary forms are utilised. By chronicle and narrative, by statute and commentary, by pastoral idyll and canticle of love; by parable and sermon, dialogue and drama, proverb and aphorism, chant and psalm; by prophecy and apocalypse; by poetry—epic, lyric, elegiac; and, as if to leave no manner untried, by that strange *journal intime* attributed to the wisest of kings which takes us through all the disillusionments and disappointments of the man of the world to the threshold of the house of God—by each and all of these the tale of human nature is unfolded. Sometimes with great tenderness, sometimes with sorrow and indignation, sometimes with satire and sarcasm, the divine afflatus, penetrating where it lists, has laid bare the spirit of man, so noble (as Pascal has told us in immortal words) and yet so base, so luminous and yet so blind, potentially so holy and yet, on occasion, if we track it to its darkest recesses, so ineffably foul. Here is a strange story—full of wonder and terror. Shall we say that it is always without discrimination for every eye?

Contrast it for a moment with the new biographical literature with which the Church united it. There all is sweetness, even in sorrow, and fullness of light, even against a background of uncomprehending darkness. Not upon all Humanity but upon One Figure only is the eye of the reader fixed; and that Figure His who called Himself both the Son of God and of Man. In four biographies, in a dozen commentaries and studies, in a mystical vision of His Kingdom militant and triumphant, the Person of Christ is discovered in all its meaning. Are we not bound to make sure that every eye shall see at least its outline, not deflected by polemics, but as it was handed down by those who first beheld Him?

The Church, confronted with the charge of these two literatures—the one inherited, the other specifically her own—acted with a wisdom that, if all these things had not been so prejudiced by controversy, might perhaps have been styled consummate. Without forcing the pace or causing offence to Jewish prejudices she raised the books of the New Testament to the same level of honour as the Old, and in the fullness of time, focussed the attention of the Christian believer upon them by drawing as a general rule both parts of the Scripture read at Mass from their pages. Then, in an appropriate hour, the Pope of the day commissioned the best scholar of the time to prepare by revision and comparison of texts such a version of the Bible in the vulgar tongue, so far as the world could be said to have one, as might merit the stamp of authority; and this St. Jerome, with manuscripts before him that no longer survive, in a grand manner accomplished. The canon of Scripture was not, however, closed, nor did the Church close it for a long while afterwards. But, when at Trent, more than eleven centuries later, the tale of the sacred books was exactly told, the Tridentine Fathers significantly avoided the curious error of leaving a long gap of empty God-forsaken years between the Old and New Testaments. Discontinuity —the idea of a discontinuity of divine inspiration or spiritual guidance—would appear on the face of it to be one of the surest marks of unhistorical Christianity ; and the recognition of the Alexandrian canon of the Jewish Scriptures (or, which is the same thing, of the so-called Apocrypha) is not only in line with the practice of Our Lord but indicates incidentally the historical sense of the Catholic Church.

The book which was thus finally consolidated and to which in this its Vulgate rendering a guarantee (not, indeed, as is sometimes ignorantly supposed, of absolute textual accuracy, but of authentic substance and freedom from mistakes calculated to cause error in doctrine or ethics [1]) was ultimately accorded at Trent, satisfied the needs of Latin Christianity in the Dark Ages. The treasures of Scripture lay open ; and men were free to take of them what they would and could. New problems, however, were bound to emerge as time went on, as new nations grew into being or were brought into Christendom, and as Latin itself became the exclusive property of the educated few. We find these difficuties troubling the peace of the two greatest of the mediaeval Popes. Though vernacular offices and a vernacular translation of part of the Bible into Slavonic had had a place in the conversion of the Slav peoples, we find Gregory VII in 1079, not perhaps without an

---

[1] The reader will find Vega's contemporary explanation of the intention of the Tridentine decree conveniently set out in Mgr. Forbes's article in *The Bible : its History, Authenticity and Authority* (Sands, 1926), p. 123.

eye upon the indeterminate position of the Slav countries between the Roman and Byzantine civilisations, resisting any further advance in that direction, on the ground that it would lead on to a demand for a Slavonic Bible and this in its turn to irreverence and error amongst those whose learning was too little not to be dangerous. And a hundred years later or more we find Innocent III, confronted with the socially subversive interpretations of Scripture of the Waldensians, wrestling with the dilemma—which his letters on the subject enforce by the ancient and authoritative admonition not to cast pearls before swine—that, on the one hand, " the desire of understanding holy Scriptures and zeal for exhorting in accordance with them, is not to be reprehended but rather commended " and, on the other, that " the secret mysteries of the faith ought not to be explained to all men in all places, since they cannot be everywhere understood by all men, but only to those who can conceive them with a faithful mind."

There precisely lay the difficulty, accentuated—tremendously accentuated—by the fact that in that still illiterate age the dissemination of the Bible meant in practice for the most part the dissemination of isolated words or passages which were learnt and quoted without their historical context or their complementary setting. About such as use Scripture so, earnest and honest souls as they doubtless often are, it is a great Anglican bishop and scholar who has said the last word ;—

It may be objected that devout students of the Bible have often proved the sternest fanatics. But the answer is easy. They were fanatics because they were students not of the whole Bible but of some fragment of it to which all else was sacrificed.[1]

There were Catholics in the Middle Ages, like the

[1] Westcott, *The Bible in the Church*, p. 13.

Brethren of the Common Life, who saw all that was to
be said for disseminating the Scriptures broadcast, and
other Catholics, like the bishops of the South of France
and North of Spain, who saw all that was to be said
against it; and these two schools could alike find support in Innocent's classical letter on the subject. Time
and place and circumstance govern such matters as they
govern other similar matters in secular statesmanship;
and we shall, perhaps, not feel, on any large view of the
subject, that it is of vital consequence to our philosophy
whether those Bibles " fair " and " old " and " written
in English " to whose existence in the hands of " good
and Catholic folk " Blessed Thomas More bears witness
in his Dialogue, were, as Cardinal Gasquet supposes, of
Catholic origin or, as Miss Deanesly maintains, no more
than " the Wycliffite text with the prologue omitted." [1]

Englishmen might judge the whole question more
easily if they could rid themselves of the belief that
Rome has cause to fear a dispassionate study of the Bible.
On the main issues between Catholicism and Protestantism she had in point of fact everything to gain from it.
No reasonable man who regards the Old Testament as
the Word of God can possibly suppose that a hierarchy
or sacrifice or ritual is displeasing to the Deity; no
Christian who calmly considers the terms of the Petrine
commission is likely to relieve himself of the suspicion
that Christ would never have delivered those tremendous
words if they were to serve no better purpose than to
mislead the most part of Christendom for fifteen centuries; nor, again, is a candid examination of the sixth
chapter of St. John's Gospel calculated to encourage the
opinion that the doctrine of transubstantiation is a fable
fondly imagined. It was not of the trained legal intelligence of More or the finely balanced criticism of

[1] Deanesly, *The Lollard Bible*, p. 15.

Erasmus that the Church had good reason to be afraid, but of those whose judgment was warped by partial or political or acquisitive aims. We are too far removed from Waldensians and Lollards and Fifth Monarchy Men to regard their ideas with anything but a mild surprise, but if we come into contact with the agitator who exhibits Christ as a wild revolutionary, the Communist who, with a sublime disregard of the point of the story of Ananias and Saphira, affirms that the New Testament is opposed to private property, or the Christian Scientist who deludes the credulous into neglecting the aid of the skilled physician, we may begin to see how difficult is this question of placing a book, invested with divine authority, at the mercy of every private interpreter.

Interrogate the evidence that hits us, as the phrase is, in the eye, when we look at the empty niches or defaced screens of the old English Cathedrals, of what the Puritans with their zeal made of the First (or, as the Anglican Table has it, of the Second) Commandment; consider the joyless Sabbaths which the Evangelicals with their piety substituted for the Christian Sunday ; deplore that loss of *joie de vivre*, which, as Mill observes, is always to be found where the wave of Puritanism has passed ; or, again, take that passage at the beginning of " The Light that Failed " where one of the great masters of English fiction and English psychology has sketched the character of Dick Heldar's doubtless well-meaning guardian [1]; and what dangerous catchwords the " Open Bible" and the private interpretation of it begin to appear!

[1] " Her religion, manufactured in the main by her own intelligence and a keen study of the Scriptures, was an aid to her in this matter (viz. the home-training of Dick Heldar). At such times as she herself was not personally displeased with Dick, she left him to understand that he had a heavy account to settle with his Creator ; wherefore Dick learned to loathe his God as intensely as he loathed Mrs. Jennett ; and this is not a wholesome frame of mind for the young."

"It was noticeable," says the same great novelist just quoted, in speaking of two army chaplains, " that whenever the Church of England dealt with a human problem she was very likely to call in the Church of Rome." [1] And it is precisely a problem in humanity, not an academical thesis, that we have to do with here. Talk as we may about the advantages of the open Bible, nothing is more apparent than that the Bible makes large demands in respect of historical perspective and religious thought before we begin to understand it, nothing is written larger upon the face of history than the necessity of protecting young, ignorant, and, in periods or countries of small education, even average Humanity, from the singular constructions that private persons read into its teaching. The policy of the Church in dealing with the problem was to insure that the milk of the Word should be taken before the meat. This was the extent of her offence—or, as some may think, the measure of her wisdom.

The mission of the Church, as we have to remember if we would understand all her mind, was both to the wise and the unwise, the learned and the ignorant ; and from both she asked the same thing—that regard for established, authoritative judgments which is the beginning of scholarship and the first condition of receptiveness in the study of all great works of literature or, for that matter, of art. Of the student, indeed, she asked something more than this temperamental conservatism. Of him she required a thoroughness of investigation and fullness of deliberation that left no place for the mere pleasure of saying some new thing. Paradox had no charm for her, nor platitude any terrors. She saw no reason to suppose that the latest opinion embodied of necessity the soundest knowledge. Her aim was truth,

[1] *Kim*, by Rudyard Kipling.

not novelty; and she moved, in consequence, if she moved at all, only by the slowest steps, insisting at every turn upon the most rigorous proof and the most rounded conclusions.

These things again have been made a reproach to her, and with a certain fatuity the World has assumed that in every " conflict with Rome " the rebels are in the right. To discuss distant controversies lies beyond the limitations of this paper; let one controversy, and that the most recent, suffice to point the moral of all. The tale of the Modernist Movement is now a story of twenty years standing; and the very names of its protagonists are beginning to be forgotten. Yet in its time it was supposed to threaten the Church with disruption, and there were those, doubtless, who thought to see in it the day of her final visitation.

The Movement had both its critical—or perhaps more accurately higher-critical—and its philosophical sides. The former was concerned with the authenticity of Scripture in general and of the Pentateuch in particular; the latter appeared to be content to throw writers, records, divine inspiration and attested fact into a melting-pot out of which the Christian believer might extract what comfort he could from the conception of truth as an evolutionary flux and of dogma as a mixed blend of fact and fiction. There was a distinction to be drawn between the temper of the more moderate critics and that of the more advanced philosophers—a distinction conveniently reflected for us in the memorials on the one hand of the late Baron Friedrich von Hügel, of whom none that knew him will care to speak without giving God thanks for the existence of so grandly generous a soul, and, on the other, of Father George Tyrrell. This distinction was not neglected by the ecclesiastical authorities.

A Biblical Commission was appointed to consider certain exegetical and critical issues raised by the progress of the Higher Criticism. Its conclusions, whilst they did not promote the theory of verbal inspiration, were in the main conservative as regards the vexed question of the authorship of the Pentateuch and consequently failed to satisfy certain Catholic students, of whom Baron von Hügel was one. An exchange of letters on the subject took place between him and Dr. Briggs, a Protestant scholar, interested in Christian reunion and the recipient of a personal assurance from the Pope that the findings of the Commission would bear no infallible character.[1] Nothing, in fact, in the attitude of the Church authorities towards the issue was in conflict with the principle of sufficient evidence; nor have they in the past, as the controversies concerning the authenticity of the Areopagite writings and of the text relating to the Three Heavenly witnesses show,[2] ultimately resisted the considered pressure of Catholic scholarship. " Even now," as the Baron rather unkindly points out in his letter to Dr. Briggs, " Catholics have not had any solemn condemnation of Pentateuchal criticism and the Protestant Churches have had three." [3]

Most of us, Catholic or Protestant, as it is well sometimes to remind ourselves, are in no position to form a valuable or even competent private opinion upon this particular subject at all. Whatever we believe about the matter we have perforce to take from authority. But there has been at least enough contradiction of the Higher Criticism in the evidence of the Monuments to

[1] Briggs and Von Hügel, *The Papal Commission.*
[2] On this see, for example, Dr. Arendzen's remarks on pp. 52, 53 of *The Bible : its History, Authenticity and Authority.*
[3] Briggs and Von Hügel, *The Papal Commission and the Pentateuch*, p. 56. The three solemn condemnations referred to are those of Colenso, Robertson-Smith, and Briggs himself.

give us pause, and enough variety in the ideas of the Higher Critics to make us recall the advice of one of the most saintly and scholarly of the Deans of St. Paul's [1] not to make the mistake of supposing that a position assailed is a position lost. The Church, desiring to prove all things and to hold fast that which is true, has done no otherwise.

The Biblical Commission had dealt, not without respect, with Modernist criticism. The philosophy of Modernism, striking as it did at the vital distinction between fact and fiction, claimed the notice of a higher authority. Disappointed in many things, the Modernists had been fortunate in one. Fogazzaro, in a novel that ran through Europe, had attempted to confound the Curia with the conception of a saint ; and behold a saint, so far, at least, as common opinion could make him one, sat upon the throne of St. Peter. The life of Pius X has lately been written by M. René Bazin and included in that series of biographies which enforces its title of " Les Grands Cœurs " with the inscription " C'est le propre des grands cœurs de découvrir le principal besoin des temps où ils vivent et de s'y consacrer." Let those who make of human character a royal road to judgment, look first upon the portrait there depicted and then turn back to the volumes in which Miss Maud Petre has described the turgid career of Father Tyrrell ; and they will be at no loss to know what Modernism was not and what it was. Not, of course, that a reasoned answer to that strange attempt to discredit objective truth is wanting ! He who runs may read it in his own common-sense ; and he who stays to ponder in the famous Encyclical *Pascendi*, where also there is presented a statement of the heretical position so scrupulously fair as to draw from Tyrrell himself the remark that, if one

[1] R. W. Church.

had not known the author of this exposition of Modernism for a subtle scholastic, one might have been tempted to take him for "a traitor in the orthodox camp."[1] It is superfluous, however, to labour the hopelessness of a position, whose intellectual defects were apparent, not only to the Pope, but even to such rationalists as Dr. Rashdall and Dr. Inge,[2] and whose chief apology has been disproved by the recent revival of scholastic philosophy in France under the leadership of M. Maritain.

It is time to pass on to the second division of the subject : the relations between the Church and secular literature. To the present writer at all events there seem to be few more extraordinary delusions than the popular belief that ecclesiastical influence operates to cramp high imagination and fetter the flights of the human spirit. Let those who doubt the capacity of Catholicism to fill the soul with the richest flowers of beauty take their stand above Florence, on the hill of San Miniato or of Bellosguardo, and, as they gaze at that purest and most marvellous product of the ecclesiastical civilisation of the Middle Age and review in thought all that it signifies and all that it contains, ask themselves in all candour whether there exists anything with which it may be compared, unless it be the lost splendour of ancient Athens. The weight of intellectual strength and æsthetic talent that lies concentrated in that single city is enough to make ridiculous the ignoble efforts of those who delve in mediæval morasses in the hope of covering the mediæval Church in mud. Only let a man take the highway along the hill-tops and all the richness of that time will spread out before him.

We are concerned in particular with Literature. It is

---

[1] *Times*, Sept. 30, 1907.
[2] See for Dr. Inge, *The Quarterly Review*, April 1909, pp. 571–603.

the great Florentine poet who lays bare the ultimate motive of all Christian writing, however imperfectly it be realised in practice ; who speaks of that new style wherein thoughts are set forth under the inspiration of love or, as the commentator has it, wherein we seek, not to say things beautifully, but to say beautiful things truly.[1] It is Dante again who, in passage after passage of trenchant criticism of Popes and Cardinals, shows how free was opinion to rebuke sin in high places, how clear was the distinction in the mediæval mind between the great seats of spiritual authority and those who filled them and—it might perhaps be fair to add—how little the authorities themselves resented attacks upon their order as distinct from attacks upon Christ and the Church. It is in Dante again that we may see, as well by the strange intermixture of Pagan and Christian figures as in the more definitely philosophical parts of the poem, how liberally the Church had, in the long run, dealt with the wisdom of the pagan world ; pondering it, purifying it, reconciling it to herself—a thing, now that it has been done, seemingly obvious and simple, but at the time requiring so remarkable a largeness of mind as to reduce to absurdity the charge that the Church is by nature narrow or intolerant. Where, as in the universities, there existed a fair field for study and combatants with head-pieces sufficient for the fray, there is, indeed, evidence enough to show that theological discussion was free and comprehensive. Consider St. Thomas's treatment of a familiar problem. " It seems that God does not exist," says the disputant in the Summa, " because . . . if . . . God existed, there would be no evil discoverable ;

[1] Purg. xxiv. 52–4 :

> Ed io a lui : " Io mi son un che quando
> Amor mi spira, noto, ed a quel modo
> Che ditta dentro, vo significando.

93

but there is evil in the world. Therefore God does not exist." [1] Forcible repressions of opinion certainly occur, but during the Middle Ages only, as Acton has been at some pains to point out,[2] where the safety of Society or the State was held to be endangered. And there in all ages we must expect to find them.

The Reformation introduced a new state of affairs. There was civil war in Christendom—a civil war whose drums and trumpets are still too often heard. The breach of Christian unity, against which it was of the very essence of Catholicism to contend to the last, brought in its train the hard necessities of warfare. The censorship which had originally come to the Church through the State and had in a measure entered into its ecclesiastical system at the Council of Nicæa stiffened into the Roman Index. So also in England the Anglican Church, at the very moment when, under Elizabeth and Charles I, it was, as some of its most ardent members consider, most truly, itself, adopted, owing to a like pressure of circumstance, the drastic expedient of the Court of High Commission. And in each case the motive of the authorities was doubtless the same—an anxiety, not as to the soundness of their cause but as to the sufficiency of public knowledge to discredit the criticism of it. Nobody, of course, can estimate how much was lost to literature by these alarms. But the words of Erasmus, who was anything but blind to the faults of the Catholic clergy, may well indicate in what direction judgment should lean throughout that long, disastrous era of internecine war in Christendom, the beginning of which he saw and deprecated: "I abhor the Evangelics

---

[1] I owe this illustration to Mr. Cecil Chesterton, whom I recollect to have heard use it many years ago. I have shortened the stages of the argument. It will be found in full in the *Summa Theologica*, Part I, Q. II.

[2] Acton, *History of Freedom*, p. 150.

because it is through them that Literature is everywhere declining and upon the point of perishing." [1]

In England, at all events, it would appear to be true to say that the operation of the Penal Laws, rather than any repressive attitude on the part of the Roman Curia, took from English Catholics for a time their power to " pull their weight " in the majestic galley which carries the genius of Humane Letters down the stream of time. They did not fail their country in literature between the Reformation and the Revolution, nor have they done so from the era of Catholic Emancipation onwards till the present day. Even if we dismiss as unsubstantial the shadowy claim of Catholicism—not, however, as two distinguished Catholic writers of the last century, Richard Simpson and W. S. Lilly, have shown without its curious plausibilities—to possess the soul of Shakespeare, [2] no one will challenge the Catholic title to Southwell and to Crashaw ; delicate spirits, holding open, amid the fierce warfare of their time, the fast-closing door between England and the Holy See. Before that door was finally closed the Church could point to greater names than these. Dryden was hers by good conviction, [3] and Pope by right of birth. And to Dryden, it has been said by one high authority, that " the debt of later English prose is inestimable," [4] and of Pope, by another, that " with him the classical spirit in English poetry reached its acme." [5]

These debts of English Letters were, unfortunately, repaid by the maintenance in England of a penal code

---

[1] Quoted in the *Encycl. Brit.* article on Erasmus. *Cf.* his observation in Ep. mvi : " The triumph of the Lutherans is the death of good learning. Wealth and wives are their real objects "

[2] See W. S. Lilly, *Studies in Religion and Literature*, i.

[3] Those who doubt it should look at the late Sir Adolphus Ward's observations on the point (*Camb. Hist. of English Literature*, viii. pp. 45–47).

[4] *Camb. Hist. of Engl. Lit.*, viii. p. 56.   [5] *Ibid.* ix. p. 89.

described by the late Regius Professor of Modern
History at Oxford [1] as " not much less atrocious " than
that Irish code which Burke characterised as " a machine
of wise and elaborate contrivance . . . as well fitted for
the oppression, impoverishment and degradation of a
people and the debasement in them of human nature
itself as ever proceeded from the perverted ingenuity of
man." [2]   In the circumstances Catholics may be excused
if they had little to show during that time in a sphere
where education means so much and love of England
so much more.   As soon as the ban was removed, the
old intellectual vitality of English Catholicism burst out
again.   Lingard, indeed, had led the revival of Catholic
letters in this country, even before it was due, by the
massive volumes in which, with an admirable freedom
from bitterness, he told the story of the Reformation
as it really was—volumes which themselves were a
marked influence in promoting the cause of Emancipation and upon which an authority whose dispassionate-
ness will not be called in dispute was able, nearly a
century later, to pass this judgment :

It is not unjust . . . to say that the history of the Reformation, or that of a particularly complicated section of it,
was never written with more discretion than it was by him.
On the one hand he refused to shut his eyes, like some other
judges of conservative tendencies, to certain aspects of the
conflict—the dark side of monasticism, for instance.   On
the other he declined to launch forth into discussions of the
general consequences of the English Reformation. [3]

The book was attacked, as any good book on a
controversial subject is pretty sure to be, from both sides
—by Anglicans like Southey, eager to prove the Church
of England all they took it for, and Catholics like

[1] Prof. H. C. Davis.   [2] See the *Camb. Modern Hist.*, x. p. 620.
[3] Sir A. W. Ward, *Camb. Hist. of Engl. Lit.*, xiv. p. 55.

Bishop Milner, who wished to make out the pre-Reformation Church in England purer than it was. Yet it served to vindicate the capacity of Catholics to write accurate and dispassionate history and, incidentally, through the refusal of the Roman authorities to condemn it at Milner's instance,[1] the desire of the Papacy that history should be so written.

This honourable effort to extenuate nothing that deserves to be condemned in the chronicles of Catholicism was apparent, almost to a fault, in the life and writings of the eminent and learned Acton. There was an entertaining humour in his protest that a great Anglican bishop [2] had, in his " History of the Papacy," let the Popes off too lightly. Certainly, Acton, with his stern resolve to bring the rulers of every Christian century, without extenuation of circumstance, before the bar of Christian ethics, and his scrupulous fear, so eloquently confessed in a fine fragment of his writing,[3] of unduly favouring his compatriots or co-religionists, was in no position to throw his mind into the common stock and afford to English Catholics just the kind of assistance which, at the moment, would have been most acceptable to them. Yet in the retrospect—if I may be allowed here to discharge a personal obligation—there seem to me to have been, within living memory, few more cogently persuasive careers than his. Here was one acutely sensitive to every lapse from charity and freedom on the great stage of ecclesiastical affairs. Here was one of whom it might have been said, as it was said of Friedrich von Hügel, that he gave one the idea of being ready to follow truth wherever he found it. Here was one whose first considerable literary enterprise—" a

---

[1] *Camb. Hist. Engl. Lit.*, xiv: p. 56.   [2] Creighton.

[3] The document found amongst his papers after his death in which he gives in an imaginative form the ideals at which he aimed. It will be found on pp. xxxviii and xxxix of the volume called *The History of Freedom*.

quarterly," it has been claimed, " far surpassing, alike in knowledge, range and certainty any of the other quarter-lies, political or ecclesiastical, or specialist which the nineteenth century produced " [1]—had failed, not indeed, as has been alleged, owing to any direct censure from Rome, but through a certain temerity or want of tact which obscured the real service it was rendering to English Catholicism by its frankly dispassionate treat-ment of matters hitherto discoloured by apology. Here was one, again, who had spent his strength in opposing the Infallibility decree of 1870 in the, as time proved, totally erroneous conviction that it would promote political to the prejudice of spiritual influences in the policy of the Vatican. And yet here, too, was one who could write that " knowledge has a freedom in the Catholic Church which it can find in no other religion " [2]; who could say that he had never thought of doubting any one of the Church's dogmas ; who could protest that the Catholic Communion was dearer to him than life itself ? [3] No recent career in this country so well exemplifies the ultimate compatibility between the nobler meanings of liberty and authority ; none shows more clearly that, with men of the finest intellect and fullest knowledge, an Englishman's cult of freedom is no invincible bar to Catholic unity as Rome conceives it.

Between these two great historians there towers, in order of time, the figure of Newman. His vital con-tribution to the truth of history had indeed been antici-pated, though in a purely intellectual manner, by Gibbon who, with a flash of genius altogether extraordinary at that time in England, had as a boy perceived the

---

[1] *The Home and Foreign Review. Cf.* with this estimate of its value by Figgis and Laurence that of Matthew Arnold : " Perhaps in no organ of criti-cism in this country was there so much knowledge, so much play of mind " (quoted in *Lord Acton and his Circle*, p. lxxvii).

[2] *History of Freedom*, p. 461.   [3] *Ibid*. p. xxvi.

historical fallacy in the Anglican position and caused a priest to receive him into the Catholic Church. Newman repeated the discovery but invested it, as it deserves, with all the charm of poetry. Intent, as his early intimates knew,[1] upon the quest of Christianity in its first beginnings, he gradually realised that the original design and essential features of the Primitive Church must be sought, not through any imagined reconstruction of the sixteenth century, vitiated inevitably as this must be by a thousand anachronisms, but rather by penetrating to the core of the only existing fabric possessed both of unassailable antiquity and unbroken development. He set forth the philosophy of organic evolution as applied to the idea of a historic church in his Essay on Development ; all the romance of his quest appeared later in his famous " Apologia."

The two essential qualities of Catholic Literature, as of all literature that deserves to move the spirit of man, are truth and beauty ; and Cardinal Newman, by virtue of his singular gifts stands between those, like Lingard and Acton (and, one might add, his own scrupulous biographer, Wilfrid Ward) who reflect Catholicism in the mirror of a logical and accurate prose and those who catch its hymns of colour in the poet's prismatic glass. As the Church was well served during the last century by certain pre-eminent lovers of truth, so also by certain pre-eminent votaries of beauty. There was Aubrey de Vere, very much a scholar and very much a gentleman ; there was Faber with his high songs of praise ; there was Coventry Patmore, the poet of married love ; there was Francis Thompson with his mastery of sound and colour ; there were Lionel Johnson and Gerald Manley Hopkins and Alice Meynell. Nor does ability now begin to fail us. Cardinal Gasquet and Dr. Butler

[1] Church, *Occasional Papers*, ii. p. 473.

have their place among English historians. Mr. Belloc takes rank with them and also with such gifted writers of poetry and prose as Mr. Chesterton and Mr. Baring ; whilst to any mention of these three makers of *belles-lettres*, it is obvious to add that of two brilliant dialecticians—Father Knox and Mr. Woodruff. All these—and others I should have liked to name both in England and Ireland—whilst they have done something to restore English literature to its proper place in Catholic civilisation, afford sufficient evidence of the versatility of Catholic writers to convince even the most sceptical that Catholic talent is neither hampered nor constrained. But as to that Father Knox has already said the last word :

> I had been encouraged to suppose and fully prepared to find that the immediate result of submission to Rome would be the sense of having one's liberty cramped and restricted in a number of ways, necessary no doubt to the welfare of the Church at large, but galling to the individual. . . . As I say, I was quite prepared for all this : the curious thing is that my experience has been exactly the opposite. I have been overwhelmed with the feeling of liberty—the glorious liberty of the sons of God.[1]

Doubtless, however, if our critics choose to have it so, Catholic writers are still in a manner circumscribed. When all allowance has been made for individual vagaries and personal idiosyncrasies, they are still bound by order and authority—by the order inherent in beauty and the authority implicit in truth. To them, but with a deeper meaning than the poet dreamed of, it has been whispered that

> Beauty is truth, truth beauty—that is all
> Ye know on earth and all ye need to know.

Shall they, then, be blamed if, in a world confused by

---

[1] *A Spiritual Æneid*, p. 247.

a thousand philosophies and a country rent by ecclesi-astical dissensions, they set forth, with as little challenge as may be, the merits of coherent and lucid thought and of a culture whose monuments are the glory of every art—they, the heirs of all the Christian ages, and their title, if such considerations move us, fully proved by time ?   Shall they not rather be ashamed if they sit all the day silent, nursing in selfish contentment their treasures of truth and beauty ?   Yet, because Truth may come to seem no more than a cold bath of logic and Beauty repel by frozen regularity, the last and loveliest word of all, as between those who find in Catholic literature the true lights of the world and those who take it for a vain phosphorescence cunningly contrived, is Love.

THE CATHOLIC CHURCH AND SCIENCE (1829-1929)

BY Sir BERTRAM C. A. WINDLE, F.R.S., Sc.D., Ph.D., of
St. Michael's College in the University of Toronto

V

THE CATHOLIC CHURCH AND SCIENCE

IT is more than improbable that any living person can remember the time when it was not assumed as a common place that between revealed religion and its exponents on the one hand, and science and its exponents on the other, there at least is—some would say must be—deadly enmity, and, in addition, that the bitterest—again some would say the ablest—opposition to science comes from the Catholic Church. I think that is a fair presentment of what is in the minds of a very large number of English people, readers of the daily paper and perhaps not much else, who think about the matter at all.

Was that the state of mind one hundred years ago? If not, how and why did such a state of affairs as we see to-day come into existence? Those are the chief questions with which this article will concern itself.

For the position one hundred years ago we have fortunately excellent evidence, for it was in 1835, which is quite sufficiently near to our date of commencement, that Wiseman—then Rector of the English College at Rome—delivered in the hall of the Palazzo of Cardinal Weld in Rome his course of lectures on " Science and Revealed Religion," which received so much attention and ran through several editions after publication. That which I have at my side is the fourth (English) Edition and appeared in 1851. It is described as by Cardinal Wiseman, for such he was at the time, having become first Cardinal Archbishop of Westminster. It is quite probable that Catholics in England, not to speak of those outside that Church, have rather hazy ideas of Cardinal Wiseman, perhaps centreing round the not over-engaging portraits of His Eminence, which are so often to be seen. It may, therefore, be news to them that at an early age Wiseman was recognised as one of the leading scholars of the world. His " Horae Syriacae " appeared in 1827, when the future Cardinal was no more than twenty-five years of age ; it was at once hailed as a work of great learning and gave him a European reputation. But not merely in Syriac and linguistic studies—he was indis-tinguishable from a native in at least six languages—was Wiseman a great scholar. He had a very remarkable knowledge of the science of his time as is exemplified in the lectures of which I am speaking. There, then, we may expect to find an answer to our first question : what was the state of affairs between science and religion one hundred years ago ? *Parva componere magnis*, it fell to my lot two years ago to write a book on similar lines, that is to say, discussing the " Church and its Relations with Science " which appeared in the Calvert Series published by Macmillans, of New York.

I have been comparing the two for the purposes of this article, and this remarkable fact appears that of all the matters which I found it necessary to touch upon only a very few and those, almost without exception, minor considerations find a place in Wiseman's two volumes ; and of the great mass of learned matter there to be discovered, ninety-nine per cent. passed without notice in my book. Am I to plead guilty to neglect of duty in my book ? Not at all ; the subjects of import-ance had completely changed in the century which extends between the two publications. Let us look for. a moment at Wiseman's book. The first two lectures covering one hundred and thirty-five pages are devoted entirely to the study of languages, a subject which the author was especially interested in and well able to handle. But to-day, except perhaps in relation to exegetical matters, it would hardly be thought of in connection with religion and certainly in no way enters into any sort of dispute that it may have with science.

The next two lectures, " On the Natural History of the Human Race," followed by the last two in the first volume, " On the Natural Sciences," look as if they ought to contain much controversial matter, and the topics in question occupy a large part of the space in my little book. And, as a matter of fact, here we do come on some things that even to-day are under discussion, but surprisingly few. To begin with, Wiseman based his ethnological studies, which were extraordinarily wide for a man of his age and special line of life, on Blumenbach's catalogue of skulls—a valuable but long out-of-date work—and on what is known as Camper's angle, which is a matter which interests physical anthropologists to-day little if at all. And what the writer is really concerned with is the unity of the human race then, though not now, a matter of dispute. Hence his controversy is merely one of historical interest to-day.

When we get to the Natural Sciences we find a section devoted to another extinct controversy, the real or apparent death of Christ upon the cross. There were persons who suggested that He deliberately feigned death in order to lead up to a sham resurrection, but with such utterly negligible people Wiseman does not waste time.

But it appears that it was then urged that He was not dead but in a faint or some such unconscious state, recovering from which he arose and left His sepulchre. I can remember, when a young graduate, that a man, then of some note in the scientific world, the late Dr. Samuel Haughton, F.R.S., preached and published a sermon, of which he sent me a copy, on this very subject. But that is more than forty years ago, and I do not remember that this point, which to anyone familiar with Pathology is grossly absurd, has crossed the controversial horizon since that time and, therefore, suppose it to be, as it should be, a dead issue.

But there is one point at any rate of first-class interest to-day and that is the evolutionary theory of Lamarck, which appeared in his " Philosophie Zoologique," which was published in 1809 and was carefully studied by Wiseman—an excellent instance of his omnivorous reading.

He describes Lamarck's derivation of man's body from an animal ancestor as a " degrading theory " and dismisses the idea on scientific lines but in no way alludes to any difficulty raised by the Biblical account. The fact is that the evolutionary controversy was but a cloud the size of a man's hand on the horizon at the time, and Wiseman neither was nor could be expected to be aware of what was coming.

Yet it is interesting to note that he actually got hold of the great factors on which the evolutionary theory and controversy came to be built. " For," he writes, " we have proved both from analogy and from direct examples : first, that there is a perpetual tendency, I might say, a striving, in nature, to raise up in our species "—he is discussing man for the time being—" varieties, often of a very extraordinary character, sometimes approximating, in a marked manner, to the peculiar and specific distinctives of a race different to that in which they arise ; and, secondly, that these peculiarities may be communicated through successive generations, from father to son." It is the evolutionary theory in a nutshell, and it is most interesting to note the evidence which he brings forward for his contention, plain proof that he possessed a highly scientific mind.

In the portion of these chapters devoted to geology there are evidences of old controversies, for example, that concerning the meaning of the " days " of creation. Criticising a work which had demanded the rigidly literal interpretation of the word he says : " I do not advocate the prolongation of the days to periods ; but I think it very wrong to call men infidels for doing so, when only such erroneous grounds are given to the contrary. The terms used to express the sun's standing still, are just as literal and express as those used in the history of creation ; yet no one hesitates to take them figuratively, because demonstrated laws of physics compel us to do so." [1] His discussion of the topic of the Flood is vitiated by the ignorance of the day, for quite naturally it is founded on Dean Buckland's then very important but now almost forgotten work " Reliquiae Diluvianae," which appeared in 1823, and with which Wiseman was well acquainted, as he was with the first edition of Lyell's classic work " The Principles of Geology," which made so great an impression upon Darwin, and indeed on the scientific world generally, and which appeared in 1830–33.

We now know that by far the greater number of phenomena, such as boulders, perched rocks and the like which, Wiseman, following Buckland, relied upon, were really the relics of the last glacial period, of which at the time nothing was known. Buckland was the prophet of what has been called the diluvial hypothesis, which declared for the action of flood waters. The world of learning had to pass subsequently through the drift hypothesis which attributed these things to deposits formed by icebergs and floating sheets of ice

---

[1] The use of a term of unindicated length, instead of a day of twenty-four hours as a translation of the Hebrew YOM is legitimised by the Church since the time of Wiseman.

before it arrived at the conclusions, which do not look like being shaken, respecting the action of glaciers. So much for Wiseman's first volume. As to the second, it is occupied with Early History, Archaeology, and Oriental Literature, and need not detain us. Before leaving the Cardinal, however, it may not be amiss to note that his attitude to possible new discoveries was precisely what Pope Leo XIII afterwards enjoined on Catholics, the traditional attitude, so very different from what is attributed to those of the Faith. Referring to the then supposed dates of early occurrences he wrote : " But suppose it should be *proved* that all the phenomena I have described belong to an earlier era, should I regret the discovery ? Most assuredly not : for never should I fear, and consequently never should I regret, any onward step in the path of science." And he proceeds to state that if an accurate geological chronology should yet come to pass showing how much earlier events were, than uninstructed persons had taken them to be, he would resign his present ideas " without a struggle."

So much for Wiseman's interesting book. It shows clearly that whilst there were small disputes perhaps of general warfare between religion and science it may fairly be said that there was none of great importance.

That there is to-day and has been for many years we are all well aware, and have now to seek the explanation of how this has come to pass.

Let us first of all examine the century-old positions of the two present antagonists beginning with religion. And here we may count out the Catholic Church in England for—with one exception yet to be fully dealt with—she was out of the picture. She was just emerging from the catacombs and from more than three hundred years of more or less brutal oppression, and she was far too busy in licking her wounds and repairing her breaches, bodily and otherwise, to have time to spare for such difficult controversies as were now to become apparent. And as far as the great non-Catholic majority of the population were concerned it is probably not unfair to say that, so far as they thought about the matters at all, they more or less accepted the Usherian chronology and the Miltonic notion of the creation as given in " Paradise Lost."

As to the scientific side, it had been very little affected by Lamarck, and the same may be said of Chambers'—at first anonymously published—" Vestiges of the Natural History of Creation," which appeared in 1844. And when the new ideas of Darwin and Wallace were made known the leaders of biological science, such as Sir Richard Owen, were little prepared to welcome them.

Into this comparatively placid pool there fell two very disturbing stones, the ripples of whose fall have very little diminished even to-day. Let us first of all consider the earlier in time, though the later in actual effect—the science of Prehistoric Archaeology, whose father was a Catholic priest—not by any means the only one who has occupied such a position of honourable paternity—Father McEnery, for many years chaplain at Tor Abbey, near Torquay, who from 1825–1841 when he died, carried out constant personal investigations at that famous spot Kent's Cavern.

He published nothing during his lifetime, and at his death those who cleared up his affairs appear to have destroyed some of his papers, the only wonder being that they did not make a bonfire of the whole lot, for no one at that time could have supposed them to contain anything of interest except to the owner. Fortunately, the bulk was preserved, and still more fortunately they fell into the hands of a sympathetic and understanding local antiquary, the late Mr. Pengelly, who published an abstract of them in 1859 and the entire matter ten years later. But prior to this publication Boucher de Perthes, in excavations at Abbeville, had found rude flint implements in 1838 at which, for some years, the scientific world turned up its nose in true scientific scorn. In 1858 Hugh Falconer, a distinguished English geologist, visited the spot, saw the specimens, and was much impressed.

He induced Prestwich, another geologist, and John Evans, a leading antiquarian, to visit de Perthes in the following year, and their adhesion to his views converted the scientific world. Since that time it has become abundantly evident that the Usherian chronology—never accepted by the Catholic Church—was wholly inaccurate and inadequate, and indeed the same may be said of that which is read in the " Martyrologium Romanum " in religious houses in the Catholic Church. The Church has not expressed any opinion formally on Biblical Chronology, but Archbishop Sheehan tells us that " it is now generally admitted that the Bible teaches nothing definite on the matter," and that the age of the human race " may be left to the investigation of scientists." [1]

It is perhaps not out of place to note the important position which Catholic priests have taken in the domain of Prehistoric Archaeology since the time of McEnery. Passing over others who are dead the acknowledged doyen of the subject to-day is the Abbé Breuil, who has a good second in Fr. Obermaier. The vastly important

[1] Here and elsewhere under the name Sheehan, I am quoting from *Apologetics and the Catholic Church*, a work by the Coadjutor Archbishop of Sydney, Australia, written when Dr. Sheehan was a Professor at Maynooth, at the request of the Irish Hierarchy, and for the use of Catholic children in Irish schools. It has the imprimatur of the Archbishop of Dublin ; has never been challenged ; and may consequently be taken by me as a mean of orthodoxy.

discoveries in China made by the Revv. Pères Licent and de Chardin are known to every student of the subject, nor is there any greater name in ethnology, including its prehistoric branch, than that of Fr. W. Schmidt, S.V.D. It will be at once understood how disturbing an influence the discoveries above alluded to must have had, and they would have had much more had it not been for the fact that it was only by degrees that the ideas spread; that they were more or less confined to scientific circles; and that they were overwhelmed by the much greater sensation which has now to be considered. But this may at once and definitely be said that they did not and have not troubled Catholic minds, as indeed must be obvious from what has been set down above.

Whatever disturbance there may have been over this question of the date of man's appearance on earth, it was not only less than but also later than that which arose after the publication of Darwin's " Origin of Species by Natural Selection," in which were set forth the views independently arrived at by himself and by Alfred Russel Wallace. This book appeared in 1859, and " The Descent of Man " in 1871, after a fifth edition of the first-mentioned book had been issued.

This is not the place to describe the conflict which arose, led from the Anglican side by Samuel Wilberforce, the then well-known Bishop of Oxford, who very unjudiciously pitting himself against Huxley at the meeting of the British Association in Oxford in 1860, laid himself open to and received as severe a reproof as any public man has experienced.

What we are concerned with here is the origin of the myth—held as fact by so many to-day—that the Catholic Church is inexorably opposed to this theory. Before entering into that history, it seems advisable to set down here plainly what the attitude of the Church is in this matter. I notice that on at least two occasions the present Dean of St. Paul's has told the world that the theory of evolution has been condemned by the Church. It is the only channel through which that condemnation has been made known, and it seems, all things considered, rather a curious one to have been selected. As a matter of fact there is not one word of truth in the statement. The Church has perfectly well recognised methods of expressing her opinions, formal and less formal. There has been no formal pronouncement one way or the other, and as regards the less formal, the attitude is entirely of the opposite kind. By less formal I allude—with the utmost respect—to statements covered by imprimaturs, that is, by official permissions to publish certain statements, after those statements have been declared by a competent censor appointed for the purpose, to contain nothing contrary to Faith and Morals. Even works with such imprimaturs have got upon the Index of Prohibited Books no doubt, but if after the passage of some years no challenge has been made in connection with such a book it may certainly be felt that its pronouncements are orthodox. Such a work is that of Archbishop Sheehan's, already alluded to, and with confidence, therefore, may be quoted what he says on this subject : " The Church, while teaching as of faith that God created the living things from which all existing plants and lower animals are descended, leaves us free to hold either the theory of Permanentism or the theory of Theistic Evolution. According to the former, God by a direct act created each species separately : according to the latter, He caused some or all species to develop in course of time from one or more directly-created stocks, or from inanimate matter." [1] And, to complete the

[1] Vol. ii. p. 43. There follows a condemnation of Materialistic Evolution where God's action is denied.

matter on the question of the origin of man's body, the same book states [1] : " If the proof were forthcoming to-morrow that the body of the first man was evolved from the lower animals, it would not be found to contradict any solemn, ordinary or official teaching of the Church." After further stating that the use of the theory of Evolution as a working hypothesis is free from the slightest objection, the book goes on to state that until science can bring forward irrefutable proof—as she has not yet done—that the body of man was so evolved, the Church, in continuation of her invariable policy of not changing her views unless it is obvious that such change is necessary, will accept the " traditional and obvious interpretation of the second chapter of Genesis, that the body of Adam was created directly by God." All this is so clear and direct that it ought to be needless to point to the books by Canon de Dorlodot, Fr. Wasmann, S.J., the present writer, and others which have appeared under imprimatur in the past few years, and in which similar statements have been set down, to show what ignorant and ridiculous rubbish has been uttered about this " condemnation " and about the attitude of the Church in this matter generally.

That matter being cleared up, let us return to our quest. There is no sort of doubt that the originator of the myth was one man, and that man none other than Thomas Henry Huxley, and the way in which it originated was as follows. In 1871 Professor St. George Mivart brought out his " Genesis of Species," which rapidly went to a second edition. Its author was a Fellow of the Royal Society and a man in the first rank of morphologists, on the same plane as Huxley, and he devoted the greater part of this book to a purely morphological and scientific criticism of Darwin's idea,

[1] Vol. ii. p. 51.

a criticism which produced considerable effect ; one, too, which he was perfectly competent and most entirely entitled to make. The latter part of his book was directed to showing that in so far as the theory was looked upon as a *method of creation by God* it received not merely no condemnation but rather support from the writings of the earlier fathers, particularly St. Augustine of Hippo, and from later writers like Suarez the well-known Jesuit scholastic. Any rational man would have supposed that the Darwinian camp would at least be gratified at this defence of their orthodoxy : was such the case ? Not a bit of it. Huxley was at once up in arms. His line of argument seems to have been something like this : " Mivart is a Catholic. Mivart has attacked the theory which Darwin has set forth and of which I approve, and Mivart has done this because it is contrary to Catholic teaching, and if he says it isn't, I'll show him that it is." There follows the well-known tale of how Huxley " tore the heart out of Suarez during a summer afternoon spent in the library " at St. Andrew's University ; how he published what he supposed to be his demolition of Mivart ; how he and Darwin (who never doubted Huxley's capability for demolishing anybody) exulted over the matter. Are not all these things written in the correspondences and memoirs of the time ? [1] As to the orthodoxy of Mivart's view there is no doubt. I knew him well for a time, and before disease had—as I think—caused a change in his attitude, not towards science and the Church but towards other things, I once asked him what reception his book had received at Rome when he told me that the then Sovereign Pontiff had sent him the honorary degree of Doctor of Philosophy as a token of his feelings towards the book.

[1] The reader will find the whole story set forth by the present writer in the *Dublin Review* of a few years ago.

As to Huxley and Suarez, I have never taken the trouble to look into the matter, since it is one of small consequence, but I know enough of Suarez and of scholastic philosophy which it is my business to teach, to feel sure that Huxley, with his complete ignorance of the intensely technical language of that philosophy, could not possibly have comprehended what he was reading, however much he imagined that he did, and I am sure that he honestly felt that he did. He wanted to find a certain teaching there and he found it. He is not the only man who has found in a book, not what it contained in the opinions of those qualified to express an opinion, but what he went out to find. At any rate, from that time Huxley never ceased to proclaim in and out of season that the Catholic Church was the deadly enemy of evolution and of all scientific progress, and even went so far as to exult the more over evolution *because* it was something that the Church would have nothing to do with, an ignorant and not very philosophical attitude.

Huxley was a man of great intellectual powers. He could write excellent English and speak it too. He had many admirable qualities—no one denies it—and he exercised enormous influence in England and did, in fact, not only make science respectable, as someone remarked, but even caused a large number of people who did not know much about it to regard any attack on science—even on what passed for such at the moment —as almost *lèse-majesté* and actually to believe that

> " When science has discovered something more
> We shall be happier than we were before."

an attitude of mind characteristic of those buoyant days before it became obvious that science was capable also of discovering quite a lot of things which can make us much less happy than we were before, as exemplified in the late war. We Catholics to-day are indebted to Huxley for the opinion which some of our fellow-countrymen hold of us to-day as enemies of science and in particular as stubborn opponents of the theory of evolution.

Huxley had his adjuvants, as the medical phrase runs, for he was assisted by two books of which something must now be said, since they have exercised great influence in creating the myth to which I have been drawing attention. The first of these is Draper's " Conflict between Religion and Science," first published in 1874. Its main thesis may be summed up in the statement of its writer : " It has come to this that Roman Christianity and science are *recognised by their respective adherents* as being absolutely incompatible ; they cannot exist together ; one must yield to the other ; mankind must make its choice—it cannot have both." I have italicised certain words because they exhibit the animus and the ignorance of the writer. Being a chemist by profession he must have been aware of the existence of such a man as Lavoisier, often called the Father of Modern Chemistry, who was slain by the materialists of the day, announcing that they had no need of men of learning, with his crucifix in his hand, a fervent son of that very Church denounced by Draper. But that is but one of scores, nay hundreds of similar inaccuracies which have been pointed out time after time and make it astonishing that a respectable firm should republish, in a series containing so many distinguished works, a book of this kind without one word of excuse or explanation.

It would have been necessary, in any case, to mention their names in an article such as this, but here is as good a place as another to remark that Pasteur and Mendel, the two greatest names in biology of the past half century or more, were both of them " respective adherents " of science and of the Church so ignorantly denounced by Draper.

The other book is one of quite a different type, for White, its author, was after all a man of some erudition, and though he commits himself to a number of absurd and inaccurate statements, the worst perhaps is that in which he speaks of Draper's book as " a work of great ability." He is less ignorant than that author, but his whole thesis is based on a mistaken notion. That new discoveries have been always and everywhere attacked when made known is a commonplace. We know that it has been so in our own times and in those before them, *teste* Jenner *et al.* And we know that the attacks have come from contemporary men of science— from whom else could they have come? But long ago there were few men of science even of learning who were not clerics, and when that was the case the opposition to new ideas naturally came from clerics because there was no other source from which it could come. To talk, however, of such a state of affairs as the war of religion with science is as absurd as it would be to describe the undoubted opposition which Darwin met from Owen and others of his contemporary scientists as the war of science with science.

My space is limited and the question of the attitude of the Church to science can only be looked at here from one aspect. I have tried to deal with it more fully in another place,[1] where I have carefully examined the cases where the Church is supposed to have acted as the enemy of science. On the general point I shall, therefore, say no more.

What I am concerned to show is that, contrary to what is commonly believed, at least during the past hundred years with which this article is concerned, and

[1] *The Catholic Church and its Relation to Science* (Macmillans, 1927).

more especially during that time of strife which is often described as the Darwinian controversy, the Church in England—and abroad, though I am not concerned with that—has not been the active nor even passive opponent of the progress of science which she is represented as being. That should, I venture to hope, be clear from the facts which I have stated. That through the work of its sons, and I may add daughters, the Church has had some share in the progress of science during that period, I could also show were this the place to make the effort.

A HUNDRED YEARS OF CATHOLIC MUSIC

BY ERNEST OLDMEADOW

VI

A HUNDRED YEARS OF CATHOLIC MUSIC

I

A Wrong Conclusion

A Catholic flock with neither Bishop nor cathedral is doubly orphan'd. While the Bishop is a Father in God, his cathedral is the Mother Church of the diocese. To house the Bishop's chair of teaching and jurisdiction is the prime purpose of the cathedral; but *Ecclesia Mater* is in Canon Law also *Ecclesia Matrix*, and not the least of her functions is the Caecilian task of inspiring and refining Sacred Music in her daughter-churches.

In 1829, Catholic Emancipation was won by a light-shunning little community which had neither a hierarchy nor any cathedral churches. From this fact a wrong inference has been drawn as regards Catholic Music. Many people imagine that the Penal Laws were wholly to blame for the prevalence, a hundred years ago, of secularity in the music of the Church. They picture the Vicars Apostolic—England's makeshift for a Catholic Hierarchy in those days—looking on with impotent despair at the spectacle of divers Ambassadors' Chapels in which the chaste musical and liturgical ideals of the Vicars themselves were mocked and set at nought.

This notion of the Embassy Chapels, in the Eighteen-twenties, and of the Vicars' attitude towards them is almost wholly mistaken. The chapel in Sardinia Street, for example, had been taken over by Bishop Douglass as early as 1799, and the Sardinian Embassy had been turned into a presbytery where four or five priests ministered to the Catholics (7,000 or so) within their prescribed area. The old chapel (one of Inigo Jones's buildings) had been doubled in size and the mission was self-supporting. And this was not the only Embassy Chapel where the Vicars were masters for all practical purposes. Therefore we must dismiss from our minds the delusion that the Kings of Spain, Portugal, France, Bavaria and Sardinia, to say nothing of the Doge of Venice, were flouting the austere liturgical tastes of the Vicars Apostolic by " making a joyful noise before the Lord " with that most expensive form of noise, orchestral music.

The Vicars, it is true, could and did put down a firm foot whenever musical proposals too far outran Catholic propriety. For example, only a year or two before Emancipation was voted, Dr. Poynter stopped a suggested Requiem for Weber (the great *Freischutz* Weber, who died whilst on a visit to London), because it threatened to be more of a concert (with a majority of Protestant performers) than a truly religious service. But, speaking broadly, they heard the Embassy choirs and bands with indulgent and even approving ears. They knew that the Ambassadors' oratories had originally been more courtly than churchly. But these chapels, where royal birthdays, accession-days and death-days could be pompously celebrated, had also been for a long time, to all intents and purposes, public Catholic churches. The English Kings, in tolerating Catholic Embassy Chapels—as an act of courtesy not as an admission of right—winked at the frequentation of these foreign oratories by native English Catholics ; indeed, it was no secret that the Pope had begged sundry Catholic Kings to attach larger chapels to their Embassies in London.

To cheapen the Vicars' venerable memory on the

ground that they condoned music which we now deplore would be unreasonable. These fine men were pastors, teachers, administrators first; and aesthetes a long way afterwards. How could they be expected to stand far ahead of their times in musical taste? The Viennese church music—by which we mean those compositions wherein only the words distinguished a Mass from an opera—was the vogue not only in England, where the song of the Church had so long been stifled, but even in those thoroughly Catholic countries where no Reformation or Revolutions had torn up the music and scattered or persecuted the musicians. Haydn and Mozart and a swarm of third-rate imitators filled the ecclesiastical as well as the theatrical bill. Weber had written some Masses in a hurry, but without letting his good and sincere music get into them. In France many Bishops permitted huge orchestral displays in church. In Courts and other musical centres of the German-speaking countries the Proper of the Mass was dropped and truly liturgical music was almost unknown. The way for Gounod was being made straight.

Two big reasons fortified the Vicars in their acceptance of the current church music. First, the Gordon Riots were fresh in their minds. They had learned that music in Catholic worship somehow soothed the savage breasts of No-Popery mobs. Low Masses without music had stirred the worst suspicions. What was this sinister " mutter of the Mass " and why did the Papists kneel through it in still more sinister silence? Beholding the back-street temples of this voiceless mystery-cult with dread, Protestants too often set fire to the humble Catholic buildings. But when music was heard issuing from a Mass-house the mobs were mollified. Here, they thought, must be a place of worship of some sort, after all; and, although regular Mass-hearers were a traitorous, superstitious and hell-destined pack, how could you be sure, when you met a fellow citizen coming out, that he had not been present merely as a lover of music? Thus many a worshipper worshipped, so to speak, behind a choir-screen, and was spared persecution.

Second, this "attractive" music at Mass was important to the finance of the Missions. The singers and players cost a good deal, but they brought in more than they cost. Many a budget was balanced with the cash of open-handed non-Catholics who would never have entered the chapels to hear sermons but were irresistibly drawn by the musical exhibitions about to be described.

II

WHAT THE MUSIC WAS

Long before the year of Emancipation, the Catholic Chapels held a distinguished place in the musical life of London. Musicians of distinction had acted as their organists and choir-masters, including the two Webbes, Paxton, Danby, the amazing Wesley and Vincent Novello. These men were proud of their posts. For instance, Novello was absent from the Portuguese chapel organ-bench only once in five and twenty years.

For the tolerable execution of intricate and florid compositions, the choirmasters had to maintain a standard of vocal excellence and musical proficiency to which few of our 1929 choir-singers could rise. The old clefs were still in use, and the accompanist had often to play from a figured bass. Infinite pains had to be taken by the choir-masters for, no doubt, a choir-boy was a choir-boy, even under the Georges. By the way, it was through Webbe's conscientiousness in training choir-boys that the now world-famous firm of Novello arose. In 1793, Webbe (of the Sardinian Chapel) announced that he would " give instruction gratis to such young gentlemen as present themselves to learn the church music." Among the young gentlemen came an Anglo-Italian boy, Vincent Novello. Later on, when Novello had himself become a Catholic chapel-master, a demand arose for a printed " Selection of Sacred Music as performed at the Royal Portuguese Chapel " ; and it was on the appearance of this work that the name of Novello was first heard as a publisher of church music.

Catholic readers at the British Museum ought to find leisure some day to handle these first Catholic publications of Novello. They are not merely ambassadorial but royal. The pair of thick and heavy folio volumes cost only twenty-six shillings : yet the engraving is after a sumptuous fashion. As for the contents, these are mostly in bad styles, with ever so much Rossi. A few of the numbers are still popular in Catholic choirs, such as Mozart's lovely *Ave Verum* and the inextinguishable *Inclina ad me* of Himmel, which is marked *andante supplichevole*. Among the respectable items may be named two compositions by that neglected master Caldara—his *Miserere* and a *Laboravi in gemitu meo*. There is plenty of Samuel Wesley, although he had relapsed into quite blatant Protestantism after some years of sincere or insincere obedience to the Pope. One of the Wesley pieces is a *Domine, salvum fac Regem nostrum Georgium*, with a very long and elaborate *Gloria Patri*. The younger Webbe is represented by a *Pater Noster* which concludes not with *sed libera nos a malo* but with *quia tuum est regnum*, etc. [To young Webbe's work Novello has appended a note explaining that Catholics do not conclude the Lord's Prayer with a Doxology.] Of course *Adeste Fideles* is in the Selection and is described simply as " The Christmas Hymn." We have here a clue to the puzzle why the tune of *Adeste Fideles* should be put down in ever so many hymn-books as " Portuguese Melody," an attribution which astounds Portuguese musicians. Probably it was at the Portuguese Embassy Chapel in London that this canticle first became popular, and it was taken to be a product of Portugal.

Although the Georges spoke German, there was no German opera in England. Weber's reforming work was to have only posthumous results. Italian *bel canto* was the rage. This helped the popularity, though not the liturgical austerity of the chapel services. The stars who shot every year into the firmament of London's Royal Italian Opera were Catholics and they cheerfully gave their services on Sundays to one or other of the Catholic choirs. This attraction brought many Protestants to Mass and to Catholic preaching ; but the price paid was high. Pugin, writing later, was indignant at the irreverent behaviour of Catholic choirs. He had seen an organist reading a Sunday newspaper during service ; and, worse still, he had seen an operatic gentleman and an operatic lady walk complacently along the church to the choir-gallery like man and wife, although neither Church nor State had had anything to say to their relationship.

Plain-chant and polyphony were not wholly despised. That Vespers and Compline received more attention than in our own day may be gathered from another of Novello's lordly folios which was prefaced by the words : " A complete Copy of the Musical part of the Evening Service having long been wanting in Catholic choirs, the present Work has been undertaken to supply the deficiency."

Holy Week had some of its musical due. The faithful came to church with Holy Week books in Latin and English and the musicians were provided with engraved copies of Palestrina's *Improperia* and with simple settings of such texts as the *Jerusalem* in Tenebrae. But, speaking generally, the weakness of the choirs was on the liturgical side and their successes were won in musical fields which are now-a-days out of bounds.

In the domestic chapels of the Catholic nobility and gentry attempts were made to follow the Embassy model. Disraeli's *Lothair*, dealing with a somewhat later period, ascribes solemnity and poignancy to the Holy Week music in a great Catholic house and it is well known that Protestants were often moved deeply by the ceremonies in private chapels. Speaking broadly, however, the domestic music was on Embassy lines.

III

What Might Have Been

The musical ideal of the Catholic Church is that all the faithful shall join with heart and voice in her public offices. The best means to this end is the so-called Gregorian Chant, which justifies both meanings of its Latin name *planus* by moving smoothly and by speaking plainly. When the precentor chooses the right pitch for the particular congregation around him, nobody has to strain after a high note or struggle down to a low one ; indeed the compass of the chant is that of ordinary human voices. The music being sheer melody, to be sung in unison, it is possible to print very cheaply ecclesiastical song-books (the Kyriale being the most familiar example) containing nearly a score of Masses and other music, and to sell them for a few pence a copy. But it is not to be supposed that the plain chant repertory has been finally settled. Gifted composers could go on writing new " Gregorian " music without limit. Indeed, one hears in France and other countries plain chant

Masses, suitable for singing by all the people, which are not in any official music-book of the Church.

When Emancipation gave the signal for a new era of Catholic life in Britain, it was most desirable that congregational singing should be everywhere encouraged. Even before 1829, Protestants had proved that men, women and children could be brought to churches and chapels without trouble provided they were allowed to " have a good sing." For example, Wesley's sermons soon ceased to be read except by those on whom they were imposed as a theological test ; but Wesley's Hymns were everywhere loved and sung. Later on, the big "Revival" movements again showed what singing could do. Mr. Moody would not have been much without Mr. Sankey. Although the book has many detractors to-day, *Hymns, Ancient and Modern* gave incalculable help to the Anglican awakening throughout the Victorian reign. But Catholics have not even yet come anywhere near the ordinary Protestant standards in this matter ; and it is commonly said, even by our friendliest critics, that Catholic congregations sing worse than any others.

To blame our leaders of a hundred years ago for not promoting and achieving a vigorous plain chant revival in all the Catholic churches and chapels would be absurd, seeing that the chant was at a low ebb even in Catholic countries, and that the mostly corrupt versions available in print were cumbrous and costly. But we may justly heave a sigh over the fact that other ways of inducing the faithful to sing in church were not tried with vigour and perseverance. The disastrous facility with which hundreds of thousands of Catholics have picked up and memorised the top line of Turner's *Mass of St. Caecilia* proves that our great-grandfathers and great-grandmothers could have learned the simpler, stronger and more dignified strains of unison Masses, not necessarily composed in the plain chant idiom, supported by the organ or some humbler chest of bellows and pipes. And they could have learned the common psalm-tones as easily as their brethren of the Established Church were learning Anglican chants. As for translations of our Breviary hymns, we are often told nowadays that these are too solid for ordinary folk to sing ; but let anybody look at some of the hymns and tunes which were effectively used in the eighteen-thirties, even in the village chapels of untutored Methodists, and he will agree that our Breviary hymns were practical. The Wesleys described their hymn-book as " a body of divinity " as well as a book of sacred hymnody. Many of their compositions were versified theology, very different from the ditties of the frothy revivalists who came later, and they were sung to solid tunes, some of which were derived, although the singers did not know it, from those choral melodies which would have made their way even if Luther had never been born. Catholics could have done what Wesleyans did if there had been somebody to set their feet in the right way.

What robbed the Emancipated Church, a hundred years ago, of its goodly heritage was the perverse and ruinous notion that every Catholic church with a musical instrument in it must have a show-choir to imitate the performances of the Embassy Chapels, of St. Mary Moorfields, of Somers Town, of Islington, and of the other Catholic churches where a musical establishment was kept up. Before the Reformation our Catholic forefathers did what Pius X, of glorious memory, urged our own generation to do : that is, they all helped to sing Mass. The Ordinary was theirs ; not the monopoly of a dozen or twenty parishioners perched up in a music-gallery. Nothing has operated with more deadly force to keep down Catholic music in the British Isles than the performing choirs. As most of their members have been volunteers it is usually considered ungrateful to depreciate their efforts, but the fact remains that, while there has been terrible efficiency in their discouragement of congregational singing, only in rare cases has there been a compensating excellence of musical achievement on their own part. The praiseworthy exceptions which will leap to many minds do not disprove the rule. And, worst of all, this type of choir, instead of improving musical taste and raising musical standards, has produced a plentiful crop of die-hards who stealthily oppose the liturgical wishes of the Roman Pontiffs and strive to perpetuate the unholy alliance of sacred texts with secular melody and harmony.

So much for the congregational singing which might have been but was not practised by the Emancipated Catholics. It remains to be added that, while Holy Church desires the participation of her children in the Ordinary of her Missa Cantata, elaborate and artistic vocal feats are admissible and even desirable, so long as they are churchly in style. The Church finds room for the most skilful musicians and would have them match the achievements of her painters and architects and sculptors, giving to Almighty God the best that human genius can offer. It is here that polyphony comes in. And here again we may heave a sigh over what did not happen after Emancipation.

The Catholic Church in England under King George III could boast the adherence of polyphonic composers not inferior to any who were writing in the strongest and richest Catholic lands. Take the case of Webbe. In many a Catholic choir to-day this composer is represented on Easter Sunday by three compositions—*Vidi aquam*, *Regina Coeli* and, at the evening Benediction, a tune for *O Salutaris Hostia!* There is almost nothing in the *Vidi aquam*. The *Regina Coeli* is downright bad. The Benediction tune is beautiful and seemly, but its homophony is without distinction. Yet Webbe, in his secular works, had shown himself a true polyphonist, able to produce madrigals in an almost Tudor style. As for Wesley (a son of the truly great poet Charles Wesley and father of " Wilderness " Wesley), during his years as a professing Catholic this extraordinary man had written music to Latin words in an ecclesiastical style immeasurably superior to anything done by his anthem-writing Anglican contemporaries. But this Georgian polyphony of English Catholic composers ran to waste. Rossini, with his flashy *Stabat Mater*, found us an easy prey ; and Gounod wound us round his little finger. The show-choirs rose to their showiest : their tenors shook shakes, their leading ladies trilled trills, and, a little later on, Mendelssohn's *Lauda Sion* was thought to be the most lofty and severe of Church Music. Yet there might have been unison singing from every throat and celestial polyphony from a few divinely favoured choristers.

IV

THE GOOD FIGHT

In this brief essay it is not possible to epitomise, in order and proportion, Catholic musical history since Emancipation was won.

With a doggedness worthy of a better cause, the showy singers have held their forts against doughty onslaughts. Many a bishop pleaded earnestly for the ejection from our holy places of singing *theatricali more et scenico strepitu*, as Benedict XIV had called it, and urged the bringing back of the Church's own chant ; but these wise pastors knew that they must make haste slowly. Archbishop Ullathorne cautiously said to one of his priests : " Use the chant if you are sure it will do more good than harm." Later on, Dr. Walsh, Archbishop of Dublin, who was himself an organist and had compiled practical manuals of Gregorian, did not feel that he was strong enough to impose truly ecclesiastical music throughout his diocese, with the result that, while Palestrina and the polyphonists were being sung in the pro-cathedral of Dublin, many of the parish choirs were delivering themselves of the most trashy Mass-music. The Synod of Westminster tried a bold move towards reform by forbidding women singers in choirs, but it might just as well have tried to dictate women's fashions. Throughout all the colonies and dominions of the British Empire, Catholics still clung to the notion that there must be "attractive choirs" as in the old days of the Embassy Chapels, with the result that mediocre vocal displays from west galleries choked what ought to have been the hearty singing of all the faithful in the naves.

Although the defence against Reform seemed to be holding firm, assaults were being made which, in the long run, have pounded breaches in the anti-liturgical wall. A whole generation before the issue of Pius X's *Motu Proprio* on Church Music brave men were in the field. A young priest named Francis Bourne, destined to hold the highest place in Catholic England, taught Latin and the chant to boys at Blackheath. A Caecilian Society, emulating the useful though not supermusicianly work under the same invocation in Germany, was established in England ; and, although it failed outwardly, it was a demonstration against the Jericho of the show singers. Father Sankey, a convert and a musician with academic credentials, brought Palestrina to Spanish Place. At the Oscott Seminary, then a training centre for the priests-to-be of several dioceses,

Monsignor Parkinson, in the eighteen-nineties, put life into the *Schola Cantorum* and showed himself a pioneer by introducing the Solesmes redaction of the chant in lieu of the Ratisbon mutilation. A liturgical magazine was started in Dublin and, although its death-day was only two years after its birthday, it did not live in vain. Children—who are still the chief hope of the Church in this matter—began to sing plain chant Masses at Holloway and Wapping. In 1898 the mixed choir at St. Mary's, Croydon, went on strike, and were mightily surprised to find a liturgical choir in surplices quietly and effectively taking over their work. On the morrow of the *Motu Proprio*, Summer Schools of Chant drew nearly two hundred eager students to Appuldurcombe in the Isle of Wight, the temporary home of the Quarr Abbey Benedictines.

This paper began with an allusion to the importance of cathedrals as inspirers and rectifiers of sacred music. Years before the issue of the epoch-making *Motu Proprio*, a hall adjoining the unfinished Westminster Cathedral was devoted by Cardinal Vaughan to the celebration of the full Liturgy of the Church, including a daily Capitular High Mass, the whole Divine Office, and the ceremonies proper to the succeeding seasons and feasts. Dr. Terry (now Sir Richard Terry), who had been doing serious musical work as choirmaster at Downside Abbey, and had edited some polyphonic masterpieces in modern notation, was brought to Westminster as director of the music. The hall was small and almost unadorned; but a sum of about £3,000 a year was spent on the choir. Nothing could more clearly illustrate the progress of musical taste than the fact that Westminster Cathedral Hall, with a choir singing nothing but plain chant and unaccompanied polyphonic Masses and motets, proved as attractive to the musical public, both Catholic and

Protestant, of King Edward's reign as did the Embassy music under King George III.

So few of our Catholic cathedrals in the days of King George V are more than busy and penurious parish churches, in which the Bishop's Chair is placed, that Westminster's example cannot yet be generally followed. Perhaps the most remarkable experiment, after Westminster's, is that of Dr. Dunn, Bishop of Nottingham, who, a few years ago, made plain chant compulsory in Pugin's Cathedral of St. Barnabas. In the Cathedral Church of the new Lancaster diocese, Dr. Reginald Dixon keeps strictly to truly ecclesiastical music. At Southwark, where a sensation was made as long ago as 1890 by the abolition of a famous and " attractive " choir and orchestra under the baton of Mr. Meyer Lutz, the music is now on grave lines, and a Festival of Diocesan Choirs is held. A detailed account of our cathedral music in 1929 would show that there are still some laggards in the march of reform ; but, speaking broadly, " it moves."

Although the great *Motu Proprio* of 1903 resounded loudly through musical England, it cannot be said with truth that our country has vied with some other countries in obedience to Rome so far as Church Music is concerned. We still lack a Society of St. Gregory, such as has been established for years in some other lands. Lists of authorised music were drawn up for the use of some dioceses ; but the Boys of the Old Brigade went on with their solos and their worldly tunes and florid figures of accompaniment as before. Indeed, one of the saddest features of Catholic life in the British Isles during the twentieth century, so far as it has gone, has been the complete disdain of egoistical soloists and organists for everybody and anybody who has suggested to them a sacrifice of vanity and a deference to their bishops and to their Holy Father. Few indeed have been the cases in which west-gallery musicians have altered their ways out of respect for lawful authority. Where changes for the better have come they have almost all been through the dying-off of the secular practitioners or the formal imposition of a new order of things by priests alive to the urgency of Reform.

Mr. Edward A. Maginty, whose enthusiasm and industry in this good cause are so praiseworthy, has recently made reasoned estimates of the actual musical situation in England and Wales. Counting the churches at about 2,000, he fears that about 1,400 of these are musically served by small mixed choirs which, while obstructing congregational singing, are unequal even to the easy choral work which they undertake. In about 100 rather better mixed choirs, the purely vocal perform-ance is not so bad ; but the repertory is unecclesiastical. This leaves say 500 choirs, or one-fourth of the whole, which range up from tolerable to very good. In the lowest of these the boys are undertrained and there is too much Haller or Turner ; but the Proper is enunciated, to more or less simplified music. The mass-chant is heard collectively, as a sort of " community singing," in about 100 churches. Parish churches confided to Religious Orders often have adequate choirs, versed in the chant and in polyphony ; but Mr. Maginty thinks that the really good choirs in Catholic Britain are much less than one-tenth of the whole number. His estimates are mainly in respect of Sunday mornings. As for Sunday evenings, Vespers and/or Compline are sung in less than 200 churches, which is a sad falling off from the old standard. Nor have the vernacular hymns waxed as Vespers and Compline have waned. There is hardly a Catholic parish in England where the parishioners know as many as forty English hymns.

V

THE FUTURE

For the second century of Emancipated Catholicism in Britain the musical prospects are bright. Mr. Maginty's survey, sad though it is, does not describe a zero but the beginnings of a thaw. One London Catholic Editor says that almost every week brings in the good news of a parish coming over to the Liturgical Movement; and, he adds, subsequent falls from grace are rare.

The right step was taken a few years ago in publishing a cheap and good *Catholic Schools' Hymn-Book*, from which children easily learn to sing not only a wider and better variety of vernacular hymns but also the most simple and necessary Latin texts to plain chant settings, such as *Asperges me*, *Vidi aquam*, *Te Deum laudamus*, *Veni Creator Spiritus*, the Easter sequence and one or two Kyriale Masses. Simultaneously with the wide circulation of the *Schools' Hymn-Book* has come the new vogue of Community Singing; and by these two factors the problem of Catholic Church music can be solved.

Perhaps the most pressing need at this stage is a band of sympathetic and even magnetic leaders who will imitate our Divine Master as Healer of the Dumb. *Tunc aperta erit lingua mutorum*. When once a start has been made among Britain's song-shy Catholics, the new era will be on us and all around us, like long-pent waters set free. Catholics are so like unto other Britons in their natural gifts and longings that they want to sing " in the congregation " : and, when they begin, they will sing with heart and voice not only metrical hymns in their own tongue but also the liturgical texts and chants of the Church.

It has been hinted in the foregoing pages that congregational Masses will not necessarily and invariably be in the ecclesiastical modes and in the plain-chant idiom. Composers may use modern phraseology provided that secularity be eschewed. But, in the narrow space here available, it is not possible to do more than shew how stately and lovely Catholic worship might become without departing from the traditional chants.

Shared antiphonally between choir and people, and supported on the organ with the aid of an accompaniment-book such as is already available for unlearned and unresourceful players, even the most curt and plain of the Kyriale Masses can be both a dignified enrichment of the Sacred Rite and, at the same time, " a good sing." In bringing this about, use can be made of those enthusiastic women who have so long and gallantly helped in the west galleries. They can form nave-choirs, to sit either *en bloc* or in two or three groups among the people so as to give confidence and to check dragging. And, as the people grow bolder with their song and the organist makes progress in his art, moments of grandeur will become possible. The firm chanting of a plain-song melody by a big company of the faithful will give the player a *canto fermo* indeed, upon and around which he can pile august harmonies and weave an ever-changing counterpoint.

And let no one object that a gifted choir would soon rebel against the baldness and sameness of unison-chant, sung antiphonally with a lusty crowd in the nave. By taking the alternate verses in *falso bordone*, or by adding descants without excess, or by expanding into the kind of polyphony which most of them have already heard used for alternate verses of processional Latin hymns, industrious little choirs would soon find themselves wondering how they could have been content so long with the tuney melodies and banal harmonies of the Masses and

motets which they used to perform in the ungrateful ears
of muzzled congregations. On High Feasts nobody
would grumble at them for combining with an antiphonal
plain-chant *Credo* some noble polyphonic Mass, or even a
full Mass in a more modern but still churchly style. And
on every ordinary Sunday they would exercise their good
voices and fine skill in the motet which the Church permits
at the offertory.

Working on these lines a Catholic choir would be
ready for anything. At times of holiday, or tempest, or
epidemic a mere pair of singers in the choir could sustain
a decorous and not undignified interchange of solemn
chant with the faithful in the nave. The easy *tonus in
directum* would see them through the Proper of the Mass ;
and the organ (which can, of course, be played to support
the voices even in Lent) would round off and fill up the
reverent strains. Yet this most frugal of musical
programmes could be expanded into a kingly feast of
song on a high day or a holy-day—into a feast like some
great noble's in the olden time, when not only lords and
ladies and knights and squires, but also plain men-at-arms
and dairymaids and hinds and scullions ate and drank
together as one family and were glad.

CATHOLICS IN PUBLIC LIFE
BY VISCOUNT FITZALAN

VII
CATHOLICS IN PUBLIC LIFE

In considering the position of Catholics in public life in connection with the Centenary of Catholic Emancipation, it may be useful, first of all, to examine what the legal state of affairs was at the time of the Emancipation Act a hundred years ago. Catholic Emancipation is generally dated in popular opinion from the passing of the Relief Act of 1829, but in fact much of the legislation passed in persecution of the Faith had before then been repealed, at least by implication. On the other hand, the Act itself did not entirely dispose of the disabilities of Catholics. The first Relief Act was passed in 1778. Until that time the Catholic was liable to pay a severe penalty for his belief; for some there was waiting the punishment of treason, that is to say, death by hanging, drawing, and quartering. For others, the penalties of *praemunire*, or being put out of the protection of the law, so that any man was free to ill-treat, if not actually to kill, them and to steal their goods. It was treason for a priest to be within the realm, and death to anyone harbouring him. £100 was the reward for apprehending him, and £100 was given for evidence leading to a conviction for saying Mass. A second refusal to take the oath admitting the supremacy of the King in things spiritual was punishable with death. To praise a book in defence of Papal supremacy, to reconcile a person to the Catholic Church, and to know of either of these offences without reporting them to the Privy Council, was to incur the terrible *praemunire*. For hearing Mass the fine was £100 and a year in gaol. Failure to pay a fine of £20 monthly for not attending the Protestant services of the Church meant adjuration of the realm, and, if the offender in this was a landowner, two-thirds of his real estate was also forfeit to the Crown. If one convicted of recusancy was caught within ten miles of London, the fine was £100, and any " reputed Papist " could be banished to a distance of ten miles from Westminster. £100 was the fine for sending a son abroad for Catholic education. The son was disinherited by law and the landed estate of the father on his death passed to the nearest Protestant kinsman. To come into a house in which the King or Heir-Apparent was present was an offence for which the Catholic forfeited £100. If he had a horse of above the value of £5, it could be seized by the constable for the King's use. His marriage could only be with the rites of the Established Church. If he kept a school he was liable to imprisonment for life, and every Catholic was bound to register his estates and his will. He could not sit in Parliament without making a declaration denying the Doctrine of Transubstantiation, and asserting that the Sacrifice of the Mass was superstitious and idolatrous, while before using the Parliamentary vote he would be required to take the Oath of Supremacy. He must have taken the Sacrament after Service and Sermon in the Protestant Church the Sunday before being admitted to any Civil Office. He could not hold a commission in the Army or Navy, or be a barrister or attorney.

It is not suggested that these Penal Laws were rigorously enforced. The leaven of humanity in the British race made that impossible, yet there were at all times some who were ready to raise a persecution, and no Catholic but must feel that he held his life and property on sufferance.

The Act of 1778 repealed certain of the worst of these Laws, including those providing for the apprehension of bishops and priests, and abolished perpetual imprisonment as the punishment for keeping a school. It was the extension of this moderate relief to Scotland which brought about the Gordon Riots.

Then came the Relief Act of 1791, under which it became no longer an offence to be a Catholic, to be a priest, or to say or hear Mass, or to perform Catholic rites. The learned professions were thrown open once more to the faithful by this Act, and the Act of 1816 enabled them lawfully to hold commissions in the Army and the Navy.

The Catholic Emancipation Act of 1829 threw open to Catholics both Houses of Parliament, and, with few exceptions, all Civil Offices, by providing that instead of the old declaration previously required for anyone entering Parliament, taking Civil Office, or voting for a Member of Parliament, Catholics should be required to take that oath only which was provided in the Act. This was an oath which Catholics could take, notwithstanding that its terms were invidious and offensive. By giving to Catholics the opportunity of sitting in Parliament and voting at elections, the Act greatly changed their status. It bestowed on them a power with which politicians were forced to reckon, and by degrees that power has enabled Catholics to regain a position of civil and religious equality with their fellow-subjects. Three years later, for instance, they obtained an Act for putting their schools and chapels on the same footing as those of Protestant Dissenters.

In 1837 they obtained from Parliament an Act which made it no longer necessary for them to be married in a Protestant church.

In 1860 they succeeded in getting passed the Roman

Catholic Charities Act, which has been useful ever since in establishing those charities which were carried on in secret through penal times; while in 1871 the invidious Oath in the Emancipation Act was abolished by Parliament, and no oath is now required of Catholics that is not equally required of their fellow-citizens, save in the case of admittance to a few offices, of which one is that of the Lord Chancellor.

In order to pass the Emancipation Act its promoters found it necessary to cast a sop to Cerberus, which took the form of provisions for the gradual suppression and final prohibition of the Religious Orders within the United Kingdom. Though as bodies they were not recognised as legal, yet between 1791 and 1829 there was no law to prevent individual members of the Orders being here. The provisions thus enacted against the Orders were never, strictly speaking, put in force, though, from time to time, use was made of them in side issues. For instance, gifts by will to, and endowments *inter vivos* of, Communities were held to be void, and many a legacy left to them has been lost in this way. Occasionally there would be a frontal attack, as when a Protestant clergyman in 1902 applied at Bow Street for a summons against those eminently learned Jesuit Fathers—Sidney Smith, Thurston, and Gerard, charging them with the offence of being in this country. The magistrate, in his discretion, refused to summons, and the High Court declined to interfere by mandamus with the discretion he had used, while making it clear that had he used his discretion the other way they might equally have declined to interfere.

Then, again, after Parliament in 1921 had granted relief to charities from Income Tax, the relief was refused by the Inland Revenue Authorities in Scotland to a charity carried on by Benedictines, on the ground that they were still an unlawful association. It was not till the Roman Catholic Relief Act of 1926 that Catholic Religious Orders were freed from the Penal Laws.

Notwithstanding Catholic Emancipation, there remained on the Statute Book the Bill of Rights requiring the Sovereign on accession to the throne to make the declaration against Transubstantiation, with its assertion that the Mass is idolatrous and superstitious. An effort was made to relieve King Edward VII from the necessity of making it, but, much as he disliked it, no way of escape was found. The growth of Catholic liberty and of the Oxford Movement, during the nineteenth century, had made the declaration shocking to all but a few Protestant ears, and in 1910, before His present Majesty was crowned, this declaration by the Sovereign was abolished by Act of Parliament.

Catholics had for so many generations been unable to take their part in the public life of the country that it is small wonder they had for all practical purposes become nonentities; and even when greater freedom came to them it would appear they hardly knew how to take advantage of it, and continued to remain in their homes hardly conscious of the duties which were opening out in front of them, and placing them on a level with their neighbours in having the same opportunities of discharging the various public duties of a professional and public kind around them. In fact, it would seem there was a reluctance among many of them to appear at all in public as Catholics. They had for so long led a life, so to speak, in the catacombs, that when the light of day did come they shrank from it.

Tradition is a more potent thing than many imagine, and tradition taught that for a Catholic, individual effort in public affairs was a thing not to be exercised, and therefore in the Catholic body there was small initiative.

How little is it now remembered even by Catholic lawyers that only forty years before the Emancipation Act, the Centenary of which we are now celebrating, the legal profession was closed to Catholics. How many Catholic parents who are now considering a profession for their sons ever think that only such a comparatively short time ago the chance of being even an unsuccessful barrister was a legal impossibility.

The effect of tradition is illustrated by a story told of an old Catholic family as late as about the 'sixties of the last century. There were several sons in the family. The father was a good old fox-hunting squire, an earnest Catholic, who had naturally been brought up with the idea that all professions were closed to him and his ; and it never occurred to him that openings for a public career had now become available for his sons, who, like their father before them, were leading the peaceful lives of country gentlemen. But one day it occurred to one of the boys that he would like to be a soldier. It was some time before the father, and the family as a whole, recovered from the surprise of realising that after all it was possible to hold a commission in the Army.

At the time of Emancipation the number of the very poor amongst Catholics was probably comparatively small. The tragedy of the Irish famine had not yet driven to our shores the hungry emigrants of that long-suffering country.

In some few of the larger towns, especially in Lancashire, such as Liverpool and Manchester, chapels existed which, it is said, were hardly large enough to accommodate the Catholics attending them. But, outside these towns, the chief centres of Catholic life were in and around the homes of such of the old Catholic families as could still afford to keep a chaplain, and where, outside the actual household, a few retainers and tenants went to make up the small congregation.

That the position of Catholics in the public life of England has vastly changed since 1829 goes without saying, but the extent is probably realised by few.

Consider, in the first place, the position of the clergy. Whilst here and there a priest may have been known and received amongst a small Protestant circle, this was probably due to his literary attainments, or to the fact of his being chaplain to some Catholic nobleman or squire, and, consequently, acquainted with some of the local gentry of the neighbourhood. But the idea that a priest could take part in the public life of his locality probably never entered into his head or that of anyone else.

It would be interesting to know if, say, even as late as the 'seventies in any of the local annual celebrations, for example the Mayoral Dinner in a borough, the parish priest, if one existed, was ever invited to the annual banquet.

When, as a result of the Education Act of 1870, School Boards came into existence, it created quite a sensation in Catholic circles that a priest should so far emerge from the limitations of his duties to his flock as to seek the suffrages of his neighbours for the right of a seat in a publicly elected body.

In these days it is probably the fault of the priest himself, due to too-retiring a nature or want of appreciation of the good services he might have opportunities of rendering, if he does not take part in the public bodies and social functions of the locality. That for a priest to take his part in public events with the greatest advantage to the Church needs tact and judgment is no doubt true ; but experience shows that the opportunities for good arising from so doing are immense and far-reaching.

With regard to the Catholic laity, the position has been completely transformed. It can hardly be realised, especially after the experiences of the late war, that in the days of the Peninsular War and at the Battle of Waterloo, no Catholic could serve as an officer in the Navy and Army. The memorials in our Catholic schools to the Catholic officers who fell in the late war are a glorious tribute both to those who made the sacrifice and to the change in public opinion which at long last wiped out this astonishing example of narrow-minded ignorance.

But the " coming into their own " of Catholics was of slow growth, and, as an example, it may be cited that in the early 'seventies, in a regiment stationed in India, the Catholics were compelled to attend the Church of England parade, notwithstanding the fact they had previously paraded for their own Church at an earlier hour, though of course they were dismissed after the parade, and not marched to the Protestant service.

But tradition has not affected Catholics only from the point of view of their treatment by those outside the Church. It is a question even now whether the traditions of the past do not still exercise to a small, though rapidly diminishing, extent an effect on Catholics against taking their full share in the public life of the country. Here and there occasionally there seems an apathy, a sort of suspicion of handicap, a feeling that a Catholic cannot compete on equal terms with those of other or of no denomination. Sometimes this seems to be made an excuse, especially in cases of failure to get on and to achieve success. To some extent, no doubt, there is something in this. Probably it is true in the case of any minority. We remember the phrase " minorities must suffer."

Apart from any feeling amongst those belonging to the same religion, there is a good and natural tendency in human nature to befriend those to whom the word " comrade " or " colleague " is applicable. Freemasonry is an instance of this, and though it is probably true that the practical effect of Freemasonry in England is philanthropic and not religious or, as on the Continent, anti-Christian, still the fact that on account of its being a secret society no Catholic can become a member, creates amongst Masons a prejudice and, at any rate, leads in a preference to the employment of members of the " craft," to the exclusion of others, and particularly of Catholics, who, in the minds of foreign Masons, are the chief enemy.

No doubt, too, there are other ways in which Catholics are at some disadvantage.

The question of the great Public Schools may be cited. That certain social advantages are obtainable from having been at one of the great and historical Public Schools of England may be granted, though, when sifted, it is doubtful if it amounts to very much more than that when a boy makes his debut into Society he knows more people if he has been at one of the large Public Schools, a disadvantage that time soon removes.

But, assuming that there is a certain " cachet " from the worldly point of view from a school career at one of the great Public Schools, is it so very much to ask of a Catholic parent to remember what his or her forbears had to suffer for the Faith, and not so long ago, when their sons could not be educated at all in this country, and to forego such advantages as there may be in order to secure a Catholic atmosphere for the upbringing of their sons ?

There can be few Catholics who have had this

inestimable privilege who do not welcome the Bishops' prohibition against Catholics going to non-Catholic schools. Happily, statistics show the number of Catholic boys attending the Protestant Public Schools as diminishing, and of those who do attend, several are foreigners. The reason given for this improved state of affairs is that the education now given in our schools enables our boys to compete on more equal terms with those from other sclools, and in recent years there has been a gradual change from the former methods of school management and school discipline in our Catholic schools, the result of the abandonment of the foreign system to which we had become accustomed in the schools on the Continent. This has now given way to the English spirit, more suitable to the English character, and parents need no longer have any fear that by sending their sons to our own schools they will be the least less fitted to take their part in the battle of life as English gentlemen, with the added and more important element of a sound Catholic training.

In this connection, the following rather amusing incident occurred not long ago. A master of one of the great Public Schools paid a visit to the master of one of our Catholic schools, and said to him : " We don't want your boys any more than you want ours, and I am always trying to persuade such Catholic parents as come to me to send their boys to you ; but I feel as I have not hitherto had the pleasure of your acquaintance that I ought not to do so any longer without being able to say that I know you and am satisfied as to your credentials."

But, after all is said and done, and making every allowance for the prejudices and ignorance still existing about the Catholic Faith, it cannot be truly said that a Catholic has any justifiable excuse for not coming forward and "doing his bit," and doing it quite as well as one of any other denomination. In fact, in many instances, better ; and what, from a purely worldly point of view, a Catholic may lose in some cases on account of his religion is a gain to him in others, because there are those who by experience have learnt to know what his religion means to a loyal and earnest Catholic, and the sense of integrity and duty it inspires in him has created in some non-Catholic minds a feeling of confidence in employing a Catholic in a situation where special trustworthiness is required.

Consider the difference the opening of the Universities to Catholics has made in preparing and training them for public life. In fairness it must be said that this change might have come about sooner than it did had it not been for the feeling amongst some Catholics themselves that the dangers of a University career outweighed the advantages. The portals of our Universities were opened to us before we had the courage to enter in. It has been suggested that what has been permitted as regards Universities might also be allowed for the Protestant schools, but the difference is immense, and those with experience are emphatic on the paramount importance of the boy having the advantage of the Catholic atmosphere, the training, and indeed the warning, to enable him to face as he emerges into manhood the difficulties and dangers he must expect. Doubtless there was much to be said for the idea that Catholics were not yet sufficiently equipped to compete with the intellectual and moral atmosphere of University life. To Cardinal Newman, and the encouragement he gave to the Catholic laity, do we owe the position Catholics now enjoy at our great Universities. It was some time before the Ecclesiastical Authorities were won over, but an appeal on the part of the laity to Rome ended in the prohibition being withdrawn, subject to conditions as to the provision of Catholic chaplains to supervise the religious needs of Catholic undergraduates. This has proved most beneficial and successful, though more adequate financial support might still be forthcoming from parents and ex-students. But another great force has grown out of this, and that is the establishment of Halls and Houses for enabling the clergy to get all the intellectual advantages of a University education. This is being taken the fullest advantage of by our Religious Orders, and, to a certain extent, by specially selected secular clergy. An amusing story is told of a Catholic on a visit to Oxford soon after some of the Religious Orders had started having their students there. He inquired of one of the University Authorities how these Popish Priests were being welcomed, expecting to receive a far from favourable reply. To his surprise the answer came : " They are the men we want. They are not like the average undergraduate who comes here to amuse himself ; they come to learn, and we give them of our intellectual best." Experience proves that whatever criticisms there may be on our University system, there is no better preparation as an equipment to embark on a public life of any kind, be it political or professional, whether for the Bar, Diplomacy, the various branches of the Civil Services, even for the Army. The late Lord Haig was once asked his opinion as to the best way of getting into the Army, whether through Sandhurst or the University. He replied he had no doubt as to the advantages of the University, adding : " I realised at once when I joined my Regiment that I was intellectually a head and shoulders above my brother officers."

Take the change which has come in the case of those wanting to enter on a political career. Within fifty years ago a Catholic anxious to enter Parliament would have had the greatest difficulty in being selected as a candidate, let alone being elected, if selected. Now the question as to his religion is rarely asked, and it is no uncommon thing for a Catholic candidate, who calls attention to the fact of his religion being a possible difficulty, being told by the local leaders of any political party that the question of religion does not come into the picture, or, if it does, that possibly it is an argument in his favour, as being more likely to secure the Catholic vote, for whatever it may be worth, in his favour, than to alienate votes from other quarters.

It is not, however, to be supposed that this change is a favour to Catholics only, for it applies equally to Jews and other denominations.

Whether such indifference to religion is a good thing or not is open to doubt. It may be that such a lack of consideration of religion at all is not a happy sign for the good of a nation as a whole, but the fact remains that no political party at the present day refuses to consider the claims of a candidate on the ground alone of his being a Catholic.

The same applies to the question of election for all public bodies, whether County Councils, Poor Law Guardians, etc., etc.; and in this connection it is a lamentable fact that the number of Catholics, men and women, willing to come forward for election on local bodies is not larger than it is.

It is not reasonable to expect fair play for Catholic children in schools, workhouses, asylums, etc., if Catholics will not themselves take the trouble to get into a position of authority, and use their influence to the advantage of their poorer and less favoured co-religionists.

Again, as an instance of our emergence from the

catacombs, contrast not only the number but the style and architecture of our churches compared to a hundred years ago. A glance at the *Catholic Directory* for 1829 and a comparison with that of the current year, and the number of priests and churches mentioned in each, is an astonishing and consoling example of progress. At the time of the first Jubilee Celebration of Queen Victoria, the Papal Envoy was taken to see the new Church of the London Oratory, then only recently completed. On his being told it was one of the finest churches in England, he remarked it would be a fine church even in Rome. Since that date several other beautiful churches have been built or enlarged throughout the country, culminating in the great cathedral at Westminster, a worthy monument to the Faith in England, and indeed a lasting tribute to the persevering energy of the late Cardinal Vaughan. At the time he was embarking on the plans he was conversing one day with two prominent ecclesiastics, and explaining his hopes as to the great work he had undertaken. When he left the room the two elderly gentlemen shook their heads and agreed together the Cardinal was far too sanguine, and the time was still far distant when the Catholics of this country could hope for such a magnificent illustration of what a real cathedral could be.

Amongst other developments in the public life of Catholics, consider the question of denominational education, and the great and successful fight the Catholics have made to maintain the principle of definite religious instruction. The Act of 1902, though by no means giving us all we wanted, was an enormous step forward, and the position then gained was undoubtedly due to the persistent and united efforts of the clergy and laity. Even more remarkable than this constructive achieve-

ment was the repelling and final routing of the series
of strenuous attacks from 1906. That Catholics have
yet got what they want, or in justice are entitled to, is
not suggested for a moment, but to have gained what
they have, to have hurled back this series of offensive
movements, is evidence of a vigour which the Catholics
of a century ago would have regarded as impossible.
Again, look at the spread of the exposition of Catholic
doctrine both by clergy and laity in our parks and
public places—the work of the Catholic Evidence
Guild and of the Missionary Society, with its travelling
van. From these two sources alone the amount of
prejudice and ignorance removed is untold, and, let it
be added, the growing tolerance of our non-Catholic
fellow-countrymen must be acknowledged with earnest
gratitude. In this connection, too, must be mentioned
the processions and pilgrimages to various shrines so
well organised by the Guild of Ransom and other bodies.
Those who recall the days following on the Vatican
Council will remember the triumphant vindication by
Dr. Newman, not yet a Cardinal, of the civil allegiance
of Catholics.

Notwithstanding the enormously improved position
of Catholics from what it was a hundred years ago, it
may well be asked : " Have Catholics as a whole taken
full advantage of the opportunities open to them ? "
Might not much more be done in public life ? Apart
from those who do enter the professions, are there not
scores whose lives are devoted to business who have
still leisure enough to give time to work on local bodies,
to assist those struggling to maintain the Boy Scout
and Girl Guide movements, to give a few hours a week
to work in Settlements, to set an example of what can
be done with a little initiative, energy, and perseverance.
It is true we are but some three millions out of a total

of about forty-two millions in England and Scotland, and from many points of view it may be, and indeed often is, argued that we have a position and influence far in excess of what our numbers entitle us to. Is this true? Put it in another way. Considering the freedom, the tolerance, the goodwill which forty-two millions of our fellow-countrymen extend to our handful of only three millions, do we, in recognition and gratitude for this generous attitude compared to the suspicion, the ignorance, the unjust bigotry of a hundred years ago, as a whole give of our best and our utmost as a thanksgiving for this change in public opinion? If the Celebrations of this year bring home to us all we have to be thankful for compared with the trials and sufferings of those who went before us not so very long ago, then this Centenary may be the means of inspiring within us a renewed spirit for work with increased energy and devotion, recognising the generous forbearance of our fellow-countrymen who, in the words of Cardinal Manning, " were robbed of that Faith " which it is our great privilege to possess.

CATHOLICS AND PHILANTHROPY
BY THE BISHOP OF BRENTWOOD

VIII

CATHOLICS AND PHILANTHROPY

PUBLIC benevolence or philanthropy, even when promoted by government, began in this country as a voluntary act of religion. It was part of the common law that the poor of a locality were to be sustained by the Church and parishioners when they were in danger of death by want, and in 1536, when legislation seems to have made its first great effort to devise means for the relief of poor, aged and impotent people, the governors and ministers of religion of the place were to succour and keep them by voluntary and charitable alms, which were to be gathered from good Christian people by means of boxes every Sunday and festival, and every preacher, parson, vicar or curate was in his sermons, at collections and bidding of the beads, in times of confessions and at the making of wills, to exhort people to be liberal.

The voluntary and religious character of public benevolence suffered a violent shock at the dissolution of the monasteries, but it by no means ceased. Two systems developed; a voluntary system which was avowedly conjoined with religion, and a legal system which though not avowedly conjoined with religion carries traces of its religious origins and practices even to this day. Unfortunately, public benevolence, like education, medicine, law, and the military and naval services became for the Catholic aggressively Protestant.

When Catholics were emancipated in 1829 they were confronted with a double problem—the formation of an adequate system of Catholic public benevolence, which would satisfy to the extent of their resources their own religious needs, and the purification of the prevalent system of Protestant relief so that they might enjoy as freed citizens that to which they were entitled without detriment to their religious belief and practice. The struggle to solve these two problems is, in the main, the history of Catholic philanthropy during the past hundred years, but it should never be forgotten that in making the struggle and succeeding they have conferred a benefit on the country and humanity altogether disproportionate to their numbers and material means, and produced a system of amelioration which deserves general encouragement and support.

It would be useful to know how far Catholics in this country at the time of Emancipation were suffering under the existing methods of Protestant relief. There is little reliable information. Charles Butler in a chapter of his " Historical Memoirs " on " Charitable Institutions of the English Catholics for the Education of the Poor " may seem to give the impression that the Catholic poor were well provided for in their own establishments. These, he writes, " are numerous and excellently conducted." They are under the direction of the clergy assisted by numerous persons of the middle class of life "whose first and latest thought is how they can procure raiment for the naked, food for the hungry, instruction and employment for the young, comfort for the aged and the last blessings of religion for the dying." " Their exertions are happily seconded by the noble and wealthy among their brethren."

Bishop Ward in " Catholic London a Century Ago " sheds some light on these general observations. Catholic institutions as organised houses of relief were rare. Societies like the Aged Poor Society, Benevolent Society, Associated Catholic Charities, in which Charles Butler took a personal interest, gave alms to poor people who came within their scope, deriving their funds from the contributions of members, collections in the churches, or appeals at dinners ; and the Society of Charitable Sisters, a body of lay-women established by Dr. Poynter in 1814, worked in the East End and elsewhere " to distribute clothing to cover the shivering members of the orphan and hapless children of indigence and misery." But when we are told that the Church in St. George's in the Fields in 1805 had within its district four prisons, two large hospitals, several workhouses, and a Catholic population of 4000, chiefly poor, and that Virginia Street in the East End had a Catholic population of 7000, we are still left wondering whether Catholic voluntary agencies sufficed, even at that early period, to protect the poorer class of Catholics from the influences which accompanied Protestant relief.

An ominous passage occurs in a circular issued in 1805 by the Committee of Management of St. Patrick's Charity School which states that often the most deserving cases were taken out of their hands when through the death of the parents the children were sent to the workhouse where there was no provision for bringing them up as Catholics ; the Committee appealed for an orphanage and a School of Industry.

In offering an opinion on this subject much must depend on one's estimate of the size of the Catholic population in 1829. The estimate, attributed to Bishop Ward, is 500,000. If these figures are reliable, Catholics were 1 in 28 of the estimated population of England and Wales, an enormous advance on Berington's figures of 60,000, fifty years earlier, when they were 1 in 150 of the total population. It is generally admitted that the number of English Catholics declined during these fifty years, and we can only suppose that this huge increase was due to Catholic immigration, induced by the Industrial Revolution and the desire for betterment, and must have produced a big demand among the weaklings for public relief. Out-relief was common in those days and might have met most of this demand without injury to religion. But those who were forced into the workhouse or prison, or even hospital, had to contend with the determination of the officials to uphold Protestant ascendency in these institutions, and if large numbers entered, this mode of leakage, which is always with us, had already begun.

The treatment meted out to Irish Catholics transported to Australia, in which the Catholic religion was not recognised—Catholics were compelled to attend Church of England services and Catholic children were brought up as Protestants in State orphanages—is an indication of the general feeling of the ruling class in this country previous to Emancipation, and we prefer to think that, though Catholics had increased in numbers since 1780, 500,000 is an exaggeration, and that the need for Catholic Emancipation from disabilities under the English poor-law and voluntary charitable systems, which was not stressed by contemporaries, had not yet presented itself in any striking manner.

In the decade after Emancipation, Catholics were busy in providing the primary requisites for the life of the risen Church; their resources in men and material were meagre; and they had to content themselves with what private benevolence they could exercise and a continuance of those methods of public benevolence that their conditions had already favoured.

But in the list of charities in 1840 there appeared for the first time the Asylum of the Good Shepherd (Hammersmith). The new-comer requires special notice. The nun ever consecrated to the work of

fraternal charity, as distinct from education, had at long
last made her permanent home in England. She represented the ideal of practical charity as proposed by the
Catholic Church ; she asked for no payment or reward ;
she gave herself for her brethren and trusted that God
would add all other things to her. The first foundation
(1839) was of Sisters of Mercy from Ireland, the second
(1840), two Good Shepherd Sisters from France. Dr.
Griffiths, Vicar Apostolic of the London District, had
sent two English ladies to make their novitiate with the
Sisters of Mercy in Dublin with a view to their return
with some Irish Sisters to establish a Convent of Mercy
in Bermondsey ; the same Bishop encouraged the two
French nuns, who could not speak a word of English,
and who had only £40 in their pockets, to found a home
for penitent girls in Hammersmith. These nuns were
the forerunners of a host of religious men and women
who have dedicated their lives to philanthropic work in
England during the last ninety years.

On Ireland's contribution to the enormous total
there is no need to enlarge. It is as obvious as the
prosperity of Catholic charitable work in England to-day.
But we should like to say one word of appreciation for
what England owes to France, and, in a less degree, to
Belgium, for sending their sons and daughters to promote tried schemes of Catholic benevolence in this
country when English Catholics were too few, or too
poor, or too occupied to found them themselves. Not
only the religious of the Good Shepherd, but also the
Sisters of Charity of St. Vincent of Paul, the Sisters of
the Poor with their offshoot the Sisters of Nazareth,
the Sisters of the Sacred Hearts of Jesus and Mary, the
Sisters of Charity of St. Paul, the Daughters of the Cross
—all of them thriving with many houses—are due to
French or Belgian initiative.

Dr. Griffiths died in 1847. Dr. Wiseman came to London and at the restoration of the Hierarchy in 1850 became the first Cardinal Archbishop of Westminster. Miss McEntee, in her valuable and exhaustive volume, recently published—" The Social Catholic Movement in Great Britain "—thus summarises the new Archbishop's relations to the problems of Catholic poverty as they presented themselves at his accession ; " Impelled by the exigencies of the situation to pioneer work in rehabilitating Catholicism in the minds of the English people and interested by temperament in scholarly and cultural pursuits, he never gave more than casual attention to conditions with which his successor was to grapple with extraordinary success. . . . In a general way he realised the need for the exercise of Christian charity, but he did not feel called upon to be a standard-bearer of the democratic movement."

There is unintentional misconception of the situation in these words. Nothing bearing the remotest resemblance to a democratic movement among Catholics, in the modern sense of the term, existed in the times of the last Vicars-Apostolic and the active years of Cardinal Wiseman, nor was it possible. Catholics were scattered and without cohesion ; even the effort of O'Connell to democratise the Catholic Institute was a failure. The Catholic population had multiplied, largely owing to the influx of Irish men and women into Great Britain during the famine years of 1845, 1846 and 1847 and after, and the conditions under which the poorest of them lived in the great towns were appalling. To say that the Cardinal never gave more than casual attention to these conditions is a reflection upon his episcopal character which is not deserved. The truth is that Catholic poverty had reached dimensions that made it beyond the power of the Catholic community to cope with it. But the community recognised the problem and with the guidance and help of their spiritual leaders worked superhumanly to solve it.

It should be noted again that the problem was pre-eminently religious. The poor Irish people who were forced to live in squalid and miserable conditions were both spiritually and corporally starved, and it is to their everlasting credit that they preferred corporal starvation to spiritual starvation, indeed deprived themselves of what are called " the necessaries of life " to provide the deeper necessaries without which life is not worth living. As early as 1843, Mr. Lucas, the Editor of the *Tablet*, had summed up the position in the words " Provision for the Catholic Poor." " We want Priests and Churches, Schoolmasters and Schoolhouses ; and then a long train of benevolent institutions for supplying the needs of their bodily and human existence."

It is a mistake to attribute the success or the failure of a vast undertaking of this kind to any single bishop or series of bishops. All the bishops gave what leader-ship and assistance they could. The means at their disposal were of the scantiest. They preached charity sermons, wrote pastorals, encouraged religious men and women to make foundations, promoted collections, assiduously visited their flocks. Bishop Ward in his " Sequel to Catholic Emancipation " has these apposite words about the bond of union between English and Irish Catholics which was the consequence of the famine. " Those who were able left their unfortunate country and many took refuge in England. For three years there was a continual stream of immigrants arriving on our shores. They brought their religion with them and many of the English congregations increased by leaps and bounds. New churches became necessary and additional school accommodation, and the work of

every mission expanded. Happily they found pastors—
many of them of Irish descent—ready to minister to
them, whose self-denial and devotion to duty did not
fall short of that which they had experienced in their
own country. And it was soon put to a severe test, for
the immigrants brought with them the famine fever
which quickly spread. Cholera also broke out and
many of the large English towns became centres of
pestilence. The clergy attended the victims and faced
the danger with courage and devotion. Numbers of
them contracted the disease and died martyrs to their
priestly vocation. At least one bishop lost his life in
this way and some hundreds of priests."

Extracts from a personal letter written by Dr.
Wiseman early in 1850 give some indication of the
success already achieved in London. "It is hard perhaps
to describe in a letter what is going on. Externally
something can be seen, *e.g.* in less than two years we
have established—and I hope solidly—seven new communities of women and three of men, in this district,
have opened up two orphan-houses, have set up an
excellent middle-school or grammar school, containing
seventy boys already, and have opened four new missions
in the heart of the poor population, and at least seven
others in different parts. This year I have a good
prospect of four great establishments springing up in
London. Yet all this I consider as nothing compared
with what I hope is latently and spiritually being done.
The vast increase of communions, the number of
admirable conversions, the spread of charitable associations are less known though still manifest to all. I think
I can safely say that in a year, or little more, 15,000
persons have been reclaimed by the Retreats given in
courts and alleys. In one place, the very worst street
of London, we boldly planted a mission among the

thieves and prostitutes and the change was so visible that a Protestant policeman asked if it would not go on again and observed that the Government ' ought to support it.' But it is in the clergy that I have found my greatest consolation. . . . I assure you that at times I am inclined to feel low and dejected at thinking and seeing how much there is to be done which is being neglected. In one district alone we have 5000 children to educate, and accommodation for only 400. We want a thousand things which our wretched poverty prevents us from having."

This long reference to Cardinal Wiseman is in the nature of a digression. Were it not for the mistaken impression we have noticed his name need not have been introduced at all. For Catholic philanthropy for the poor is a natural product of the Catholic religion and, as the Church established itself in England, there was a strong effort in every diocese on the part of the bishop, clergy and people to provide benevolent institutions for its suffering members. The surprise, when we look at the list of charities in 1865, is what was done, not what was left undone. The movement received a strong impetus when Archbishop Manning made his appeal in 1866 to establish the Westminster Diocesan Fund for the education of 20,000 children, uneducated and uncared for in the streets of London. It met with an immediate and most generous response from the Catholic laity and has been the means of establishing orphanages, reformatories, industrial and poor-law schools in the Westminster Archdiocese, several of which are functioning to-day.

The example set in London was followed in other places and a network of these institutions, many of them built at the expense of the religious men and women who worked them, gradually covered the land. As

early as 1842 Charles Langdale had pointed out that
more schools were needed to prevent leakage, and the
discussion on the repeal of the Penal Laws (1841–6)
emphasised the sectarian manner in which gaols and
workhouses were conducted. There were not enough
clergy to minister to the spiritual needs of a sudden and
large influx of Catholics, of whom many fell out of touch
with religious influences and many others hung on their
fringe ; when they and their children entered the workhouse and workhouse school, they were in imminent
peril of renouncing their Catholic allegiance altogether.
The Catholic community were aware of the danger, but
it was impossible for them to relieve the State of the
feeding, clothing and education of a multitudinous poor,
and nothing remained but to come to terms with the
authorities and provide institutions to which those
authorities might send chargeable children to whom
they were unable to give the Catholic upbringing they
required. This arrangement, we say it to the credit of
the authorities, has worked well. The initial difficulties
have nearly all been surmounted, and, as in elementary
education, a partnership between the various public
authorities and the Catholic authorities has been evolved
which with good-will on both sides has produced an
aggregate of Catholic philanthropy which is an asset to
the country and a marvel in the Catholic Church. As
the government gradually widened its responsibility
for distress, it offered opportunities to the Catholic
community to widen theirs also, and at the present time
there is scarcely a department of benevolent activity
which is not being conducted on Catholic lines and under
Catholic auspices with government encouragement and
support. Besides the poor-law institutions already
mentioned, there come under this category homes for
physically and mentally defective children, homes for

penitents, refuges for fallen women, sanatoria for tuberculous children and adults, homes for cripples and epileptics and many others.

But its association with poor-law relief is only one aspect of Catholic philanthropic activity. A mass of Catholic destitution existed in 1866 which was outside the poor-law system, either because the sufferers could not or would not accept its assistance. Catholic voluntary effort, as we have stated, was insufficient to cope with it. Application was frequently made to Protestant voluntary agencies for relief and this often entailed a loss to the children of their Catholic faith. The Catholic community chafed under this attrition, but it was not until 1899 that effective measures were taken in London to arrest it. Cardinal Vaughan in a Pastoral Letter issued in 1895 put the position clearly. " We must hesitate before we reproach our Protestant fellow-countrymen for these losses. Many of them have spoken to us with sufficient plainness, if not with sufficient satisfaction. They have told us that it is not their intention to proselytise ; but that as the Catholic community in London make no adequate provisions for the Catholic waifs and strays who infest our slums and appear before our police-courts they, at least, must open the doors of their institutions and give them a hearty welcome. . . . In some of these cases the State, as guardian of Society, comes in with ample provision ; but in a large number of cases the State and public opinion expect us to take up the cause of our own destitute and orphan children ourselves, if we would not be privy to their becoming criminals or apostates." " It is impossible to estimate with accuracy the number of our losses. Thousands and thousands of Catholic children have been robbed of their faith in past years ; they have been immigrated ; they have been spirited from one place to another; they have been cut off from all Catholic influence; their very names have been changed and they have been sent into the world aliens to the religion of their baptism."

In 1899, as a result of this appeal, a Crusade of Rescue was organised and in 1901 was amalgamated with an older Society, the "Homes for Destitute Catholic Children." Similar organisations were established in other dioceses and a general effort was made to live up to the motto "No Catholic child who is really destitute or whose faith is in danger and who cannot be otherwise provided for, is ever refused." This effort still persists and grows. We do not say that it is as complete as it might be, but it is a noble work, nobly supported, and is the chief direct contribution of the modern Catholic community to philanthropic enterprise.

It is difficult to ascertain with complete accuracy what the results of the strivings of a hundred years are in charitable institutions, in man-power, and in numbers relieved and maintained. We are well within the mark when we say that more than 200 residential institutions, many of considerable size, exist in England and Wales at the present time; of these some 150 are Orphanages, Poor Law, Industrial and Reformatory Schools which devote themselves to the education and training of over 12,000 children. There are 29 hospitals, general and special, and 45 homes and refuges other than those mentioned above. Nearly all are under the direction of, and mainly staffed by, religious men and women who have dedicated their lives to charitable service. Space does not permit us to give a list of these charities, but we take the liberty of recommending the inquirer to "A Handbook of Catholic Charitable Organisations," compiled by the Superior Council of the St. Vincent de Paul Society and published by the Catholic Social Guild as the " Catholic Social Year Book " for 1927, in which a list and account of many of these charities are given, together with information on Charitable Associations, national and diocesan.

In this survey of the history of Catholic Philanthropy in England and Wales during the past hundred years we have refrained, as far as possible, from mentioning names. The Catholic dislikes the word " Philanthropy," and we are sure that no Catholic would care to be singled out as a Catholic Philanthropist; every Catholic is a philanthropist or hardly a practical Catholic at all. We have aimed rather at showing how a small, impoverished Catholic community under the Providence of God has struggled to express in the circumstances which followed emancipation its religious conviction that men should have love one towards another. The principal actors have not been the organisers, debaters, large benefactors, but the humble, silent, cheerful workers, who have prayed and wrought and spent themselves, each in his own place and generation, that the vision which we see to-day might be. Their names are unknown to us but they are written in the Book of Life. We are urged to these remarks in our anxiety to incorporate in this essay a short account of the operations of the Society of St. Vincent de Paul, since it was established in England in 1844. It came to us, as many another benefit, from France. Its object was to induce Catholic lay men to come to close quarters with poverty and distress, whether spiritual or corporal; to prevent it if possible; to visit it, observe it, appreciate it; actively to sympathise with it and relieve it. It was the antithesis of the workhouse system in which the community segregates its unfor- tunates and subordinates them to officialdom; the Society called upon its members to retain the distressed within the community and treat them as brothers.

Long before the world had heard of the blissfulness of the service of man, the Society was showing that there was no proper Christian life without it. It required no wealth, demanded no extraordinary exertion. While a man ate and drank and earned his daily bread, he was to exercise himself in Christian charity towards his neighbour. No work of charity was outside its scope. The Society has prospered in England, but not as much as one would like.

The report for 1927 is before us. There are about 622 Conferences in England and Wales ; the number of Active Members is 7179 ; the visits paid to families were 229,790 ; special visits were 49,344 and the cases visited were 28,532. Among the special works of the Society are the supervision of Male Catholic Probation work in the Metropolitan area ; the supervision of a Hostel at Harpenden for lads under a term of probation ; the supervision of the George Blount Home for Catholic working boys of good character ; the aftercare of Industrial School Catholic boys ; the management of a Catholic Seamen's Home and Institute at Victoria Docks, London.

It remains to say a few words of the future of Catholic public benevolence in this country. Manifestly there must be separate Catholic benevolence as there is separate Catholic education ; both are religious works and the decline of either would spell unhappiness to the individual Catholic and decline to the message and influence of the Catholic Church. Fortunately there is every sign of growth. Public opinion seems to favour an expansion of Catholic benevolence on the ground that voluntary charitable agencies should be encouraged and that a religious community has responsibility for the maintenance of its poorer members. While recognising this responsibility as part of their religious teaching Catholics are entitled to their share of the compassion of the State. The State shows a disposition to continue to give it under such conditions as to make it possible for Catholics to accept it. There has been perennial discussion as to the co-operation of Catholics in schemes or movements of benevolence supported or promoted by religious persons or sections who are not Catholic. With every scheme or movement that protests in word or deed against the Catholic religion they can have nothing to do. Happily that attitude is waning, there is a tendency to help distress or destitution without making the help a reason to injure religion, and it has been found possible for Catholics to contribute to and use hospitals and similar institutions under voluntary and non-Catholic religious management without conscientious objections. The subject bristles with difficulties and this is not the place to consider it. We venture to express the hope that while practising their own methods of Catholic benevolence, Catholics may be allowed to retain their hard-earned place as co-operators in a general system of benevolence which has in view the spiritual and physical welfare of every member of the nation.

RELIGIOUS ORDERS OF MEN
BY ABBOT BUTLER

IX

RELIGIOUS ORDERS OF MEN

IT appears that in 1829 there were in all England and Scotland only four communities of men of the religious Orders. Throughout the penal times a number of priests of the older Orders—Benedictines, Dominicans, Franciscans, Jesuits—had at all times been labouring on the English Mission; and in 1829 there were several such, working as individual priests in missions and chaplaincies in many parts of the country. But of communities of men living together an organised life under rule, there were but four : the Benedictine priories at Ampleforth and Downside, the Dominican at Hinckley, and the Jesuit College at Stonyhurst. These English communities had all been uprooted from their Continental homes by the upheaval of the French Revolution, and had succeeded in re-establishing themselves at home. Several convents of women belonging to the old Orders had similarly come back to England; but this chapter is concerned only with the men. And probably in nothing does the growth of the Catholic Church in England since Emancipation stand out more strikingly than in the multiplication of the four communities of 1829 into the multitudinous and multifarious communities of 1929. This is all the more wonderful in that the Emancipation Act was framed with provisions for bringing about the gradual but sure extinction of all Orders and Institutes of religious men by making illegal all recruiting : women were not interfered with. These disabilities remained always a dead letter, and were in practice disregarded; but they were repealed only the other day.

The first increase in religious Orders of men was the introduction into England of three Italian congregations of quite modern origin. The Rosminians, or Fathers of Charity, were the first comers, introduced by Bishop Baines, Vicar Apostolic of the Western District, at Prior Park, Bath, in 1835, when he had failed to secure a Benedictine community to staff his new college there. The Passionists came in 1842, and the Redemptorists a year later. The three new Orders were akin in spirit, scope and work; their vocation was primarily the extra-parochial work of preaching missions in the great towns and in country places, giving retreats, lectures, and so on. They introduced the Italian practices of devotion, and thereby gave a shock to the old-fashioned English "Challoner Catholics," brought up in the solid austere piety engendered by the conditions of suppression in which they had lived, out of touch with the more exuberant forms of devotion that had grown up in Catholic countries, and so looking with suspicion on novelties. The Italian Fathers on their side thought the English Catholics to be in a backwater, stagnating and infected by the Protestantism in the midst of which they lived; and they believed that the low estate of things Catholic was due to the over-caution and timidity of the Vicars Apostolic and clergy: they imagined it wanted only energy and courage, and a forward movement on the methods of modern Catholicism as in Italy—and England would soon be Catholic again. These ideas they urged at Rome, and thereby caused no small difficulties for the Vicars and the old priests. Fr. Gentili, a truly apostolic and remarkable man, the leading Rosminian, was one of those who took part in this agitation; but we have Dr. Ullathorne's witness, who knew him intimately, that at the end of his life, 1850, he recognised and regretted the injustice of these attacks on the old clergy.[1]

Among the Passionists the most prominent figure was the saintly Fr. Dominic Barbieri, famous as the one chosen by Newman in 1845, at whose hands to make his submission to the Catholic Church.

Fr. Gentili it was who gave the first public mission in England, at Nottingham in 1842, and again at Coventry in 1845, while Ullathorne was rector; and on this occasion took place the first public procession in which a statue of the Blessed Virgin was carried in England since the Reformation, as an expiation for the Lady Godiva procession going on at the same time.[2]   When Ullathorne went to Bristol as Vicar Apostolic he had Gentili to give a mission there in 1847, and another of a month's duration in 1848; " it had a great effect, and began a new order of things," says Ullathorne ; but the prolonged effort was too great and caused Fr. Gentili's death a year later.   Meantime Fr. Dominic, the Passionist, was at work giving missions ; also the Redemptorists. These three Italian congregations have been dwelt upon, as they played so great a part in the awakening of active Catholic devotional life in England, and in the infusing of new blood and new spirit into the Catholic remnant in the first years after Emancipation, before the increase and revival consequent on the accession of the converts of the Oxford Movement and the great Irish immigration after the Famine.

When we come to deal with the general subject of the religious Orders of men during the century, the best method will be to take the various Orders and Institutes in groups and briefly sketch the outline of their developments, with an indication of the spirit and work of each. and what they severally stand for.   Thus, it may be

[1] See *Life of Bishop Ullathorne*, i. p. 152.   [2] *Ibid*. i. p. 132.

hoped, will be drawn a picture of the variety, the richness, and the usefulness of the many forms of religious life offered by the Catholic Church to men.[1]

The great groups will be in historical order: (i) Monks; (ii) Canons; (iii) Friars; (iv) Regular Clerks; (v) Secular Clerks; (vi) Institutes for Foreign Missions to the Heathen; (vii) Teaching Institutes; (viii) Institutes of Brothers for Works of Charity.

I

Monks

1. Of the monastic Orders the *Black Benedictines* naturally come first. The principal group of Benedictine monasteries in England are those of the Old English Congregation which survived the break-up of the Reformation, and in a wonderful way has preserved the line of continuity with the Black Monks of Old England. The two Benedictine communities of 1829 belonged to it. The Downside community was that of St. Gregory domiciled in Doway from 1606; the Ampleforth that of St. Lawrence of Dieuleward, Lorraine, of the like date. A third community of the English Congregation, that of St. Edmund, originally in Paris, existed in 1829, but not on English soil, being established at Doway in the old home of St. Gregory's. They were in 1829 small struggling communities that had with difficulty survived the storm of the Revolution and consequent transplanting. A school was attached to each; and monasteries and schools in time took firm root and grew and thrived through half a century in a quiet unobtrusive way. The first step forward for the English Benedictines was the opening in 1860 of a new monastery on new lines

[1] A useful handbook is *Monasteries and Religious Houses of Great Britain*, by F. M. Steele, 1903.

at Belmont, close to Hereford, through the generosity of the late Francis Wegg Prosser, Esq., the Founder. It was founded as a cathedral priory, the church being the pro-cathedral of the new diocese of Newport and Menevia; it was also to be the common noviciate and tirocinium, or training house for all the monasteries of the Congregation. The conditions of housing and of the chapels in the older monasteries were such as to make impracticable a full observance of Benedictine liturgical and conventual life; and so the first four years of monastic life passed in fuller Benedictine conditions, and amid much liturgical stateliness, exercised a very elevating influence on the young monks.

In 1878 was opened a fifth monastery at Fort Augustus, the only Benedictine revival in Scotland.

As the monasteries and schools grew and waxed strong, and the elements of Benedictine life could be better carried out, a great return from the conditions of the missionary period towards normal Benedictine conditions was effected by Leo XIII, and in 1900 the monasteries of the Congregation were raised from the status of priories to the full Benedictine stature of abbeys. A few years later the noviciates were reopened in each abbey, according to the tradition of the Benedictine monastic family; and Belmont became a normal abbey. There has been a notable increase in the liturgical side of the life, so that a full Benedictine regime is now carried out in a way worthy of the houses that by legitimate descent represent the old Benedictine monasteries of England. Moreover, in 1903, consequent on the French laws affecting religious Orders, the third old community, that of St. Edmund, migrated from Doway, and established itself at Woolhampton, near Reading.

Besides those of the old Congregation, there are other Black Monk monasteries in England. In the 'sixties was established at Ramsgate a house of the Subiaco Congregation of Primitive observance, which opened a school. In 1882 Père Muard's community of the same Congregation, expelled from France, came to England and settled on the site of the old Cistercian Abbey of Buckfast, Devon. A few years earlier was established at Erdington, Birmingham, under the stress of the Kulturkampf in Germany, a community of German monks, which since the war has gone back to Germany. At a later date, again under stress of expulsions from France, two houses of the French Congregation have been established in England, the abbey at Farnborough and Quarr Abbey. Last of all came the convert community of Caldey Island,[1] 1913, which has been affiliated to the Subiaco Congregation, in connection with Ramsgate.

Thus there are now ten major Benedictine abbeys, six of them with schools attached ; and there is a day school at Ealing, London, attached to a priory dependent on Downside. The abbeys belong to three Congregations of English, Italian and French origin ; and, as should be expected among Benedictines, while they show a substantive unity in life and spirit, it is a unity marked by diversity in detail. The most characteristic work of the English Benedictines will probably be thought to be their schools. Those of the three houses of old foundation are now great modern public schools, rightly looked on as in the front rank of Catholic schools, and of the public schools of the country, holding their own well at the Universities in studies and athletics alike, and in the Services. Also, as an inheritance from their work in the English Mission as individual missioners during the long dark period of persecution and penal laws, the monks of the English Congregation have

---

[1] The Benedictines of Caldey Island have now removed to Prinknash Park, Gloucestershire.

a number of parishes wherein they live and work as pastoral priests. At Oxford and at Cambridge are smaller houses of studies, where young monks go through university courses in preparation for their work as teachers in the schools. And there has been a quite remarkable, if restricted, output of historical and religious literature to the credit of the old Congregation.

Of the monks of the other Congregations, those of Ramsgate resemble the English, in that they have a school, and also serve the parishes on the Isle of Thanet. The others naturally develop in a high degree the liturgical element of Benedictine life; some of them produce literary work—Farnborough is conspicuous for the scholarly and learned character of its productions; and most of them undertake pastoral ministrations on occasion to come to the aid of the secular clergy.

The other old monastic Orders, Cistercian and Carthusian, have each a house in England.

2. The *Cistercian* or *Trappist* abbey of Mount St. Bernard, in Charnwood Forest, Leicestershire, was founded in 1837 by that remarkable man, Ambrose Phillipps de Lisle. The Cistercian idea was a literal return to the conditions of life at Monte Cassino in St. Benedict's own day: a life of liturgical prayer, seclusion, silence and manual labour. The Trappist reform, initiated by de Rancé, carries out this programme with great fidelity; and at Charnwood Forest the monks, a small community of only nine priests with several lay-brothers, live this life of prayer, and of work on farm and fields which fills up the greater portion of the day.

3. The *Carthusian* is at the opposite pole: the Trappists live their life in common with no privacy; the Carthusian lives in the isolation of his cell, almost a hermit, coming into contact with his brethren only at the prolonged church services. This, however, Trappists and Carthusians have in common, that the extreme

austerity of both regimes justifies the purely contemplative life they lead, and their withdrawal from the external good works of the " mixed life," as exercised by Orders ranked, for all that, as " contemplative "— Benedictines, Dominicans, Franciscans. The manner of Carthusian life is well known, and there were half a dozen Charterhouses in Catholic England. Nowadays there is but one, Parkminster, under the Sussex Downs, established in 1883, as a place of refuge for French Carthusians. It now has seventeen priests, mostly French, but with a growing English element.

II

CANONS REGULAR

1. Reckoned with the monastic Orders, the *Austin* or *Black Canons* flourished greatly in Catholic England, having several large abbeys. In 1880 members of the Italian Lateran Congregation of Canons Regular came to revive the Institute in England, and set up various houses. They are mainly concentrated in Cornwall where is the noviciate house at Bodmin and several parishes served by single canons ; there are two houses in London, Eltham and Stroud Green. In the communities a monastic regime is followed. The external work is principally pastoral work, either in large town parishes, served by communities, or in country parishes served by single priests.

2. The *Premonstratensians* or *White Canons* of St. Norbert also flourished in Catholic England. They, too, have come back, from Belgium in 1870, but so far the revival has been but a small beginning. They have a - community in Manchester serving one of the large parishes ; and they serve three or four small parishes elsewhere.

The difference between canons and monks may be put thus : while monks are religious men living a monastic cenobitical life in common, to whom the clerical state is a non-essential adjunct, with the canons this is reversed : their clerical state is of their essence, the monastic element an adjunct. Canons are clerics, priests, who take on a monastic regime ; monks are cenobites who, not originally but from an early time, have habitually been in Holy orders.

III

FRIARS

Chaucer's " alle the ordres foure " of *Friars* are with us again to-day. They are Dominicans or Black Friars, Franciscans or Grey, Carmelites or White, and Austin Friars ; to them must be added the Servites. They all go back to the thirteenth century.

1. *Dominicans*, or *Black Friars*, or *Friars Preacher*. Like the other old English Orders, the English Dominicans had a house on the Continent, at Louvain, during penal times, whence issued forth a succession of priests on to the English Mission. On the suppression of this house at the French Revolution the English Province was thrown on its own resources in England, and after various vicissitudes succeeded in establishing a noviciate house at Hinckley in 1814. This was one of the four religious communities of men existing in 1829. But at that date and for twenty years more, the old Province seemed on the verge of extinction. In 1850 the noviciate was moved to better and more monastic buildings at Woodchester, near Stroud. Since that date the formation of houses with communities has gone on in steady progress, so that now the Black Friars have a great London house at Haverstock Hill ; also a house of

studies at Hawkesyard, Rugeley ; and lesser communities at Manchester, Newcastle and Leicester, serving large town parishes. A boys' school has quite recently been opened at Laxton, Northamptonshire. And most important and characteristic of all, a church and friary are in process of erection at Oxford, in St. Giles's, to be one of the great Dominican international colleges, of like standing with those at Louvain or Fribourg. At this Oxford college will be a full theological faculty, at which scholastic philosophy and the Dominican traditional theology of St. Thomas will be taught publicly to all comers. The external works of the English Dominicans are very varied. Living up to their name of Friars Preacher they give missions and retreats with great frequency, and they undertake courses of sermons as special preachers. Certain of the best equipped among them give at the Universities, both Oxford and Cambridge and the new Universities, as Manchester, courses of public lectures, frequented by University circles of all kinds, on apologetics and on philosophical and theological problems of the day, grappling with such difficulties by the principles of St. Thomas's teaching. They take a leading part, too, in more popular forms of propaganda, such as the open-air speaking of the Catholic Evidence Guild to crowds of all comers in the London Parks, or the Bull Ring in Birmingham. A considerable output of high-class apologetic and theological literature is to their credit. Their priories in the towns minister to large middle-class and working-class parishes. Their works are manifold ; and it is not too much to say that of all the religious Orders now at work in England, the Dominicans most fully realise the idea of " mission " in its primary sense of effort to bring the Catholic Faith to the knowledge of the great masses of the English people.

2. *Franciscans*, or *Grey Friars*, or *Friars Minor*. The

English Franciscans, who had laboured so faithfully in the English Mission through the penal times, unfortunately did not weather the storm of the French Revolution. On the destruction of their house at Doway they made efforts, which proved unavailing, to open a noviciate in England. In 1829 the old Province was moribund, and twelve years later it had to be wound up, only half a dozen elderly friars surviving. The restoration of Franciscan life in England came from the Continent.

The first comers were the *Capuchins*. They were one of the many strict reforms that have marked Franciscan history, and date from the beginning of the sixteenth century. The Capuchin reform has flourished vigorously, and is now one of the three great branches that exist side by side in the Order of St. Francis. It was in 1850 that Italian Capuchin friars came to England and started a friary at Peckham, South London. In the early days they did great pioneer work, notably in South Wales, under Bishop Brown, founding and nursing missions in many parts of the country, to the number of thirty-five, which, when fairly established, they handed over to the bishops, to be taken on by the secular clergy. The head house is at Peckham, the house of studies at Olton, Birmingham; in these houses, and in others at Pantasaph, North Wales, and Crawley, Sussex, there are strong communities, and there are two or three lesser ones elsewhere. Quite recently they have fallen in with the current that is carrying all the religious Orders to the Universities, and have opened a house in Oxford. It need not be said that the Italian element has died out long ago, and the Capuchins have become a thoroughly English body. In 1870 they were formed into an English Province of the Order. True to St. Francis' idea, their primary external work is the preaching of missions and giving retreats; and they lay themselves out to help the pastoral clergy by sermons and by responding to calls for supplies at need. They have had among them more than one thinker and writer of distinction in the front rank of English Catholic writers on theological and religious topics; and they have given to the world what is certainly the best modern " Life of St. Francis " in any language.

Eight years after the Capuchins came friars of other Franciscan reforms, since grouped together by Leo XIII under the designation of *Friars Minor* pure and simple. They came from Belgium, and in 1858 made a small beginning in Cornwall; they moved after a short time to West Gorton, Manchester, where in 1862 was opened a friary destined to be for many years the centre of the Friars Minor. The head house is now at Forest Gate, East London; there is still a strong community at Manchester, also one at Liverpool, one at Glasgow, and five or six more with half a dozen priests in each, most of them in the great towns where the friars serve large working-class parishes, thus carrying on St. Francis' idea of ministering to the spiritual needs of the poor; and this is their chief external work. They also undertake missions, retreats and sermons.

The third great group of the Franciscan Order, the *Conventuals*, also is represented in England; but they came much later and have taken root less firmly, indeed they only just exist. They have one small house in Liverpool and a couple of parishes, and number only eight priests all told.

The three other Orders of Friars are among us in England, but on a smaller scale than the Black and Grey.

3. The *White Friars* or *Carmelites* were strong in England in olden times, but they died out completely long ago. In 1862 the Discalced Carmelites of St.

Teresa and St. John of the Cross came to England from Spain, the home of the reform, and have a well-known and much frequented church in Kensington and a noviciate house at Wincanton, Somerset.

4. The *Augustinian Friars*, though strong in Ireland, are weak in England. They have two or three parishes in London, but no community.

5. The *Servites* or *Servants of Mary*, founded at Florence at the middle of the thirteenth century, were not in England in old Catholic times ; they first came in 1864 and have their chief house in Fulham Road, South Brompton, where a community serves a large parish. They have other small communities at Bognor and at Begbrook, Oxford, and a few lesser parishes.

Monks, Canons, and Friars are the " old Orders," coming from the Middle Ages ; we pass now to the modern Orders and Institutes, the first of which are the Regular Clerks, a product of the Counter-Reformation.

IV

REGULAR CLERKS

Regular Clerks are by their institute clerics and priests, and they are devoted to some particular work or works as their own special object.

1. By far the most important of the Regular Clerks is the *Society of Jesus*, or *Jesuits*. They have at all times since Elizabeth's reign been strong and influential in England, and one of the four communities of men in 1829 was the Jesuit College at Stonyhurst, near Blackburn, Lancashire. Stonyhurst, indeed, was a threefold community—the school, the noviciate of the Society, and the scholasticate being severally established in three houses

on the estate. The boys' school was the continuation
of the old college of the English Jesuits at St. Omer, near
Calais. During our century the Jesuits have been able
to form an astonishing number of communities for
carrying on the manifold religious activities of the Society.
There are the houses of government and formation of
the Society itself : two at the headquarters at Farm Street
in Mayfair; the noviciate at Roehampton ; houses of
studies, one in Oxford itself, and one, a year ago, a few
miles out of Oxford, at Heythrop, Chipping Norton ;
while the old house of studies at St. Beuno's, North
Wales, is now the tertian house of the English Province.

A foremost work of the Jesuits has always been
secondary and higher education. Of boarding schools,
besides Stonyhurst, they have opened others at Beaumont,
Windsor, and at Mount St. Mary's, Chesterfield. These
schools, above all Stonyhurst, have a fine record in the
army, in the professions, and in public life. But in
these days, when the cry is that the most pressing need
of the Catholic educational system is the opening of
efficient secondary day schools in the large towns, perhaps
their greatest contribution to Catholic education is the
effort the Jesuits have made to meet this urgent want :
in North and South London, at Stamford Hill and Wim-
bledon respectively, in Liverpool, Preston, Leeds and
Glasgow do they conduct large day schools with much
efficiency. The day schools are attached to large town
parishes worked by the Fathers in community, as also
are many other such town parishes, and lesser ones in
smaller centres. They give retreats in great number, and
missions, lectures, sermons ; and they organise and run
certain widespread confraternities, as the Apostleship of
Prayer, Children of Mary, Knights of the B. Sacrament.
A new departure has been the opening of retreat houses
for working men in Catholic centres, chiefly in the

North, where workmen go in great numbers to make week-end retreats under the guidance of a Father. Also should be mentioned the house at Osterley to meet the case of " late vocations," those who, having perhaps gone into business and later on feeling the call to the priesthood, find themselves debarred by lack of Latin ; they there receive the instruction that is necessary, and in this way a quite considerable number of vocations have been saved for the secular clergy and for religious Orders.

In the " Apostolate of the press " the Jesuits have been easily the first among the Orders in England ; it may safely be said that their output greatly exceeds that of all the others put together. They were fortunate in recruiting in the 'fifties a number of distinguished Oxford converts, who gave impetus to this sphere of activity. Their publications are of all kinds—spiritual books, controversial, homiletic, biblical, theological, philosophical, historical ; much of it popular, to meet practical religious needs, some of it of high scientific quality. And for sixty-five years they have produced " The Month," a high-class religious periodical.

In short, in the many-sidedness and versatility of their religious activities, the Jesuits by the very nature of their institute surpass all other Orders.

Other Regular Clerks are the Rosminians, Redemptorists and Passionists. Their work and their broadening influence on the English Catholics in the early days after Emancipation, has already been spoken of. The work of all three Congregations is much the same : missions, retreats, preaching.

2. The *Rosminians* or *Fathers of Charity* have also education as an integral part of their vocation. They have in England one large secondary boarding school at Ratcliff ; their headquarters and house of studies is at

Rugby; they are strong in South Wales, where in the early days they did good pioneering work, and so now they are established in large parishes in Cardiff and Newport; they have lesser parishes in various places, among them Ely Place, London.

3. The *Redemptorists* have their headquarters at Clapham; they have houses also at Erdington, Birmingham, at Liverpool, at Monkwearmouth, at Perth, and elsewhere. Though it is not usual with them, in England they do serve the parishes attached to most of their houses. All their houses are communities; but their special vocation being the preaching of missions, the ideal is that each Father spend the year half in community and half abroad giving missions and retreats.

4. The *Passionists* at the beginning got much prestige from the holiness and zeal of the first comer, Fr. Dominic, and from the fact that in 1847 the well known Fr. Ignatius Spencer, Lord Spencer's brother, and one of the pre-Oxford converts, threw in his lot with them—a man of boundless zeal. Their headquarters are in London, at Highgate, where they have a large community serving the parish. They are established also at St. Helens, at Broadway, Worcestershire, and at Glasgow. As with the Redemptorists, their houses are always communities, but their vocation as missioners calls them out with great frequency.

V

SECULAR CLERKS

These are secular priests living together in community, under rule and obedience so long as they abide in the community. Two such institutes in England, the *Oratorians* of St. Philip Neri and the *Oblates* of St. Charles Borromeo, claim special interest from the fact that the

English foundations were the work respectively of Newman and Manning. There are two Oratories, the Birmingham Oratory of Newman, and the London Oratory of Faber. Both serve large town parishes, and by St. Philip's special creation of the Little Oratory they are conspicuous centres of religious influence on men. Newman started the Oratory School, the first attempt to graft English public school ideas on to Catholic education. The school has had a distinguished record, and has recently been transplanted from Edgbaston to Caversham, Reading. The Oblates of St. Charles are at Bayswater, and serve the parish there, and also parishes in other parts of London.

Under the category of secular clerks fall the *Vincentians*, so-called from their founder, St. Vincent of Paul, also *Lazarists*. They were founded to give missions to the poor, but also to undertake the formation of candidates for the priesthood in seminaries. In England their chief work is conducting the Catholic Training College for male teachers in the elementary schools; they have also large parishes in Sheffield and Lanark.

VI

INSTITUTES FOR FOREIGN MISSIONS

The Congregations and Institutes for working missions to the Heathen call for a special word. Some of the older Orders, Friars and Jesuits, have a missionary side, but the definite mission to the Heathen is not strongly marked in the English Provinces.

St. Joseph's Society for Foreign Missions is the only English creation of a religious congregation in modern times, the first of Cardinal Vaughan's three religious creations. Founded in 1866, it is now well established and flourishing, and several important districts in the mission field are entrusted to it. The Mother house and college are at Mill Hill, North London.

Other Congregations primarily but not exclusively missionary, as *Marists*, *Oblates of Mary Immaculate*, *Assumptionists*, all have houses in England, the Assumptionists a school at Hitchin ; and divers foreign missionary institutes have footholds, as the *Pious Society of Missions*, *Picpus Fathers*, *White Fathers*, and many more.

VII
TEACHING INSTITUTES

We speak here of institutes whose vocation and work is primarily and essentially secondary education. The *Josephites* and the *Salesians* are clerical institutes. The former have only one school in England, at Weybridge. The Salesians are the wonderful institute of Don Bosco. They conduct large schools in Battersea, Bolton, Chertsey and Farnborough. They also have a house of studies at Cowley, Oxford.

There are non-clerical institutes of teaching Brothers. The first and most famous of these is the Congregation of *Brothers of the Christian Schools*, founded 1684 at Rheims by St. John Baptist de la Salle, now a world-wide institute. It has several secondary schools in England : in South London at Norwood, in Liverpool, Manchester, Leeds, Hexham, Cardiff, Portsmouth, Shrewsbury ; also industrial schools in Manchester and Glasgow.

Alongside of them are the Irish *Christian Brothers*, an independent branch of the same institute, in the forefront of education in Ireland. In recent times they have come to England, first at Prior Park, Bath, and in Bristol; and now they work two large secondary day schools in Liverpool, and others in Blackpool and Birkenhead.

The *Xaverian Brothers* are of later origin, Belgium,

1839; but they were the first of the kind to come to England, 1848. They now have large secondary schools in Clapham, Brighton, Mayfield, Manchester.

VIII

CHARITABLE INSTITUTES OF BROTHERS

Finally, there are throughout the land a number of Brothers of various institutes given up to charitable works of all kinds : hospitals, orphanages, homes for the aged, (asylums, but not in England) ; care of deaf and dumb, and of blind ; nursing, visiting prisons, and other great works of mercy. Of such may be named the *Alexian Brothers*, *Brothers of Charity*, and *of Mercy*, *Hospitallers of St. John of God*, and many more.

It will be of interest to end with some statistics. In 1829 there were four communities of men of the religious Orders. In 1929 there are more than thirty greater communities of at least twelve priests and upwards living a strong community life according to the nature of the divers institutes. In addition there are some forty lesser communities of six to twelve priests, where the divine office is said in choir in those Orders normally bound to choir. And there must be a dozen more communities of teaching Brothers staffing the schools conducted by them. There are, moreover, several communities of five priests working large parishes. In all, it may be said that there are now well over a hundred communities, large and small, of men bound by rule, wherein at least five are living together in common life.

Again, of the 4,800 Catholic priests of England and Scotland, 1,600 are regulars. The Jesuits come first with 400 ; the Benedictines follow with 350, 260 being of the old English Congregation; of Friars there are 160 Franciscan priests of all kinds, and 75 Dominicans; of Redemptorists, 60.

Though most of the Orders and Congregations share in the work of the pastoral clergy, the serving of parishes, especially those in which their communities are planted, still predominantly they fulfil their normal function in the church life of the country as auxiliary forces for carrying on extra-parochial activities, supplementary to the ordinary work of the secular clergy : missions, retreats, special sermons, lectures, and education in all its branches ; and some of them have more leisure than falls usually to the lot of a parish priest for the pursuit of ecclesiastical study and the apostolate of the press.

Yet, while in the foregoing sketch it is the external works and activities of the religious Orders that have been dwelt upon, it must ever be stressed that such works are in reality but secondary objects. The primary object of all religious Orders has been well set forth in a fine passage by a recent Oxford professor of ecclesiastical history, writing on the *Imitation* : " If society is to be permeated by religion, there must be reservoirs of religion, like those great storage places up among the hills, which feed the pipes by which water is carried to every home in the city. We shall need a special class of students of God, of men and women whose primary and absorbing interest it is to work out the spiritual life in all its purity and integrity, who give themselves up to the pursuit of religion in itself and by itself." [1] This is the primary function of every religious community of what kind soever, to be a " reservoir of religion." And the community through the individuals : Leo XIII once laid down that every religious Order has a twofold object, the primary being the sanctification of its members by

[1] Dr. Bigg, *Wayside Sketches*, p. 135.

198

the vows and the religious exercisings proper to its spirit ; the secondary, the carrying out of the good works it devotes itself to. Thus every religious is pledged by his state to " aim at perfection "—this is, by the renunciations of the vows, by self-discipline and mortification, to cultivate seriously the spiritual and interior life, and above all to be a man of prayer. This is substantially true of the most active Orders as of the most contemplative, though the emphasis will vary. It has to be remembered that though Dominicans are " Preachers," and though Franciscans were sent by St. Francis to minister to the needs of the poor, and though Benedictines from the beginning have been used by the Church in divers spheres of good works, still they are all ranked as " contemplative Orders," and they all stand for contemplative prayer, for meditation and the interior life, as indeed do all the Orders.

And this, probably more than their external activities, however good these may be for religion and society, is the great outstanding contribution of the religious Orders to the modern world, in England as elsewhere, in our day no less than in the Middle Ages. And indeed, perhaps more in our own day then in past ages is there the need of bodies of men who give themselves up primarily " to the pursuit of religion in itself and by itself." It is by this standard, more than by the standard of their practical utility in Church and State, that the real value of the religious Orders is to be estimated.

RELIGIOUS COMMUNITIES OF WOMEN
BY MAUD MONAHAN

X

RELIGIOUS COMMUNITIES OF WOMEN

THERE is scarcely a more impersonal word in the English language, nor one of more historic content, than " nun."

A mission is opened in England, Central Africa, China, the Fiji Islands, and immediately a request is made for nuns. Almost any will do, it would seem! All will have the same essential characteristics, and for details beyond that one is prepared to make the best of them. The harassed and lonely apostle at work in a vast district will feel comforted, for his little ones will be loved and taught, his old people sheltered and honoured, his sick and dying consoled, his sinners offered sure refuge, and above all Tabernacles will be opened and surrounded with loving care, whether it be in a desert or a jungle or a great town, and from these little spots of earth reconquered wholly to Christ the King, He will work His work in His own way, through willing instruments, however poor, just nuns.

The oneness of interests in the great army of nuns is their strongest asset, they have been mobilised for one end and honour one flag. Whatever their nationality may have been, it is known and expected that nuns should have but one allegiance, that sworn to Christ the King. For His work alone they go over all the world. For the most part they are nameless Knights, fighting with closed visor and blank shields, bearing a pseudonym for convenience, but to the great world as a whole just a nun. They are neither for nor against political parties, neither for nor against any age or time, but ready to be all things to all manner of men, that they may help them into heaven.

Saint Gertrude, of whom Our Lord said He made His home in her heart, was to her age just a nun. Saint Teresa of Avila, beneath whose statue in Saint Peter's is inscribed the words " Mater Spiritualium " was in life but a nun ; so too, even more completely, was that newest light, now shining over all the earth, Saint Teresa of Lisieux. No women have done more for the world than those who were but nuns. Some of the most outstanding names in England of our own day are those of religious.

In the battle that is ever raging between the children of God and the prince of this world, great efforts have been made from time to time, by their enemies, to get rid of these troublesome nuns. Protestantism tried to abolish them in the sixteenth century, and succeeded completely in England only. The Revolution of 1789 swept them from many parts of Europe and thought they were done with for ever. One hundred years later it was found there were 16,298 houses of religious Congregations of women in France alone ! It had been alleged that nuns were cobwebs of antiquity, and religious life a time-worn institution, unsuited to an age of freedom ! It is indeed an institution of immemorial date, and in its nature timeless. For the desire of which it is the outcome, is deeply implanted in human nature, and has been intensified beyond power of destruction by the Incarnation of Christ Our Lord.

So unprejudiced a witness as a leader in *The Times* has lately declared that " among the most powerful and persistent (of the ancient desires surviving to our own days) is that of escaping from the pressure of the masses . . . into privacy, independence and uninterrupted continuity of purpose. Everyone will not confess to this desire, but few are free from it. At its highest it urges to a life of contemplation." Hence Carmelites, Benedictines, Cistercians. " In its next degree it prompts men to lose and so to find themselves in subjection to an impersonal discipline, which some, lacking a monastery or the monastic impulse, have discovered in the forces of the Crown." The power sought for and gained in religious life could not have been more adequately explained. Those to whom the monastic impulse is not taboo have " found themselves " in the many modern congregations which, like the army, serve and fight the battles of the world, while keeping free from it through their enclosed religious life. However little that enclosure may profess to be, there is always some in a habit, a common life and ordered duties.

Wherever the Church has freedom for her normal life, there religious Orders will abound. First, women will desire to be made one thing with Christ, and then to be docile instruments in His hands to work His one great work of saving souls. That this is a labour that calls for the best of woman's gifts is not hard of proof. It has been said, and on the face of things seems true, that a large proportion of the human race never, in their mortal pilgrimage, pass beyond the stage of spiritual babyhood. Thus is it, perhaps, that countless passports are viséd for Eternal Life. But where and whenever children abound, there above all is needed woman's help. As Dr. Ullathorne once put it : " Wherever a mother is wanted by distressed and bereaved humanity, there a nun comes in."

These two desires in the hearts of women have been the sources from which multiple orders of the Church have had their rise. They have begun in such little ways : have been the dream of a girl's heart, longing to give her motherly love ; a vision, apparently beyond attainment, seen for a moment, then pursued till death ;

a little flame of hope flickering in wild storms, that somehow kept a hold on life and grew to a great light ; a longing, an ambition to scale the heights of holiness that has flowered in an unimagined glory.

They are many, but hardly enough when one considers that whole continents have yet to be won to the Kingdom of Christ, and that it is fully recognised that permanent success in the Missions cannot be attained without the help of nuns. There, above all, Convents become centres of Christian civilisation, just as in past ages among the barbarian races peopling Europe. At the end of the nineteenth century 52,000 nuns were at work in the mission fields. Though it seems a vast army, it might be wished their numbers could be multiplied.

It has, of course, been said by some that there are too many Congregations ; religious life would gain in strength and dignity and its influence increase if its forces were united in a few great orders, instead of being scattered among hundreds of small devoted bands. It has also been said that the number of religious vocations is diminishing. Though there is truth behind these statements, neither, it would seem, should pass unchallenged.

The needs to which these Institutes are destined to devote their services are still more numerous and varied than they. At times, in face of these imperious calls for help, it has seemed better and has brought a swifter succour, to enlist a little band of territorials, than to open negotiations with existing troops of the line. Hence new religious Orders. Such, doubtless, in the years to come will be the beginning of native Congregations among the peoples of Asia and Africa. Sometimes the results of such a move may not have been successful, but, as it has always been from individual efforts of this kind that the great Orders of the Church arose, it would seem none are in a position to cast the first stone of doubt on such a venture. None can see, till time has proved it, which have and which have not received a spark of a diviner life. Each fresh effort made thus throughout the ages has been a brave attempt to meet new wants, in what was hoped might prove a better way.

That the number of religious vocations is diminishing is hardly credible. It seems truer to say there can rarely have been more. But whereas a century ago, in England, girls who wished to give their lives to God in some religious Order found about eight Congregations, distributed in some twenty Convents, from which to choose, to-day their choice lies between over one hundred and forty different institutions, comprising 892 Convents. All of these, though necessarily in continual need of recruits, manage to carry on their works. They experience, perpetually renewed in their favour, the miracle of the drop of oil in the cruse. Not an ideal state of things for the eager, doubting heart of man, longing to rest in assurance on the strength of gathered stores, but one that should bring near to God, as under such conditions none can trust to their horses or their chariots, but must ever petition at the gates of Heaven, just for their daily bread.

In the rush of modern life, the multifarious activities of which tend to stifle thought, this need of prayer to give true values to work is more than ever felt. " Greater faith in the influence of the Contemplative life," each one's own contemplative life, is the universal need to-day, it has been said. " Religious have this great lever in their hands," wrote the Abbot of Sept-Fons, " and using it can rebuild, as no others can, the Christian life in their lands."

The historic associations of the word nun reach back into the furthest ages. The institution has been at all times a living monument, recalling and bearing witness to another life. The very atmosphere of a Convent has something of permanence, something of universality, and therefore of that other world. This is a source of comfort or of annoyance to those who visit them, according to the attitude of their own minds towards spiritual things. In the Great War our Catholic soldiers testified to this use of every Convent. Cast out in strange lands, they looked for them, and having found them hailed them as their own possessions, some little spot in which they had a share.

All through the History of the Church their Idylls have been written. The narrative appearing more attractive, perhaps, the further off the scene is laid. " In those distant ages," wrote Montalembert of the Convents in Anglo-Saxon England, " the nuns formed a great army, hardy and dauntless, bearing the glorious ensigns of sacrifice with magnanimous serenity and humble fervour. They confessed victoriously before the new-born Christianity of their age—the Divinity of Jesus Christ, the atonement of suffering, the immortal empire of the soul over inferior nature." But lest those on active service should be discouraged by these glowing words, one, Eadburga, writing to Saint Boniface in the stress and toil of that same life as lived, said simply : " For all these reasons [she had enumerated] and for others which could not be told in a day, not even one of the long days of July or August, our life is a burden to us ! " The confession of Eadburga and the panegyric of Montalembert can both be applied to religious women of our day.

But though religious life has always been found in the Church it has passed through many varied forms, and, as in other things, there has been, it is said, for over a hundred years a tendency to return to the primitive conception of the earlier days of Christianity. In those times religious life was much the same for women as for men. It was not until the advent of the Preaching Friars in the thirteenth century that papal enclosure was made the rule for all professed nuns by a decree of Boniface VIII. This legislation was confirmed by the Council of Trent, and was even extended to Tertiaries of the contemplative Orders by Saint Pius V. Cut off thus from all exterior work, the great monastic Orders with solemn vows and strict enclosure held their ground for long unchallenged, as the only accepted setting in which women could devote their lives to God. The modern world has found them hard to understand, but once they were as familiar as the unchanging landscape and seemed to be endowed with the same undying life. They still exist to-day, if in diminished numbers. In 1912 there were 11,679 Benedictine nuns and 5,000 Carmelites in the world. Their Convents are still the homes of silence, prayer and work that they have always been. Their utility has, of course, been questioned, but, as it has been said, the renewal of the spiritual life that has come to all classes of people through Saint Teresa of Lisieux is more that sufficient answer to such comment.

Since the beginning of the nineteenth century when the Church modified the law regarding enclosure, allowing the forces of religious life to be diverted into many channels, thus to water every soil, the number of nuns has increased in a wonderful way. The manner in which new fields were opened out to them is learnt from the story of the development of an idea which came to its re-birth some centuries ago.

Nothing is apparently more ineffective than a truth announced out of due time. Yet that it should have been uttered was necessary so that dying it might come to live, and sinking into the minds of men begin the slow process of growth and development. Those to whom it is at any time given to see further than their fellow-men, and to find ways not yet explored, or perhaps forgotten, to work God's work, have suffered, as it were, a martyrdom of mind and hope.

In the history of religious women as they are known in the world to-day there are pioneers of this sort, to whom the way was shown into vast fields of work awaiting them. They did not reach the promised land themselves, but it is they who have truly found and conquered and explored it. Their ideal it is that, grown and developed beyond, perhaps, their furthest vision, has written the lives of Mary Aikenhead and Margaret Hallahan, of Blessed Julie Billiart and Mère Blin de Bourdon, of Saint Madeleine Sophie Barat and Mother Duchesne, of Eugénie de Brou and Madame d'Houet, of Blessed Louise de Marillac and Eugénie de Smet, of Madame Jéhouvey and Jeanne Jugan, of Mother Stuart and Sister Mary of St. Philip, of Mother Magdalen Taylor and Mother Connelly, and of all Foundresses of modern Congregations, and great religious to whom the Church in England to-day is so much indebted.

At the very moment that the greater part of Europe appeared to be renouncing its inheritance and cutting itself off from the Faith, the geographical discoveries of the great explorers were revealing new harvests of souls to be gathered in, and the mind of the Church was turning with longing towards those mission fields. Apostolic men *and women* was her crying need, though at the time the worth of woman's work was at a discount. That nuns, however, should be readmitted to an active share in the work of the Apostolate, needed at that time little less than a revolution in the ideas prevailing with regard to religious life for women.

In response, as it were, to these needs of the Church, the Spirit of God, moving over the minds of men,

brought forth almost simultaneously and quite independently, two schemes for the conquest of the world
of souls.

On August 15, 1534, Saint Ignatius and his first companions set out upon their great career. In November
1535, on the Feast of Saint Catherine of Alexandria,
Saint Angela Merici founded the primitive Company of
Ursulines. " She would regenerate society by the help
of non-cloistered religious women, working within the
family circle." All works of charity were to be their
business, but especially the education of girls.

So daring an innovation attracted universal attention,
and thus was to awaken similar lines of thought in many
minds. To accept it would have been to open up the
whole field of social work at once to religious women.

So strong was the opposition of authority that the
houses of the Primitive Ursulines, after the death of
Saint Angela were, in most places and especially in
France, changed into monastic institutions, and thus
kept as their sole work the education of girls. No other
being compatible with solemn vows and papal enclosure.

But the idea, though frowned upon, had many friends;
Saint Angela's brave venture, if apparently defeated,
had, in reality, set a light upon a candlestick to be seen
by the whole world.

In the following century Anne de Xainctonge, Saint
Francis de Sales and Mary Ward, among others, hailed
it as the first glimmering of a new star in the heavens.
In the hearts of all three God kindled the same fire, an
ardent desire that women should spend themselves as
religious for the salvation of the world.

All three were arraigned before the bar of their times.
Of Anne de Xainctonge Père Coton, the celebrated
Jesuit, gave it as his considered verdict that she was
" the most extraordinary thing he had met with in his

numerous journeys in France." And when in 1605 she stood in person to plead her cause before the saintly Prior of the Charter House, the learned Prior of St. Bénigne, the Curé of St. Médard, and the Dean of the Sainte Chapelle, they could only marvel at her audacity, and the venerable Prior of the Charter House voiced their astonishment " that women could aim so high as to desire to do for girls what the Jesuits had been doing for seventy years for boys ! " She was extraordinary, for " she wished," it has been well said, " to have the essence of Religious Life, and to have that in its entirety, but of its exterior forms and secondary characteristics she would accept only such as were no hindrance to her end."

She won her cause, but like the Sisters of Saint Vincent de Paul, at the price of renouncing the name of religious, till time had explained her meaning.

The very name of the Visitation, founded by St. Francis de Sales, tells the story of a similar desire not attained. " Although," he wrote to Mother Favre, " I should have found a special sweetness in the title of simple Congregation, where Charity alone and reverence for the Beloved would serve as enclosure, I agree that we shall make a formal religious Order . . . and I make this acquiescence with quietness and tranquillity. . . . Our Lord's sovereign hand will do more for this little Institute than men can think."

Mary Ward, as Anne de Xainctonge a few years before her, was to fight for the same cause. She, too, knew what women could do, and did not think, as it has been said, " that they needed the perpetual shelter of four walls to enable them to give their lives to God." She, too, raised her eyes audaciously to the Jesuit model.

If papal enclosure seemed an obstacle to Anne de Xainctonge and Saint Francis de Sales living in a Catholic country, far more did it seem so to Mary Ward, planning her Institute for the England of 1616. Writing at the time she said : "I hope in God it will be seen that women in time to come will do much." When some had spoken disparagingly of her work, and one rash man had ventured to say that "women could not apprehend God!" (Saint Teresa had died less than forty years before), Mary Ward wrote with pitying displeasure: "Let us not be made to think we can do nothing. . . . Men are, I confess, Head of the Church, women are not to administer the Sacraments, nor preach in public Churches, but in all other things wherein are we so inferior to other creatures, that they should term us 'but women'? For what think you of the word 'but women'? but as if we were in all things inferior to some other creature, which I suppose to be man! . . . If they would not make us believe we can do nothing, and that we are *but women*, we might do great matters."

She was to see her own work crushed, but her heroic pursuit of it was a cause of its final triumph. Sixty years after her death, in 1703, Clement XI gave a Brief approving the Constitutions of the Institute of Mary, but "without approbation of the Congregation itself." This was, perhaps, the first instance of such a favour being conferred on any unenclosed Religious Society, with simple vows and general government. A century had yet to pass before the way was opened to the full development of this changed ideal. And in fact the upheaval of the French Revolution was eventually the means used by God to remove the last obstacles.

As its destructive waves passed over Europe, the existing Orders were swept away. A few nuns managed to escape to other countries ; a few found a martyr's death ; but the great majority were robbed of all their possessions and turned adrift in that unfriendly world.

While political troubles were thus rendering the

213

observance of solemn vows with all they entailed, difficult, especially for women, the last doubts in the mind of the Church as to the need and desirability of Congregations with simple vows vanished in the presence of a Europe falling back into paganism. The outlook being changed, the Holy See gradually revised the law regarding religious, and declined from that time to sanction any new Congregations with solemn vows, and even suppressed solemn Profession in the old Orders of women in France and Belgium.

With this passing of the demand for strict enclosure the chief obstacle was removed which had hindered the approbation of new Societies. This formal sanction so earnestly sought after is that by which Congregations are drawn out of the ranks of mere individual effort and given a place in the Church as one of her recognised families.

Of the new Institutions which immediately sprang up in Europe, many were to find work in England, and practically all went out on the foreign Missions, winning admiration by the magnitude and success of their undertakings even from those to whom their ideals were incomprehensible. " Madame Jéhouvey, c'est un grand homme ! " said Louis Philippe, of the Foundress of the Sisters of Saint Joseph of Cluny, when brought into touch with the work she had inaugurated among the negroes in French Senegal.

It would be impossible, in a few pages, to enumerate these religious Orders of simple vows and modified enclosure, now in England, much less to give any adequate account of the work they are engaged in. But as things are to-day this is in no way necessary. Fifty-five years ago a book published on the Convents of the United Kingdom appeared under what was then, doubtless, a most appropriate title : " Terra Incognita." To-day that title could not stand. Convent life has been explored, its history written, and its map filled in with plain and genuine landmarks, replacing the mysteries and monsters, which, after the fashion of the cartographists of old, our ancestors had sketched in places not yet visited.

Chronicles and Histories of religious Orders of women, or of individual houses of these Orders, lives of Foundresses or of distinguished members of Communities, have made known the end and meaning of religious life and explained, as far as such a thing can be explained, how that life is lived.

The Chronicles of the Augustinians of Saint Monica's, who are now at Newton Abbot, the delightful records of the English Canonesses that have appeared from Hayward's Heath, the Story of the Bridgettines of Chudleigh, and other books of the same kind tell of the pre-Reformation orders still among us, which were brought back into England by the French Revolution. These Convents, with two houses of Mary Ward's Institute, which had weathered all storms from 1680, numbered about twenty when on April 13, 1829, the Catholic Relief Bill became at last the law.

In the course of the struggle over this great question, *The Times* of February 28, 1828, wrote : " The majority in the House of Commons on Tuesday night, in favour of a repeal of the celebrated Test and Corporation Acts, is in truth what may be called a thundering event. It will sound from one end of the Kingdom to the other and the echo will be heard in foreign parts."

That event, as Cardinal Wiseman said, in an address delivered in Louvain in 1863, " was to us what the egress from the Catacombs was to the early Christians." The way being at length opened for the normal development of the Catholic Church, Convents began immediately to multiply. They may, perhaps, be classified as

Congregations of Irish origin, of Continental origin and generally cosmopolitan, and of English origin. A classification according to their works would present more difficulty, for, while some are definitely engaged in only one pursuit, such as the education of children, others embrace, under their rule, several spiritual and corporal works of mercy.

Of the Institutes more especially devoted to the latter, the first to come to the assistance of the Church in England was that of the Irish Sisters of Mercy. In an appeal, published in the pages of the "Catholic Directory" for 1839, the " Pastors of Bermondsey and Rotherhithe " begged for help to establish a Convent of this order in London. They drew a picture of the happy effects of such works in France and Ireland : " while England still," they said, " remains unaided by these sisterhoods." A year later the nuns were at work in the district which has known them ever since.

Of modern Congregations which are of Continental origin, among the earliest to find footing in the land were several devoted to the work of education. Of these the Faithful Companions of Jesus were the first to reach London, just one year after the Emancipation of Catholics. Their Foundress, Madame d'Houet, arrived friendless, as she thought, and almost penniless, to find awaiting her acceptance a large house containing a flourishing boarding school and day school ; and a dozen girls who were only waiting for a chance of entering religious life ! In this fairy-tale fashion the first house of the Order was opened at Somers Town, then an almost deserted spot in London.

This Institute owed its origin in part to Father Varin, S.J., and was one of a group of three or more which will be for ever connected with his name : The Society of the Sacred Heart, founded by Saint Madeleine Sophie Barat, which came to England in 1842, opening the house at Roehampton in 1850 : and the Congregation of Notre Dame, founded by Blessed Julie Billiart, the first house of which was opened in Penryn, Cornwall, in 1845.

Of the work of this last Order it was said in 1920 that to it we owe " in large measure the present numerical strength of Catholics in England." That so great a claim can be made is due, not only to the generosity and breadth of outlook of the order, but to the life-work of Sister Mary of St. Philip in the Training College at Mount Pleasant. It was her courage and her many-sided personality that carried it to success. Through the work done there by the Sisters of Notre Dame the Church was enabled to face the immense problem of compulsory elementary education in 1870, and to provide a sufficiency of trained teachers for Catholic schools, to save the faith of generations of children. From the earliest days of her Institute, Blessed Julie Billiart had foreseen this need of training Catholic teachers, " who would be ready to go wherever they were wanted," and she had included this apostolic work among those to be undertaken by her daughters. From the very earliest times, too, the nuns had served their apprenticeship of dealing with the intricacies of Government organisation in the department of Education. When they first went to Holland in 1807, William of Orange-Nassau, King of the Netherlands, was inaugurating a petty persecution of religious Communities in order to prevent their expansion and the consequent growth of the Faith in his land. The methods he adopted were new at the time and evidently thought to be of overwhelming force. Innumerable heart-searching forms were drawn up to disgust and bewilder teachers, especially foreigners, and diplomas had to be obtained at most limited notice after rigorous examination in Dutch and French. These would seem to our generation like the toy guns of children, accustomed as we are to the marvellous intricacy and astonishing variety of forms which emerge from every source. And as for examinations, they can frighten but few, having now been extended from adults to infants. But even in 1807 King William was mistaken in thinking that the nuns could not face his arms, nor adapt themselves when necessary to modern methods. Mère St. Joseph was more than a match for him, and steered her course so successfully through all difficulties that when in 1829, finding she had not gone, he came himself to visit her at Namur, he was so delighted with all that he saw that he conferred Dutch citizenship upon her. It was with the same brave spirit that Sister Mary of Saint Philip also won her laurels. There are now nine Catholic Training Colleges under nuns in Great Britain, all of which look with gratitude to the one that blazed the trail.

Among these religious congregations engaged in the work of education, several still have modified enclosure. This has at times been looked on with disfavour, and yet in this restless age, where aimless hurry and perpetual uproar accompany us all day long, childhood might gain if it could find a quiet spot from which "the stress and beat of human life could be for a time removed," as Mother Stuart wrote, speaking of the formative influence of the quiet of the woods and fields on child life. That something of these "halls of space and avenues of leisure" is to be found within those Convent schools, it may perhaps be claimed, and this without prejudice to the many-sided interests of the children's lives.

The ten years from 1850 to 1860 saw the Little Sisters of the Poor established in London, Manchester, Bristol, Birmingham, Plymouth, Leeds and Newcastle, so greatly was this work of loving self-devotion needed and, once known, always appreciated.

It was an event, when in 1857 the first cornettes of the much loved Sisters of Charity of St. Vincent de Paul were seen in Sheffield. In 1927 this world-famed Congregation had sixty-two houses in England. The same year that brought them to the country saw the opening of the Assumption Convent in Kensington Square. Cardinal Wiseman had greatly desired to have a house of this Order in London, that he might through it establish Perpetual Adoration of the Blessed Sacrament in his diocese.

Before the close of the century many other Communities brought their meed of help and opened Tabernacles in long-lonely districts. Among them were the Helpers of the Holy Souls, an order with an Apostolate for both worlds ; the Institute of the Cenacle, founded by Marie Thérèse Couderc ; to give retreats was the end of this Congregation of women, and it has been approved by Rome.

The Little Sisters of the Assumption were also harbingers of a new ideal, and inaugurated a work of quite special character : ministry to the sick poor in their houses. " Could companies of these Little Sisters be multiplied in all the large centres of population," wrote Cardinal Bourne in 1917, " it would not be long before home-life would be transformed and supernaturalised."

In 1891 friends were found for working girls, when in response to Cardinal Manning's appeal : " Go to my China ! " a Convent of Marie Auxiliatrice was established in the East End. In the person of its foundress, that Order had been put through a school of suffering, such as must have won for it the power to understand all sorrow.

While the greater number of religious Congregations are therefore, as in pre-Reformation times, of Continental origin, a few among us can claim their English birth.

But with the Catholicity that belongs to all such Institutions they have now gone out from England as Apostles to other lands.

Among these Congregations, Mother Margaret Hallahan's work has priority of place. Dr. Ullathorne's wish was to found a religious community devoted to active works; Mother Margaret's determination was never to be anything but a Dominican. The outcome of these two wills is known as the " English Congregation of Saint Catherine of Sienna." There were twenty-two Convents under its rule in 1911.

The year 1847 opened the first chapter in the History of the Congregation of the Holy Child, when a house was founded at Derby by Mother Connelly. It is with St. Leonard's, however, that the traditions of the Order are bound up, and from there it spread throughout England and America. Mother Magdalen Taylor's Community of the " Poor Servants of the Mother of God " owed its name to a similar Congregation in Poland, but in all else was of English origin and founded in London in 1870. " The Foundress," said Cardinal Bourne, in the Preface to her newly published life, "was one of the outstanding women whom God raised up for the rebuilding of His Kingdom in England. She is not unworthy of being associated in thought with Mother Janet Stuart and Mother Margaret Hallahan." A congregation with a somewhat similar end was founded at Nottingham by Bishop Bagshawe in 1884 : the Sisters of Saint Joseph of Peace ; and still earlier in the century, about 1851, the Sisters of the Cross and Passion began a work for factory girls in Manchester. Schools of all kinds are also in their hands. In 1877 the Sisters of The Little Company of Mary founded their twofold work of nursing the sick and praying for the dying. They already have houses over all the world.

The same may be said of the Franciscan Missionaries of Mary, an Order which originated in India in 1877 under Mother Mary of the Passion, who had left her home in Brittany at the age of twenty-one to devote herself to the welfare of the natives. She began her great venture by Exposition of the Blessed Sacrament in a lonely little chapel in the Nilgherry Hills. In 1925 her Congregation already counted 164 houses.

In 1908 an attempt was made to revive what was an old tradition connected with the name of Saint Catherine of Sienna, when a Community of Dominican Secular Tertiaries, known as that of Corpus Christi, began work at Leicester. Recruits have already gone out to Trinidad and the United States.

Many other companies should find mention here of this great army of religious women, always standing ready for service, undismayed by trouble or adventure. A friendly critic of the life of Mother Stuart wrote : " I was right in my judgment, it is Romance of the finest kind ; for the essence of romance is great love, great courage and the conquering of difficulty and danger, and of all these things the ' Life ' is full and *skalin*, as the Scotch version of the Psalm says." What was here said of one life is a true verdict on many. The romance of great love, great courage and high adventure is found in the story of every religious Order.

Nuns have been loved and made little of, praised and blamed, but they themselves are without illusions either as to their weakness or their power, to the roughness of the way or the immensity of the work awaiting them and their successors to the end of time.

THE INFLUENCE OF CATHOLIC LAYWOMEN

BY MISS MARGARET FLETCHER

XI

THE INFLUENCE OF CATHOLIC LAYWOMEN

CATHOLIC laywomen have developed their influence during the past hundred years in an atmosphere partly foreign to them. I shall, therefore, treat my subject as a story to which the general history of the woman's movement will serve as chorus. The relationship between the two histories has been so close, their interaction so important that, separated, the Catholic one would be almost unintelligible. When in 1829 Emancipation was at last granted, and Catholic women realised that henceforth they would not form part of the quarry of a slackened hunt, they knew themselves to be in many ways scarred and spent by the long chase ; and yet at the same time to be gloriously free. They had acquired a spiritual fortitude and had preserved an inner moral liberty which were not characteristics of English women at the beginning of the nineteenth century. As they looked around at the neighbours with whom, in the coming friendliness of which there were already signs, they might now expect to mix more freely, they must have wondered how much they still held in common. The French Revolution and the Napoleonic Wars, which had shaken the whole world had shaken some .obsessions from the English mind. Religion, even a non-English one could act as a buttress to civilisation and become a constitutional asset. On the outbreak of the French Revolution the English Government had welcomed and assisted some 8,000 *émigré* Priests and had not only permitted them the practise of their religion, but had allowed them to minister to the scattered English Catholics. Exiled nuns had likewise been sheltered and permitted to open in this country the schools which they had carried on abroad. The indifferentism which was then fashionable in the upper classes contributed to the growing tolerance which accepted the presence of the Catholic Mrs. Fitzherbert at Court, as the privately married wife of the Prince of Wales. Her story illustrates the tenacious character and the strong hold on moral principle of the penalised Catholic woman. Her personality won universal respect, and it would be difficult to fix a limit to the influence, both direct and unconscious which she exercised in obtaining sympathy for her co-religionists.

The Jacobite cause had long been utterly dead. When in 1824 French workmen, excavating among the foundations of a chapel in the Church of St. Germain, had chanced on a leaden casket inscribed with the Royal arms of England and the declaration that it contained portions of the body of James II, George IV ordered that it should be buried with Royal honours. The English men and women of different faiths who, in Paris, followed the Catholic rites of that funeral of a long-dead Stuart, were also laying to rest the mere ghost of a long-dead dynastic struggle.

And yet not the Stuart cause but the Catholic Faith had been the magnet which had drawn Catholic girls across the water all through the penal days, to seek education in those convents in which so many of their countrywomen were already living as nuns.

Characters have long ancestries, and we must glance both at the distant and the immediate past if we are to understand those of the Catholic women of 1829.

From the time of Elizabeth onwards from the most remote inland districts outwards to the coasts had run those well-trodden but uncharted ways to Catholic liberty. No country seat, no isolated farm, no tavern, no humble home where Catholics dwelt but was known and counted upon. Young women set out on perilous journeys with strangely disguised escorts and with high courage. The English families have kept their chronicles, the Convents abroad have kept theirs and have preserved them through wanderings and exiles. Together they form an epic in which, towards the end, is recorded the return of many an English nun fleeing from prison and pursuit on the Continent to the shores of her own country now turned from persecutor to protector. Nor had English Catholics been entirely deprived of the means of educating their girls in their own land. From the time of Cromwell down to this day a school has been maintained at York by the English nuns of the Institute of Mary. The Convent chronicles relate by what subterfuges, through what perils, and by grace of what local sympathy this end was achieved. Hammersmith, too, always a centre for Catholics, sheltered during the same period a school kept by the same Order, until, after the Revolution, it passed into the hands of French Benedictines. By the beginning of the nineteenth century at least five other boarding schools for girls had been opened by exiled orders. By means of young women of the upper classes who had been taught in these schools, education was spread to the girls of the less well to do through small private schools in towns, or in villages near the country seats of Catholics. The penalty for this zeal was imprisonment for life, small wonder then that these little schools avoided publicity and that it is only here and there that published records allude to them. And what of the education itself, in what did it differ from that in the country at large? It would seem at all points to have had the advantage. On the secular side languages were better taught; needlecraft had been preserved as a traditional art, history included that of Europe. It provided above all an intensive spiritual culture, and developed that power of mental

227

concentration only to be secured by the practice of meditation. It was an age of discipline and repression for the young, but in the convent schools the girls breathed an atmosphere of supernatural peace, whether they lived under the shadow of danger or shared in the innocent gaiety of the cloister, fidelity to the things of God was equally the cause.

It was very much a religion of the Four Last Things which survived the penal days in this country. One stripped of sentimentality, of all sensuous aids, all exotic devotions. It was a religion most faithfully observed. The little band of English Catholics had developed a civilisation peculiarly their own; that of rural England without its provincialism, its insularity. That of a conservative England, played upon by the spirit of old France, a little blighted by Jansenism. These country people of the upper classes, during the winter months, frequented the embassy chapels in London and diplomatic society. Yet in their hearts they remained unflinchingly English, treasuring in their homes the relics of martyrs, their own kinsfolk, and caring for the spiritual interests of their humble neighbours while awaiting better days.

The Protestant scheme of society had made too narrow a provision for women. Under it her sole destiny was marriage. Her upbringing was directed to equipping her with what the taste of the times demanded in a candidate for that estate. Even the wordly counted a little religion, if it were tactful and accommodating, as among the adornments of a woman. In those days women, together with the entire working-class population, were expected in the sentiment of the Anglican Catechism to order themselves lowly and reverently towards their betters. Protestant philosophy offered no outlet for a superabundance of women, and England, in sending her men-kind out over the world, retained a much larger number than matrimony could absorb. The great mass of these were without solid education, without independent means, and without freedom. The once essential household industries were rapidly disappearing from the more prosperous middle-class homes which, adopting the aristocratic tradition, forbade all renumerative work to its women. This unmarried class formed a shadowy third estate in social life, which was held in little honour, but which provided auxiliary service for the family.

To the great reserve of energy stored up in these quiet but unsatisfied lives came the seeds of revolution. Brought across the Channel by free-thinking spirits at the beginning of the century as the "Rights of Women" and the "Equality of the Sexes," the gospel rapidly found adherents amongst those who had little sympathy with the general revolutionary programme upon which it had appeared. The soil was most prepared exactly where conditions of life were becoming intolerable, in a country with a population in which the sexes did not balance, and in which the religious outlook was restricted to the limited horizon of the reformers! The English mind was favourable for the early culture of a claim which, although revolutionary in a social sense, was, in an ethical one, virtually a demand for an extended application of Christian teaching. The distaste for speculative thought which characterises English women, their practical good sense and instinct for order, led them to concentrate on a first step of immediate service in bettering their conditions. Leaving aside the logical conclusions of moral free-lances and ignoring the sexual licence indulged in by some of the advocates of women's freedom, they entered upon a campaign for securing better education for their sex, and thus obtained the key to the whole position. The forcing of that door is by now an oft-told tale, and cannot detain us here. Meanwhile, Queen Victoria, applauded by the growing moral earnestness engendered by the Evangelical movement throughout the country, had set her court in order, and had made conjugal fidelity a popular ideal. The middle of the last century saw the culmination of Protestant influence in social life. Protestantism had been living on its moral capital and was unconscious of its powerlessness to lead should ethical guidance be called for in changed conditions. Women on the contrary were becoming confident and courageous, and it was the pioneers of the Feminist movement who often provided the incentive which the Protestant church failed to give. Thus, though the Victorian outlook reverenced " good " women, it was essentially class-bound and lacking in justice. The women's movement was essentially democratic in that its solicitude embraced the entire sex. Thus the 'sixties which first saw public examinations opened to girls, saw a woman's public championship for the human rights of the prostitute.

The multiplication of religious Orders of women in this country during the earlier half of last century only concerns us in so far as their presence contributed to the shaping of the lay mentality. In this they played a notable part. Three elements must be welded into one whole if an effective laity were to be secured—the descendants of English Catholics, converts, and Irish emigrants. Parish life had yet to be developed, a social life did not exist. In these circumstances convents became centres of extra-mural influence. The incoming Orders were, until the 'seventies, almost without exception of French origin. In some cases they were after-Revolution foundations designed to meet the educational needs of a half-paganised youth and to revive the weakened faith of older women. With this view they were accustomed to organise sodalities and retreats for the laity, and to interest themselves in individual converts. Those were days of autocratic parental authority when a father felt justified in casting out a daughter penniless from the home if she became a Catholic. Instincts of the old hunt lay in the subconscious mind, and so late as the 'forties and 'fifties the common people felt it legitimate sport to throw stones at Catholics on their way to Mass. Habits of aloofness are not easily overcome in such circumstances, and the convents alone afforded for their lay guests the sympathetic and stimulating atmosphere in which their spiritual life could unfold. To say that a French spirit pervaded the revival of Catholic life in this country is not to accuse it of being a foreign spirit in a nationalist sense. In after-Revolutionary France Catholics were, to a great extent, withdrawn from public life and from a society with which they had little sympathy. They developed their own culture which was predominantly spiritual, and which was perfectly adapted to meet in this country all the needs of a people which had not attained a corporate life. The incoming converts who were finding their way to the faith through opposition and prejudice were usually women of character who, for the most part, entered religion and strengthened the English elements in the Orders. Others contributed to the building up of a Catholic literature, and took a leading part in works of charity and the development of parochial social service. It would be true to say that up to the close of the last century the quiet but steady development of lay women's activity and influence was on the traditional lines of Continental Catholic benevolence and that this period culminated in the erection by Cardinal Vaughan of an English Branch of the Association of the " Ladies of Charity " founded by St. Vincent de Paul in 1602. Individual women here and there were towards the end of the last century entering civic life, becoming guardians, school managers, and so forth, that they might watch

over the interests of their co-religionists. The poorer
element had been enormously increased by the successive
Irish immigrations culminating in that of the great
potato famine of 1849. We have seen that the English
Catholic remnant was steeped in the supernatural, the
convert was versed in apologetics, to these was added
the tenacious spirituality and high combative courage of
an Irish element. Starving and destitute the Irish sought
these shores in such numbers as to constitute a problem
for government, and to tax Catholic charity to the
utmost. But their coming was a great spiritual asset,
and one which will be increasingly understood as the
fabric of the social order which has been built by
Protestant hands fails to resist the assaults of paganism.
For these emigrants were of the same blood and the
same spirit, as those left behind in Ireland, who died by
the roadside, their mouths stuffed with grass to stay the
pangs of hunger rather than drink the soup proffered
by government agents as the price of apostasy. The
women of that trek eastward had a great capacity for
motherhood and were capable of unbounded sacrifice.
Whether they have prospered or have continued poor,
they remain in this country the faithful upholders of
Christian marriage and the Christian family. Of these
three component groups of Catholic life that of converts
rapidly increased towards the end of the century.

Meanwhile all the contributory streams tending
towards woman's emancipation from convention and
baseless tradition were converging into one insistent
demand for the franchise. The little rills irrigating
distinct areas were become a stream in spate. In the
closing years of the last century the political aspect of
the movement occupied so much public attention that
the formation of very important women's societies at an
earlier date and which are still doing valuable work, is

apt to be overshadowed. These societies, which were formed with a view to securing particular ends, became schools of political training and the means of developing a civic sense in their members. We single out one in particular, because of its unconscious share in bringing National Catholic Women's Leagues into existence.

In 1888 a group of leading women in this country, members of various societies for the protection and education of women, in conjunction with a similar group in America, decided to promote international gatherings in order to extend and strengthen the woman's movement. Thus the " International Council of Women " came into existence. In 1895 various women's societies in England, which were occupied with some form of social service, were gathered into an organisation known at first as " The National Union of Women Workers " (now as the " National Council of Women ") for the purpose of holding annual conferences. These unofficial women's parliaments could claim to exercise a substantial influence on public opinion, their debates were reported in the general Press, their resolutions were forwarded to government departments. Naturally, their atmosphere was predominantly Protestant, although Jewish societies were admitted. Direct mention of religion, which was not recognised as having authority to lay down social principles, was excluded from debate. Courtesy to all was practised in these neutral assemblies, and subjects were treated only up to the point at which they could be dealt with on common ground. Women's interests and the humanitarian outlook of the late Victorian period provided the binding cement. An atmosphere of achievement, of security, and of confidence in the future pervaded these platforms. It was believed that Anglo-Saxon women had a message to deliver ; and they certainly had an aptitude for organisation to communicate.

If on some rare occasions a challenge by free-thought was given in these English conferences, it obtained a shocked and very brief hearing. The waters of security closed over the incident. No one looked for any writing on the wall. But when the attempt was made to impose English platform procedure on International assemblies, unforeseen difficulties occurred. Feminism in proportion to its adoption by revolutionary and anti-religious parties had been, if not altogether distrusted, yet very cautiously adopted by the people of Catholic countries. Catholic and anti-clerical refused to share the same platform, because both were sufficiently logical to recognise that their creeds formed the roots of mutually destructive social systems. On the Continent it was the case of a church claiming to teach and to lay down moral principles for acceptance or refusal. The situation abroad, therefore, was very different from that in this country. It was found impossible to advocate a merely abstract claim for women's equality with men when in practice all its supporters put forward by way of argument the highly controversial changes and reforms which, in their opinion, would ensue. The practise of urbanity and tolerance was inadequate where antagonistic aims were involved. In 1904 this International Parliament of women met in Berlin. It was attended by a number of Catholic women interested in the feminist movement. They at once took in the situation. Here was a new force, a new power in the world, but one which was not necessarily Christian. There was no mistaking the capacity and zeal of these women, but the Conference was individualistic and opportunist in tone, and by the necessities of the situation must continue to be so. Their answer was the formation of the National Catholic Frauenbund.

Meanwhile in this country towards the end of the

last century the tranquil waters of Catholic life began to stir. Some force was working beneath the surface. Hitherto the religious life of all three elements in the social body had been intensified by some form of suffering. Now a generation had grown up without this experience. New types of converts were coming into the church, women practically free from parental control and economically independent. In the course of training for professions they had seen the trend of much in the world of youth which was away from Christianity. The young were not merely drifting out of religious practice as their parents had done, they were eager crusaders in the cause of " new thought." The outlines of the inevitable ultimate struggle between Catholicism and a new paganism were beginning to be visible. As seen from without, the Church had appeared to these newcomers as the guardian of all the rights for which women were striving, the protector of a healthy feminism within the framework of Christendom. Arrived within, they found a people who it seemed to them were side-tracked from the main road of national effort, who were making of life a quiet ante-room of Heaven, and who knew nothing of the need outside of what they had to give—that supernatural vision, that tenacity to principle, which their whole history had fostered.

A small group set to work to try to persuade Catholic laywomen that a great opportunity of corporate influence lay open for them. That organised as a National society they could take their place in women's conferences, as the upholders of Christian social principles in their integrity. As a first step a quarterly magazine was published, a voluntary venture without any commercial aim, in order to provide a means of propaganda. It not only soon attracted an interested group of Catholic women in this country but established sympathetic correspondence with those abroad who were engaged in the same task. A great many changes which have since been secured were urged in its pages, notably the removal of the embargo against Catholic women entering the Universities of Oxford and Cambridge. After two years of preparation the Catholic Women's League came into existence, encouraged and protected by the Archbishop of Westminster, afterwards H.E. Cardinal Bourne. Its first executive committee contained an equal number of members of old Catholic families and of converts, and as far as possible all conditions of life were represented. For, above all, the movement was to be democratic in this sense that the relationship of its members would not be that of a giving by the more fortunate classes to the less fortunate, but that of comrades working side by side for social reconstruction on Christian lines. Its promoters foresaw something of the rapid development in the social education of the industrial classes and their increasing share in civic life which is apparent to-day. Not only was this League to leave party politics entirely alone, a matter comparatively easy for unenfranchised women but, what was more difficult, it was to leave all efforts for or against the franchise to specialised societies to which Catholics could and did adhere according to their views. So far as public work was concerned, the aim of the new undertaking was simple enough, namely, to uphold Christian ethics in a period of rapid change and vital challenge. Within the Catholic body lay the formidable task of preparing laywomen for the multiple forms of social service in which they should be sharing, of arousing their interest in the reforms already secured through women's influence, and stimulating a healthy education. A period of intensive work must be entered upon if the new organisation was to attain the requisite standard of efficiency. Not only must the art of public speaking be mastered, procedure must be acquired, a practical organisation devised, and varied studies undertaken. Moreover, the general membership must be familiarised with the virtues needed for " team work," in which they were quite unpractised. It was essential that a corporate social conscience should be engendered. Personal intercourse could alone do this in the case of a thinly scattered people. Provision was made at the outset for the holding of frequent committees and councils to be composed of delegates from all branches and sections, as they should be formed. In no other way could the more populous Catholic north with its greater heritage of tradition and its simpler social life have been welded with the preponderately convert south with its closer links with general national life. The acceptance of this new movement within the Catholic body was very gradual. To many it appeared merely as a version of the social disorder beyond the Church's borders ; as the enemy creeping into the fold. With two or three exceptions however, the Bishops accorded the freedom of their dioceses to the movement, several were its warm champions. The approval of parish Priests came more slowly, and the progress of the work can be likened to that of water, which finds its way only where an uneven ground permits.

In 1907 Catholic women, including nuns, came up to the old universities, and henceforth, with the rising standard of secondary education, the number of women entering professional life and the various social services, official and voluntary, steadily increased. The Catholic Social Guild made its appearance in 1909 with a view to promoting social study among the youth of both sexes, mainly of the industrial classes, thus increasing the number of young workers fitted for corporate social work.

In 1910 the Catholic Women's Suffrage Society was formed by a group of women who wished to give corporate Catholic support to the claim.

By the end of the first ten years of the century Catholic laywomen were venturing well out upon the high road of modern life. Meanwhile, on the Continent the Catholic women's movement was rapidly spreading and modern methods were being adopted on all sides. Proposals came from the recently formed French League for the formation of an international federation. An inaugural meeting was held in Brussels during August 1910 at which the Leagues of ten European countries were represented. A federation was agreed upon and a provisional constitution approved. This was further developed at a meeting held in Madrid during the following year. To that of Vienna held in 1912 the Holy Father Pius X, who had noted the movement with interest, sent a request that a report of the proceedings should be submitted to him. At the last pre-war meeting held in London in 1913, by which time the number of affiliated National Leagues had increased to 40, the Holy Father was officially represented. At this meeting the constitution received its final form, and the federation under the title of *l'Union Internationale des Ligues Catholiques Féminines* was officially recognised by the Holy See. Already it had been possible to discern the subtle action of international intercourse, broadening here, deepening there, extending knowledge and infusing zeal. At home Catholic women, though absorbed in the struggle for efficiency and self-development, remained essentially unspoiled, in that they placed spiritual welfare far above physical comfort or material security. They still thought in terms of eternity. In this they often taxed the patience and outstripped the comprehension of the more materially minded of those with whom their work might bring them in contact. In this difference lay, and still lies, their power both to influence and to antagonise.

During the war all the efficiency which has been acquired was put to the test and Catholic women as a corporate body took their full share in the National effort. The success of this work, the stress laid on the spiritual needs of those for whom it was undertaken went far to reconcile to modern methods those Catholics who had hitherto held themselves aloof. When, in 1917, a limited franchise was granted to women and thus new duties were imposed even on the unwilling, Catholic women joined organised societies and undertook public work in greater numbers. Notably did they help forward the work of the newly-established Catholic Evidence Guild for teaching Christian doctrine at open-air meetings. All dioceses were now open to this laywomen's movement and parochial barriers began to fall rapidly.

In 1919 Pope Benedict XV notified his wish that the *Union Internationale* should renew its sessions. Many difficulties lay in the way—the absorption of the leaders of constituent Leagues in after-war problems at home, fatigue, poverty, limited train services, and so forth. However, in 1921 a preliminary meeting was held in Cracow, and in July of 1922 a full conference took place in Rome. Over fifty Leagues were then represented, including those of Canada, the United States and South America. It was in many ways a changed assembly. Formerly it had been concerned with the voluntary social effort of women whose knowledge of the actual conditions of life was in some countries and in some directions a limited one. War had now stripped the veils from the social sores of life. Where revolution had swept women had been enfranchised with a stroke of the pen, there were those present who sat in the

Parliaments of their own countries, and who had taken a share in repelling the attempt to overthrow the Christian basis of civilisation by means of the legislature. Information brought to the conference of the varied methods of attack was first hand and well documented. Catholic defence and counter-attack were the subjects of discussion, spheres of influence had become national. At the end of the sessions H.H. Pius XI appointed a Cardinal protector to the Union.

At home Catholic Englishwomen found themselves in a much more baffling position in the matter of outside relationships than that of their sisters of countries in which the struggle between the Church and a new paganism was open and clear-sighted. After-war England had thrown off most traditions but had retained one delusion. It still believed that there was some alchemy in English approval, which deprived any practise or precept of its power for evil. Christianity, for great masses of the people, had come to mean no more than a vague benevolence; anyone was a Christian who chose to cover his or her private opinions with the label. Numbers of women, slightly intoxicated with their own material efficiency, became self-constituted social reformers. With dangerous impulsiveness they accepted new proposals which seemed to promise immediate benefits of a material kind. A whole new outlook on life had come to the surface. The binding cement of Protestant Victorian ideals had utterly crumbled away. Propositions such as increased facilities for divorce, the mechanical prevention of birth, the merely companionate nature of marriage, the proposal to give an equal status to the legitimate and the illegitimate child, all of them items of the well-planned anti-Christian attack elsewhere, were in this country being welcomed with an almost innocent irresponsibility by women who had never studied

Christian principles or pondered their consequences. It almost seemed that their island security had played the part of a nursery wall, cutting them off from reality. In the midst of this Catholic women are standing four-square, doing their utmost in their civic work and public relationships to influence and enlighten public opinion. They are strengthening and developing protective work for girls and women against immoral propaganda, and they are endeavouring to develop an intellectual defence and even a counter-attack. All trace of hesitation and of false timidity has disappeared. The widespread nature of the peril has done much to unite all classes.

In making these somewhat sweeping claims we do not lose sight of the fact that adherents of organised work are always surrounded by a margin of the indifferent or that there are a number of individualists in any community who yet do effective and influential work though unable to co-operate with others. But the movement which set out to create a National Catholic laywoman's influence cannot be said to have failed, when it now numbers 116 branches and sections the delegates from which in assembly constitute in effect a Catholic woman's Parliament. It is a parliament, too, with a certain amount of executive power, since every branch and section is able to give some measure of effect to its resolutions. If its numbers are small, some thirteen thousand, those of the *Union Internationale*, of which it forms part, attain to over twenty million. So much for corporate influence. The sphere of the Catholic woman's direct personal influence is proportionately enlarged. She is fully enfranchised and is eligible for Parliament. She now fills the Mayoral office, sits on Municipal Councils, and on the Magistrates' Bench. She is adequately represented in all professions and callings.

At the beginning of the last century we found

Catholic women standing crippled and isolated in the midst of a securely established and innately hostile Protestant society. They had remained essentially English, and were wholly Christian. To-day, greatly increased in numbers, they have become an integral part of national life. They stand wholly Christian and essentially English in the midst of a crumbling Protestant society, ready to spend all they have of gifts and of influence in helping forward the reconstruction of all things in Christ.

STATISTICAL PROGRESS
BY REV. HERBERT THURSTON, S.J.

XII

STATISTICAL PROGRESS OF THE CATHOLIC CHURCH

SEVEN years after the passing of the Catholic Emancipation Act, Henry, fourth Duke of Newcastle, a Tory die-hard of the more extreme type, moved in the House of Lords for " returns of all Roman Catholic chapels, with the dates of their erection, also returns of all monastic establishments, distinguishing whether for monks or nuns, together with the number in each ; also for returns of all Roman Catholic colleges and seminaries in England and Wales, distinguishing those which belong to the Jesuits ; and also of the number of Roman Catholics in 1799, and their progressive increase down to the present time." In introducing this motion the Duke stated that Popery was alarmingly on the increase in Great Britain ; that in 1835 there were 510 Roman Catholic chapels in England ; while, sixty years before there had been only thirty. " In addition to this, eleven new churches were building ; and at Kidderminster and Dover, Protestant chapels had been turned into Popish chapels. There were also eight Popish colleges and seminaries, the object of which was manifest." Commenting upon this utterance in its next issue, the *Dublin Review* showed no inclination to repudiate the allegations made. " We can assure his Grace," said the writer, not improbably Wiseman himself, " that he has underrated the number of new churches now in course of erection : they are certainly not less than forty, not to speak of four or five which have been opened this year. The number of our British colleges amounts to nine."

On referring to Hansard, one discovers that the report, which the *Dublin Review* had probably obtained from *The Times* or some other newspaper, was not entirely accurate. The Duke had read to their Lordships an article in *The Newcastle Journal*, and in it there was question, not of England merely, but of Great Britain, so that Scotland was included. The estimate of 510 chapels, therefore, was pretty near the mark, though in England and Wales the total in 1829 (Emancipation year) had been less than 400. But whatever the increase in numbers may have been, the vast majority were still very tiny buildings, and many of them were only the private chapels of Catholic gentlemen to which the public were admitted. From the account in the *Dublin Review* it would seem that the return asked for by the noble Duke was agreed to with some modifications, but I have been unable to find any trace of it in the official index of Parliamentary Papers. On the other hand, a week before the discussion in the Lords, an address in the Commons demanded a return of the number of registered Dissenting Meeting-houses and Roman Catholic chapels in England and Wales. This was duly made, and on July 14 of the same year, 1836, it was ordered to be printed. For statistical purposes, however, the document is utterly worthless, and we may perhaps conjecture that the failure in this case was the reason why the fuller inquiry asked for by the Lords was not proceeded with. A letter had apparently been sent out to each of the Clerks of the Peace in the different counties and to the Town Clerks in the urban districts ; but the results were very disappointing. While a few of the Clerks thus addressed had taken evident pains to obtain information and to provide a tabulated statement—the Town Clerk of Norwich is conspicuous in this class—the great majority of the replies are quite ludicrously baffling and laconic. Many answered that they had no record of any chapels having been licensed in their district; others declared that they were unable to distinguish between Dissenting meeting-houses and Roman Catholic chapels, others again implied that the Justices at quarter sessions sometimes issued a licence and sometimes did not trouble about it. The majority of the returns seem to have been made in two lines, followed by the Clerk's signature. Thus, for example, in the case of the county of Northampton :

Number of licensed Dissenting Meeting-houses 195.
Number of Roman Catholic chapels -   - none.
                                   CHARLES MARKHAM.

One of the most quaintly worded replies is that returned from Bewdley (Worcestershire), then a town with about 4,000 inhabitants.

The return from Bewdley as respects the number of meeting-houses is four. A Roman Catholic chapel the return for is nil.
                                   W. N. MARCY.

Still, even from these very unsatisfactory materials a certain amount of useful confirmation may be obtained of the data furnished from the Catholic side by the *Laity's Directory*. We may take as a case in point the borough of Cambridge where, for the last thirty years, one of the finest Catholic churches in England has confronted the visitor as he makes his way from the station towards the great University centres. Strangely enough, Cambridge was the *alma mater* of some of the most ardent converts to Rome in those early days before the Oxford Movement began, of such men, for example, as Kenelm H. Digby, Ambrose Phillipps De Lisle, and the Hon. George Spencer.[1] Of De Lisle, or Lisle Phillipps, as he was called

---

[1] There are notices of the first two in the *D.N.B.* ; of the third a very full account is given in *The Life of Father Ignatius Spencer, C.P.*, by Father Devine.

at that time, it is recorded that when a student at Trinity in 1825, he and his friend Kenelm H. Digby, used to ride over to Ware every Sunday morning, a distance of 25 miles, in order to hear Mass and receive Communion. Quite in accord with this story we find in the *Laity's Directory* for 1829 the following entry headed Cambridgeshire :

Sewston Hall, near Cambridge, Rev. E. Huddleston. The late venerable Bishop of the Midland District had long entertained the design of establishing a permanent mission in the town of Cambridge ; which measure was strongly recommended by the celebrity of the place, the daily increasing number of resident Irish Catholics, and the fact of there being no public chapel in the whole county. Influenced by the same weighty reasons, the present Vicar Apostolic of the District, the Rt. Rev. Dr. Walsh, has determined to act upon the intentions of his illustrious predecessor ; and under such high sanction the Rev. Edward Huddleston, who has been appointed to this arduous and destitute mission, appeals to the piety and generosity of the Catholic public in support of a measure at once so auspicious to religion and so creditable to the Catholic cause.

Nevertheless, some thirteen years elapsed before the town of Cambridge possessed a Catholic chapel of its own. In the return of 1836 the Town Clerk reports " there are not any Roman Catholic chapels in Cambridge," and the Clerk of the Peace for the county remarks : " there is only one Roman Catholic chapel in this county and I do not find any entry of a licence for that."

The fact was that though the Duke of Newcastle, in the speech above referred to, encouraged their Lordships to believe that a sum of £400,000 " had been remitted from the Continent to this country and Ireland for the purpose of promoting Popery," the progress of Catholicism in rural areas was all along very slow. In the towns, development was much more rapid, and the very natural enthusiasm of those Catholics who witnessed this growth was often taken in bad part by the Evangelicals who lived in apprehension of a plot to overthrow the British Constitution and introduce Romanism. The Catholic journals of the time contained a good many self-congratulatory notices in the tone of the following extract :

Times have changed very much, and we are not insensible to the exertions of those liberal, enlightened statesmen that brought about the change. We have now a large chapel at Moorfields, which all the world frequent, and where for years the truths of *religion* have been without fear announced. The Borough chapel, near the Belgian ambassador's chapel, was some forty years since opened in a narrow dirty lane ; the best term it deserved was that of a wooden shed. It contained about two hundred ; and in every respect was a most miserable dwelling for a house of sacrifice. The new chapel in the London Road, which was substituted for the old one, holds about one thousand ; but the congregation belonging to it is nearly twenty thousand. East Lane Chapel, Rotherhithe, near the site of the once princely abbey of Bermondsey, can number from two to three thousand of a congregation. Virginia Street, once an hospital for foreign sailors, was at first nothing more than a room for the priest. This has swelled into one of the most capacious chapels in London, and the few that knelt and prayed in the priest's room to hear Mass has increased to the ten thousand of the actual present congregation. The congregation of Lincoln's Inn Fields is ten thousand at least. Warwick Street Chapel, most repair to it, not for the prayers, but for the music. Spanish Place Chapel has a congregation of six thousand.[1]

This passage was selected among others by the writer

---

[1] I take this from *Fraser's Magazine*, March 1839, p. 264. The only reference given is to " the *Catholic Magazine* at the close of 1834 " ; this seems to be incorrect, but the quotation is no doubt authentic. Strange to say, almost every one of the buildings here mentioned has now disappeared, having been replaced by a more spacious edifice.

of two articles in *Fraser's Magazine* (March and April 1839) in illustration of the " vaunting " spirit of Popery, and to stimulate his Protestant countrymen to use their best energies in counteracting it. There can be no doubt that the party whom he represented were seriously alarmed. In the October of the previous year (1838) a similar article had appeared in the influential and very widely-circulated *Blackwood's Magazine* under the title of " The Progress of Popery," and this seems to have been at once reprinted in pamphlet form by the Protestant Association. They must have sold well, even at 3d. apiece, for copies still dated 1838 bear the imprint " ninth thousand." The *Fraser's Magazine* articles were accompanied with a map of Great Britain dotted over with tiny black crosses, each of which was meant to indicate the location of a Catholic chapel. In Lancashire, Middlesex, and Stafford they are so numerous that they look as if they were meant to indicate forests. Neither was this the first attempt made to bring the rapid diffusion of Popery home graphically to a too indifferent public. A similar map had been issued in 1833 by the " Reformation Society " with a marginal letterpress in which attention was drawn to the fact that the number of Catholic chapels in England and Wales had, in ten years, grown from 358 to 423, and those in Scotland in like proportion.

There can be no doubt that after the passing of the Catholic Emancipation Act this matter of church accommodation, at any rate in the towns, was taken in hand very vigorously. In 1840 there were 469 churches and chapels, and by 1850 these had further increased to 581. In 1890 there were 1,335 Catholic places of worship open to the public, and in the present year, 1929, there are 2,183, of which 1,546 are registered for marriages. With regard to the number of priests no very precise information is available for the early years of the nineteenth century. The *Laity's Directory* supplies no alphabetical list, and the question is complicated by the presence in the country of a good many survivors of the French *émigré* clergy. One would be led to suppose from a list of those who had signed a certain " Form of Declaration of Catholic Communion " printed in the *Laity's Directory* for 1830, that there were no less than 89 French priests who were still available—at least for the purpose of saying Mass. But we do not know how many of them were infirm, or incapable of missionary work owing to their ignorance of the language, and from time to time, no doubt, opportunities offered by which a certain proportion were able to return to friends and relatives in France. Probably in 1829 the 395 chapels in England and Wales were served by rather fewer than 500 Catholic clergy. In 1850 there were 788 priests, in 1890 there were 2,478, in 1929 there are 4,310. Of course, it must not be forgotten that during the century 1829–1929 the population of England has nearly trebled. It was still a little short of 14 millions in 1831 ; it is now considerably in excess of 39 millions, despite the appalling decline of the birth-rate in recent years.[1] But even since 1890, during which time the population has increased by a third, or, in other words, in the proportion of 3 to 4, the Catholic churches have increased almost by two-thirds and the Catholic clergy have increased by rather more than two-thirds, *i.e.* by more than the proportion of 3 to 5. This, it is plain, seems to mark progress. It would imply that, while other denominations are demonstrably losing ground, the Catholic Church is not only keeping abreast of the increase of the population, but distinctly gaining upon it.

[1] Already in 1926 the population of England and Wales, according to the official estimate of the Registrar-General, was 39,067,000.

Shortly after the delivery of the Lincoln judgment in 1890 the then Archbishop of Canterbury (Dr. Edward Benson) published a pastoral letter which seemed intended to allay for the benefit of Evangelicals any suspicion of Romanist sympathies which the terms of the earlier pronouncement could have excited. He declared his conviction that despite all that had been said of the menace of Ritualism, Englishmen at large were in no danger of being led to the Church of Rome. " It has been shown," he wrote, " that in all these years she has effected here a multiplication of edifices and institutions, but not of souls ; that she makes no statistical progress. No, the ancient Church of England is with us. I do not fear that the new Italian Mission will make anything of our clergy or people." Mr. Gladstone, when in 1894 he published his pamphlet on " The Vatican Decrees," had also said something very similar, and it must be admitted that there were considerations which seemed to show that in spite of a more efficient equipment and organisation, the Catholic Church in the preceding half century had lost quite as much as she had gained.

That these views were based upon a misunderstanding of the true position of affairs will, I believe, be made clear to anyone who studies the facts of the case fairly and impartially. In times of exhilarating progress an optimism is apt to prevail, which, especially under the stimulus of persuasive oratory, paralyses the judgment, so that men very readily assume that to be true which their partisan sympathies regard as desirable. This tendency was, as I conceive, at the root of a very ill-founded belief that the Catholics in England shortly after the passing of the Emancipation Act already formed nearly a tenth part of the existing population. It is, perhaps, not quite certain whether it was the fears of the No-Popery alarmists or the enthusiasm of the newly-

emancipated Catholics which contributed most to the
propagation of this crazy idea, but it is in any case likely
that the two influences reacted upon each other. I
cannot find that the Vicars Apostolic gave any kind of
encouragement to the extravagances here referred to.
Bishop Briggs in making his report to Rome in January
1839, estimated the number of the faithful in the Northern
district at about 180,000, and his Vicariate was by far the
most Catholic of the four. Bishop Griffiths, in a similar
report to Rome dated June 1837, claimed only 157,000
Catholics for the London district. On the other hand,
those in the Western district, according to Bishop Baines'
very detailed report submitted in 1840 did not exceed
25,000.[1] For the Midland district no official statement
at this period seems to have been preserved, but
Bishop Baines, the Western Vicar Apostolic, who
travelled about England a good deal and was keenly
interested in a new redistribution scheme of the Vicariates,
regarded the flock of his Midland colleague as only half
as numerous as that of Bishop Briggs in the North.[2]
This would give us a total of a little over 450,000 for the
whole of England and Wales, or—allowing a margin for
Catholics settled where no chapel existed—let us say
roughly half a million.

Now it was just at this time that the articles, already
referred to, appeared in *Blackwood* and in *Fraser's
Magazine*. The first of these, after pointing out that
there were 43 Roman Catholic chapels then building, and
that, whereas forty years before no single popish college
existed in the country, " there were now ten, as well as
sixty seminaries of education, besides chapel schools,"

---

[1] All these figures will be found in Mazière Brady's *Episcopal Succession in
England, Scotland and Ireland*, vol. iii. pp. 201, 280 and 316. They were
extracted from the original reports in the Roman archives.

[2] See Bishop Baines' letter to the Cardinal Prefect of Propaganda, printed
in Bishop Ward's *Sequel to Catholic Emancipation*, i. p. 235.

proceeds further to state with all the emphasis of capitals :

It must be remembered that the Roman Catholic population of Great Britain is now very little short of TWO MILLIONS, and that there is, as we have shown, great wealth among their leaders.

I have not been able to trace this estimate of two millions any further back, and I believe that the writer in *Blackwood* was the father of it. Naturally it caused a sensation. *The Times* took the matter up, and inevitably the discussion elicited comments on the Catholic side. For all those who were interested in " the Association of Prayers for the Conversion of England," which had shortly before been organised in France by the Hon. and Rev. George Spencer, afterwards a Passionist, such an assurance of the progress of Catholicism was a valuable aid in the propaganda they had undertaken. Hence we find prominence given to it in the *Catholic Magazine* for January 1839, where the editor among other observations remarks :

We are inclined to think, but are not quite sure, that our number is overrated when reckoned at two millions by the writer in *Blackwood*. We are certain, however, that if our numerical strength be not yet so great, it must become so ere long, as the conversions to our faith, acknowledged by the better informed among our opponents, satisfactorily prove.

Naturally, the same estimate was taken for granted in the two alarmist articles which appeared shortly afterwards in *Fraser's Magazine*, but, almost equally as a matter of course, it was improved upon. *Blackwood* had used the phrase " very little short of two millions in Great Britain." In *Fraser's* we now read that " the number of Roman Catholics in *England and Wales* is estimated at two millions," and the lesson is driven home by the further statement :

It would be impossible exactly to ascertain the number of Roman Catholics except under the authority of a Parliamentary Order, but if the number is about 2,000,000, then they are nearly twenty-nine times more numerous now than they were in 1780, while the population of the country is only double what it was in that year.

These articles, like that previously referred to, were reprinted by the Protestant Association as a pamphlet, and in this way the legend obtained further currency, figuring shortly afterwards in a speech delivered by O'Connell at a Catholic meeting held on July 15, 1839, in the Freemason's Hall.

Have we not a right (he said) to come forward and to claim for all—not for Catholics alone, but for the Protestant Dissenters, for every class—the right to be free from the control of the State in the management of their religious education ? (Hear, hear and cheers.)   Have not the Catholics the right to demand this ?   How many are we ?   We are 7,000,000 in Ireland (cheers).   They say we are at least 2,000,000 in Great Britain.   I believe that it is not exaggerated.   In Liverpool we are 100,000 ; in Manchester, 70,000 or 80,000.   However, say only a million and a half—we are 8,500,000.   What other persuasion has so many attached to it ?   Not the Presbyterians ; they are only 3,000,000.   Not the Wesleyan Methodists ; they are but about 300,000.   Not the Established Church ; they are but 7,000,000.   And when one talks of the Established Church it is hard to say who belong to it.   I know a most respectable family in Dublin stated to belong to the Established Church : the eldest daughter frequents the Derbyites ; the other the Calvinists ; the third the Established Church ; the father does not go anywhere, reminding one of Paddy's description of a " bitter good Protestant " (which in Ireland means an Orangeman) : " He ates meat of a Friday, hates the Papists, and goes nowhere of a Sunday." (Laughter and cheers.)

But the discredit of this over-estimate, though it seems to have originated on the Protestant side, fell upon the Catholics. A Church of England journal, the *Ecclesiastical Gazette*, in the middle of 1840, published an indignant protest leading off with the following characteristic sentence :

As the Roman Catholics still continue to assert, or to intimate indirectly, that their number in Great Britain amounts to about two millions, and as it is evident that this is an enormous exaggeration made to serve a particular purpose, it seems desirable to ascertain as early as may be their real numerical strength.

Accordingly the writer in support of his protest drew attention to the small number and very diminutive proportions of the Catholic places of worship and more especially laid stress upon the Registrar-General's figures for the working of the new Marriage Act, which had come into operation in 1838. The number of Catholic marriages returned was only 1,629, and this corresponded, so he argued, to a total Catholic population for England and Wales of 223,987. Still this was certainly too small an estimate. The truth was that the Catholic layfolk, many of them poor and uninstructed, had not yet realised that it was possible, or at any rate that it was a matter of strict obligation, for them to be married according to their own ritual. The additional fee which had to be paid to the registrar for witnessing the marriage acted as a deterrent. Hence the inference deduced from the small number of Catholic marriages sinned as much by defect as the estimate objected to had sinned by excess. In any case, one argument which can now be framed seems unanswerable. If there were only 1,629 Catholic marriages in 1838, and in 1924 there were, according to the Registrar-General's returns, 16,286, the Catholic population must have multiplied tenfold in the interval, while the population of the country as a whole has not even trebled. But we may readily admit that in 1840 the controversialists on both sides were very much at sea in this matter of statistics, and the *Catholic Directory* for that year affords curious proof of the differences of opinion which prevailed ; for while on one page data are supplied which would seem to correspond to a total of less than 700,000 Catholics, the editor, in another place, expatiates on " the religious aspect we now behold in Great Britain —a Catholic population of nearly two millions in a country where the Catholic religion and name were almost extirpated."

In the year 1851 a sort of " census of religious worship " was attempted in England by counting all those who, on Sunday, March 30, attended the morning and evening services in the churches and chapels of all denominations throughout the country. Such an enumeration was bound to prove unsatisfactory from the point of view of reliable statistics, for in the case of the Catholics more particularly, many of those who went to Communion at an early Mass were present again at the High Mass and thus were counted twice over. At the same time, the official who edited the results in 1854 was probably not far from the truth when he expressed the opinion that " the total number of persons professing Roman Catholicism in England and Wales cannot be less than 1,000,000 and probably exceeds that number." The total population at that date was as nearly as possible 18 millions. The Registrar-General's returns showed that 4.8 per cent. of the marriages were celebrated according to the rites of the Catholic Church. Roughly speaking, this would imply that about a twentieth of the population were Catholics ; for though it is true that mixed marriages were numerous, and these, being for the most part celebrated with Catholic ritual, gave the

Catholics more than their share, still there were many marriages irregularly contracted in Protestant churches by careless and easy-going people who nevertheless had no idea of apostatising from the creed in which they had been brought up.   One definite element in the situation which cannot be ignored is the fact that in 1851 the Census returns showed that over 500,000 people then residing in the country had been born in Ireland.   Now certainly the vast majority of these were Catholics, even if they were far from fervent in the practice of their religion, and there was also a pretty large alien contingent of Italians, French, Belgians, etc., most of whom had duly received baptism in their childhood with the forms of the Roman ritual.   To these we have to add a considerable number of converts, the first fruits of the Oxford movement, who had already in 1851 made their submission to the Holy See.   There seems, therefore, little ground for quarrelling with the estimate just mentioned of 1,000,000 Catholics in 1851, but it must also be remembered that a considerable proportion of these were recent immigrants driven over to England by the Irish famine and the miseries it brought in its train.   They did not, for the most part, make this country their permanent home, but passed on to America or Australia, as soon as friends were able to supply them with sufficient money to pay their passage in an emigrant ship.   At the census of 1851, 29 people out of every thousand enumerated in England and Wales had been born in Ireland. At the census of 1921 the Irish-born numbered only nine in every thousand.

What, as regards our Catholic population, is the present position of affairs ?   The question is one of great difficulty, owing to discordant views as to what constitutes a profession of Catholicism, to the unreliability of returns which are based, not upon enumeration but upon general impressions, and especially to the unknown factor of leakage, the loss to the Church of those who, having received Catholic baptism in their youth, gradually drift away into infidelity or indifference. There can be no question that the number of these last is very large and that the process is greatly facilitated by the multiplied distractions and amusements of modern life, as well as by the tendency to forsake the country and to congregate in towns. The negligent in new surroundings fail to make themselves known to the clergy and get lost. One cannot be blind to the fact that a certain amount of the church-going in old days was due to the dullness of life. A man was led to attend church services, because such attendance was something to break the monotony of existence. But having set foot in church even from the least worthy of motives, he was often prompted to say his prayers and heard an occasional sermon which helped him to keep the commandments. Nowadays the cinema, the concert-room, and the motor char-à-banc are powerful rivals to every place of worship, and the careless soon lose the habit of church attendance. All religious denominations suffer in greater or less measure. We cannot be surprised that there is leakage. None the less, despite the leakage, there is good evidence that the Catholic Church in this country still continues to make statistical progress—not only absolutely, but even relatively to the increase of the population.

And first of all there is the positive and, as I think, quite reliable evidence of conversions, the returns made from every diocese of those who after a period of instruction and, in a sense, of probation, have made their profession of faith and have, for the most part, received conditional baptism. Since 1914 these figures have been printed annually in the *Catholic Directory*. It may be of interest to repeat the totals here. The first group deals with the conversions from 1912 to the end of the War, the second with those since the beginning of 1919.

Year	Converts	Year	Converts
1912	6,511	1919	10,592
1913	7,184	1920	12,621
1914	9,034	1921	11,621
1915	9,367	1922	12,406
1916	8,501	1923	12,796
1917	9,018	1924	12,355
1918	9,402	1925	11,948
		1926	11,714
		1927	12,065
Total		Total	
1912 to 1918	59,017	1919 to 1927	108,118

The two groups together yield a total of 167,135 converts received during a period of 16 years, and consequently an average of rather more than 10,000 a year. Scotland, it is to be noted, is not included in these lists. Many, of course, of those who have entered the Church during this period have since died. Some few have gone back or lapsed into agnosticism. But the vast majority remain with us as active and fervent Catholics. Those who being baptised and educated in the Faith afterwards fall away are for the most part the careless and the pleasure-loving. The converts who replace them are, as a rule, keen in their zeal for religion and it rarely happens that their change of creed does not involve some measure of personal sacrifice.

But the factor upon which I am inclined to place most reliance as evidence of the statistical progress made by the Catholic Church in England during recent years is the returns of our infant baptisms. In 1927, the last

year for which the figures are available, these amounted
to 65,176. Let it be noted in passing that the number
is in no way exceptional. There were 65,411 in 1925,
67,565 in 1924, and 68,445 in 1923. Now the total
number of births in 1927—we are, of course, speaking
always of England and Wales—was 654,969.[1] It must at
once be evident that if 65,176 of these infants received
baptism at the hands of a Catholic priest, the Church can
claim very nearly a tenth part of the coming generation
as formally entrusted to her religious keeping. If one
argued crudely, one would be tempted to infer from this
that very nearly one-tenth part of the population made
profession of Catholicism. As the estimated population
in 1926 was 39,067,000, this would mean that the
Catholics in England and Wales numbered well over
three and a half millions. I am not so sure that this
would be an exaggerated estimate, if we were content to
count as a Catholic every man and woman who would write
themselves down R.C. if they had to fill in this detail in
a census paper. But clearly there are deductions to be
made. In the first place there are a very considerable
number of mixed marriages. If the promises made by
the non-Catholic party in such a contract are faithfully
adhered to, all the children will be baptised Catholics,
though the inference that all their family belongings are
Catholics would be quite unjustified. Of still greater
importance is the question of birth restriction. This, it
is to be feared, is not unknown even in Catholic families,
but it is quite well understood even by the most uneducated that the practice is condemned by the Church, and
consequently the number of children born to Catholic
parents is undoubtedly in excess of the average which

[1] In as much as the total births for England and Wales decreased from
694,563 in 1926 to 654,969 in 1927, the proportion of Catholic infants has
increased rather than diminished.

prevails among parents of other denominations. Unfortunately, one can only state the difficulty and leave it. No sort of test is possible of the allowance which should on that account be introduced into our calculations.

Next in importance to the baptism returns are the statistics for Catholic marriages. These come to us from two sources, the registers of the churches in which the marriage takes place, and the official returns of the Registrar-General. For some years past the former, like the infant baptisms and the conversions, have been printed annually in the *Catholic Directory*. The latter, so far as concerns the form of the celebration of the marriage, are only computed every five years, and the latest statement we possess is that for the year 1924. With regard to this last, the editor of " The Registrar-General's Statistical Review of England and Wales for 1924 " remarks (p. 134) " Roman Catholic marriages have continued their considerable increase in proportion noticeable since 1909," and he adds that " the northern industrial counties, particularly Lancashire, are the stronghold of Roman Catholic marriages." This is the more noteworthy, because, as is well known, dispensations for mixed marriages are very rarely accorded in that region. Now in 1924 the total number of marriages in England and Wales was 296,416. Of these, 16,286 were returned by the Registrar as having been celebrated in Catholic churches. This implies that 55 marriages in every thousand were Catholic marriages, and if we applied the same proportion to the population as a whole we should be led to the conclusion that 2,045,000 were sufficiently earnest in their practice of Catholicism to wish to get married by a priest of that denomination. On the other hand there would be a reduction to be made for the mixed marriages, for the family connections of such a pair will presumably be half Protestant. When, however, we compare the Registrar-General's figures with those returned by the Catholic clergy in the *Catholic Directory*, we notice a great and very significant discrepancy. According to the Registrar-General the number of Catholic marriages in 1924 was 16,286; according to the clergy returns the Catholic marriages numbered 20,394, a difference of more than 4,000. A similar disagreement is manifest on all the other previous occasions when it was possible to confront the figures of the Catholic registers with those of the state officials. In 1919 the Registrar-General could only vouch for 19,078 Catholic marriages, whereas our own registers showed 21,751. Or, to take an example on a more limited scale, in 1912 the Registrar's return for the two counties of Cheshire and Shropshire, which form the diocese of Shrewsbury, recorded only 416 Catholic marriages. But the number sent in by the clergy themselves was 476. A prejudiced critic might easily suppose that there was deliberate falsification or, at any rate, gross negligence on the part of the parish clergy who sent in these figures; but the explanation is quite simple. The excess of 4,000 entries in the Catholic registers for 1924 is simply the record of *marriages put right*. The parties had previously contracted in an Anglican church or civilly before the Registrar, and afterwards, repenting, had gone through the ceremony before the parish priest of one of them, thus validating the union in the eyes of the Church. It must be abundantly plain then, that the Registrar-General's returns can by no means be trusted as presenting the sum total of all the Catholics who contract matrimony, and if we assume that the real figure was nearer 20,000 than 16,000, we should obtain a ratio of something like 7 per cent. of Catholic marriages which would correspond to a total population of Catholics numbering close upon three millions.

Everything, of course, depends upon the definition we adopt of what we mean by a Catholic. If we only include under that term those who " fulfil their Easter duties " and normally hear Mass on a Sunday, the estimate of 2,156,146 which stands in the *Catholic Directory* would probably be even excessive. The compiler appends a footnote, referring especially to the estimates of the Catholic population in each diocese, to the effect that " these figures in many cases cannot be accurate." And, indeed, when we notice that in the instance of three such dioceses as Westminster, Southwark and Salford, the same estimate has remained unaltered for the past eleven years, it must be evident that no more has been aimed at than a very rough approximation. But if, on the other hand, a Catholic be understood to be one who would not repudiate the description himself, who was willing to have his children baptised in the faith and would probably welcome the help of a priest on his death-bed, the evidence seems abundantly to warrant the conclusion that there are at present rather over than under three million souls who, subject to a less rigid interpretation of the term, could fairly be described as Catholics. The population of England and Wales has not much more than doubled since 1851, and if we may take one million as a reasonable estimate of the expansion achieved after 21 years of Emancipation, the development of Catholicism during the last 80 years has rather more than kept pace with the natural increase to which the vital statistics of the country bear witness.

THE OUTLOOK

BY G. K. CHESTERTON

XIII

THE OUTLOOK

WHEN we really wish to know how the world is going, it is no bad test to take some tag or current phrase of the Press and reverse it, substituting the precise contrary, and see whether it makes more sense that way. It generally does; such a mass of outworn conventions has our daily commentary become. An excellent example occurred recently concerning the prospect of Protestantism and Catholicism. The editor of the *Express*, a literary man of deserved distinction, summed up the matter by saying that he had no prejudice against Catholicism or Anglo-Catholicism, that he had every respect for them, but that England (evidently including himself) was solidly Protestant. This is a very neat and convenient statement of the exact opposite of the truth. I have most friendly feelings to the gentleman in question; and it is without the least animosity to him that I say that what is sincere and alive and active in him is Anti-Catholicism and nothing else. What is really working in the world to-day is Anti-Catholicism and nothing else. It certainly is not Protestantism; not half so much as it is Pelagianism. And if the religion of modern England is to be called Protestant, there is at least one other adjective which cannot conceivably be applied to it. Whatever else it is, it is not solid Protestantism. There might perhaps be a case for calling it liquid Protestantism.

Now this marks the chief change of the century we celebrate. The political circumstances of the final Tory surrender to Emancipation were, of course, complex. Emancipation seemed to some a sort of mongrel and

monster, produced by two opposites ; the survival of
the Old Religion and the principles of the French Revolution. But in such things there are complex harmonies
as well as contradictions. In some ways the ultimate
quarrel of Rome with the French Revolution was rather
like the recent quarrel of Rome with the French Royalists.
It was resistance to a pagan extreme ; but there had been
not a little Catholic sympathy before the thing reached
that extreme. There had been countless liberal clerics
in the first movements of the reform ; Pius IX had begun
by being the reverse of reactionary ; and the atmosphere
was such that the gigantic protagonist of Catholic
Emancipation himself, the great Daniel O'Connell,
could combine passionate Ultra-Montanism with the
largest political Liberalism without any division in the
simplicity of his mind or the general humanity of his
ideals. Those who hated him both as a Radical and a
Roman Catholic would have seen no inconsistency in
those two hateful things. The truth to seize about all
that earlier situation is that the bigotry was on the other
side ; in one sense the theology was on the other side.
We cannot see it clearly in the statesmen ; for they were
either free-thinkers or opportunists. Wellington met
his Waterloo ; but he was a good soldier and, therefore,
retreated when it was futile to stand. But if we look at
the mass of the people, we find a real religious resistance
—because there was a real religion. That resistance is
now only found in America, where just such a Democrat
as Daniel O'Connell is still threatened with political
exclusion solely for being a Catholic. In some points the
Americans are a hundred years behind the times.

But this sort of purely political exclusiveness will not
be the chief problem of the future. Whatever be the
relation of Rome to the new world, her authority will
not be transferred to Dayton, Tennessee. The political

effects of the political emancipation are relatively simple
and in a sense the easiest part of the speculation. Everybody knows that Catholic Emancipation has never led,
and never will lead, to the direct political disasters
that some foretold. The Duke of Norfolk was never
actually caught in the act of imitating Guy Fawkes ; and
Lord Russell of Killowen seldom if ever invited a
Spanish Armada to these shores. Outside certain local
Puritan fevers, chiefly in America, there is no reason to
suppose that the world will be so unreasonable as to
repent having elected Catholic Mayors or sent out
Catholic Ambassadors. The cant about a foreign
allegiance is still heard ; but that is because a cant can
long outlive a cause. Men who are wide awake are
well aware that the Catholic internationalism, which bids
men respect their national governments, is considerably
less dangerous than the financial internationalism which
may make a man betray his country or the revolutionary
internationalism which may make him destroy it. It is,
of course, possible that, under the pressure of Catholic
conversions, the world may return to older and rougher
types of persecution ; but it is not immediately probable.
But when we turn from the political to the spiritual
prospect, we find a change which is exactly represented
by the reversal of the journalistic maxim mentioned
above. We must realise what England has become,
under all titles and terminology, if we would make a
guess about what she is next destined to be.

If we want to measure the distance between the
date we celebrate and the day in which we live, between
Catholic Emancipation and its consequences after a
century, we shall find the newspaper quotation very
important. If we wanted to describe the conditions a
hundred years ago in this country, we could not do it
better than by saying that *then* England was solidly

Protestant; or the Protestantism of England was solid. And we shall still better understand the modern change if we ask what is meant by that solidity. It had a very definite meaning, which has now so completely disappeared that even those who most frequently invoke it are least able to imagine it. There is nothing like that sort of solid confidence to-day. It meant this : that the types and ranks of society really and sincerely interested in religion did really and sincerely believe that Protestant religion had been proved superior to Catholic religion. It was strongest in the middle class, especially the wealthier middle class ; but that middle class had been steadily growing stronger and wealthier, as was natural in a specially mercantile and capitalist community. It covered a multitude of healthy, hard-headed and even clear-headed professional and commercial men ; I say " even clear-headed " because, though the English had the name of not being logical, they were far more logical in those days than they are now. If they sat longer over their wine, they argued longer over their politics ; they did not live on hurried cocktails and hurried headlines. Their mercantile politics might be narrow ; but the number of them who could expound some connected thesis, such as Free Trade, was very large. And as their politics consisted of certain definite theories, right or wrong, so their religion consisted of certain definite doctrines, true or false. If you had asked any such Protestant why he was a Protestant, or what he meant by being a Protestant, he would have instantly stated or explained those doctrines ; just as a Free Trader would explain Free Trade. There were Englishmen, of course, for whom the whole business was vaguer or more indifferent ; but they did not make the tone of that solid mercantile England. The populace made the Pope a guy, just as they made Guy Fawkes a guy ; but the poor were at the best treated like children and left, like children, to make a guy or a game of anything. A great part of the higher aristocracy had been quite sceptical and pagan throughout the eighteenth century, or even from the seventeenth century; but the same tact and informal secrecy, which keeps such a class together, kept it from any public insult to the Protestant religion of England. And that religion was a religion; it was Protestant, and it was national; that is, it was the religion of the normal citizen.

Now if you had asked an educated English Protestant in 1828 why Protestantism was right, or why Popery was wrong, he would not have had the smallest difficulty in answering. Of course the first thing to be emphasised would have been what has since been the first thing to be doubted or denied. It was the literal inspiration and inerrancy of the Hebrew Scriptures, and sometimes even of the English translation of those Scriptures. It was the view that still lingers in provincial corners and is called Fundamentalism.

At the beginning of the nineteenth century, practically all Protestantism was Fundamentalism. But it is a great mistake to suppose that the true Protestant of history had nothing better to do for men than to throw a Bible at their heads. What he valued was the theological Scheme of Salvation supposed to be set forth in that work; as the Free Trader valued Adam Smith as the instrument of a theory. Of that theological theory there were two main versions; one, universal in Scotland and very prevalent in England, that God chose some to receive the benefits of redemption and rejected others even in the act of creating them; the other, that men could accept God but only by accepting this theological scheme of salvation, and that their good works had no effect on the result. This was the great doctrine of

Faith independent of Works, which was so universally recognised as the chief mark and test of Protestantism that we might almost say that it was the whole of Protestantism, except indeed where Protestantism took the very fiercest form of Calvinism. It is not a question of making points against Protestantism; this was the chief point that could be made for Protestantism. It was especially the popular point; the most persuasive point; the most sympathetic point. From this idea of instantaneous individualist acceptance of the Atonement, by a pure act of faith, came the whole system of appeals on which this form of Christianity relied. That was why it was so easy, so personal, so emotional; that was why the *whole* of Christian's burden fell off at the foot of the Cross. There were no degrees of sin or details of penance; because works were not in question at all. That is why they needed no Confessor or Sacrament of Penance; because there was nothing *they* could do to diminish sins either hopeless or already abolished or ignored. That was why it was wicked to pray for the dead; for the dead could not be anything but instantly beatified by dogmatic faith alone, or lost for lack of it. That was why there could be no progress or further enlightenment in the life to come; or in other words no Purgatory. And *that* was what was meant by being a Protestant; disapproving of prayers for the dead; disapproving of progress after death; disapproving of any religion that relied on good works. That was the great Protestant religion of Western Europe, of which we would speak as respectfully as we would of the virility and equality of Islam; and a hundred years ago it was normal and national. It was, in the newspaper phrase, solid.

To-day, as a national and normal thing, it has utterly vanished. Not one man in twenty really dis-

approves of praying for the dead. The War, in killing
many million men, killed that one pedantry and perversity.
Not one man in twenty is either a Calvinist or an up-
holder of Faith against Works. Not one man in twenty
thinks he will go to hell if he does not instantly accept
the theological theory of redemption ; perhaps it would
be better if he did. Not one man in twenty believes the
Bible infallible, as real Protestants believed it infallible.
Of all that wonderful system of religious thought,
thundered against Rome in so many sermons, argued
against Rome in so many pamphlets, thrown out scorn-
fully against Rome in so many Exeter Hall meetings and
Parliamentary debates, nothing remains. Of all that, as
it affects the forward movement of the educated classes,
and the future of the world, nothing remains.

But there is something that remains. Anti-Catholicism remains ; though it is no longer Protestantism,
any more than it is Albigensianism or Donatism. And
that is the factor we must grasp and estimate, if we are
to estimate the outlook to-day. Protestantism is now
only a name ; but it is a name that can be used to cover
any or every ism except Catholicism. It is now a vessel
or receptacle into which can be poured all the thousand
things that for a thousand reasons react against Rome ;
but it can only be full of these things because it is now
hollow ; because it is itself empty. Every sort of
negation, every sort of new religion, every sort of moral
revolt or intellectual irritation, that can make a man
resist the claim of the Catholic Faith, is here gathered
into a heap and covered with a convenient but quite
antiquated label. When the journalists say that there is
solid Protestantism, all they mean is that there is a pretty
heavy reluctance or resistance in the matter of any return
of the English to their ancient religion ; and this, up to a
point, may be quite true. But the heap is a hotchpotch ;

the resistance is not a rational resistance, in the sense of having a clear and commonly accepted reason; and in so far as it has a prevailing colour it is quite the contrary colour to that which prevailed in Protestantism. It is even more against Calvinism than against Catholicism; it is even more insistent on works than were the Catholics; it would make a future life far less final and more purely progressive than did the Catholic doctrine of Purgatory; it would make the Bible far less important than it is to a Catholic. On every single point on which the Protestant attacked the Pope, he would now say that the modern spirit was a mere exaggeration of the Popish errors. In so far as there is such a vague modern spirit, common to all these things, a spirit that may be called either liberality or laxity, it never was at any time the spirit of Protestantism. It came from the Revolution and the Romantic Movement, indirectly perhaps from the Renaissance of men like Rabelais and Montaigne; and ultimately much more from men like More and Erasmus than from men like Calvin and Knox. When the Protestant orators in the present crisis repeat rather monotonously, " We will not lose the freedom we gained four hundred years ago," they show how little they share the religion which they defend. Men gained no freedom four hundred years ago; there was no particular freedom about creating the Scottish Sabbath or preaching nothing but Predestination or even yielding to the Tudor Terror or the Cromwellian Terror. But it is arguable that they gained freedom a hundred years ago, as Catholics gained it a hundred years ago. It is tenable that such freedom was the expanding effect of the American and French Revolutions and the democratic idealism which came with the nineteenth century and seems in some danger of declining with the twentieth. Above all, it is arguable that they have a certain kind of freedom *now*; not because they are Protestants, for they are not ; but because they are anything they like and nothing if they like that better ; because they are theists, theosophists, materialists, monists or mystics on their own. How much such freedom is worth, or how much chance it has of bearing any fruit in anything positive or creative, is another matter ; but in order to anticipate the next phase, it is necessary to realise that this phase is one of negative liberty, not to say anarchy. Whatever it is, it is not Protestantism ; and whatever it is, it is not solid.

This is the truth symbolised in the remark on the Prayer-Book Debate : that a crowd of Free-Thinkers and Nonconformists and people of any opinions dictated the affairs of the Church of England. I am very proud of the fact that Catholics abstained from doing so and avoided a very obvious piece of bad taste. But the fact itself contains fine shades that have hardly been noticed. It is not sufficiently realised that even a congregation at the City Temple, or a crowd come to hear a Dean or Canon in St. Paul's Cathedral, is often, in fact, almost as mixed and dubious in religion as the members of the House of Commons. Many Nonconformists are not conforming to Nonconformity ; and a churchman often means only a man who never goes to chapel. Such differences exist in the same sect or even in the same man. If we would grasp the modern problem, we must simply take at random some fairly typical Englishman and note how little he really *is* anything. He has, let us say, been brought up a Congregationalist and drifted away ; he is by normal and rather negative habit an Anglican ; he has become by unanswered doubts and vague popular science an Agnostic ; he has often wondered if there is anything in being a Theosophist ; he has attended one or two séances and might be persuaded to be a Spiritualist. *That* is the man we have got to deal with ; and not some rigid Protestant labelled Methodist or even some rigid Atheist labelled Materialist. It is that man whom we have to set out to convert, after a hundred years of relative political liberty have left the old Protestant England far behind us and the new Catholic England still far away.

It is only fair to say, of course, that events have falsified almost as much the prophecies of those who promoted Catholic Emancipation as of those who resisted it. Many Liberals hardly disguised the idea that to emancipate Catholicism would be to extinguish Catholicism. Many thought they were tolerating a dying superstition ; some thought they were killing it. It is the other superstition that has been killed. But there are always new superstitions ; or, to put it more moderately, new religions. And a general estimate of the chances will see them chiefly affected, I think, by the presence of these new religions side by side with that very ancient thing called Agnosticism. The real interest of the speculation is in the question of which of the two will turn out to be the really formidable opponent of the Faith in the future.

We know what is really meant by saying that the Church is merely conservative and the modern world progressive. It means that the Church is always continuous and the heresies always contradictory. We have already noted it in the case of Protestantism ; and the men who now completely contradict Protestantism, even in order to contradict Catholicism. But one effect of this contrast between continuity and bewildering variety is that the Church is generally seen in the light of the last heresy. The Church is supposed to consist chiefly of the things which that heresy happened to disapprove. So much of the Protestant tradition still remains that a great many people suppose that the chief marks of

Catholicity are those which stood out as stains in the eyes of the last school of critics. Romanism is supposed to be made up of Popery and Purgatory and the Confessional, with the queerest things thrown in, such as incense and rosaries and the images of saints. But these were often the things most important to Protestants, not most important to Catholics ; and not most important to the other opponents of Catholics. A Mahommedan would not connect Rome with Purgatory, because he himself believes in Purgatory ; a Buddhist would not connect her with images, because he himself has images ; an old pagan would not have been horrified at incense, because he used it himself. In the same way the new religions will not attack the old religion for the old reasons. A Christian Scientist will not assume that all stories of miraculous healing must have been frauds. A Spiritualist will not assume that all supernatural messages received through men must be impossible. It will be an entirely new list of charges or challenges that will come from the new mystics, who have imitated so many of the old marvels. In so far as the new religions become the leaders of the opposition, a new class of controversies will arise ; with the faith-healers, for instance, upon the mystery of matter ; with the psychic investigators upon the influences of evil. All this will bring us further and further from the special Protestant problems ; and a hundred years hence the Church may look to her enemies something utterly different from what she looked like a hundred years ago. She will look different because she will be the same.

But if no new religion becomes important enough to be the main issue, the immediate change will be much simpler. The two centuries will probably have completed the full transition from Protestantism to Paganism. The Church will be facing once more her first and her most formidable enemy; a thing more attractive because more human than any of the heresies. This condition that can only be called Paganism is not easily defined and has often been misrepresented. In one aspect it may be called practical materialism without the narrowness of theoretical materialism. The Pagan looks for his pleasures to the natural forces of this world; but he does not insist so strictly upon dry negations about the other; he has commonly admitted a vague borderland of the unknown, providing him with possibilities of inspiration or of awe which are forbidden to the cheap, modern atheist with his clockwork cosmos. The worshippers of the Unknown God could at least build an altar, though they could not inscribe it with a name. But I fancy that men who have once been Christians, or whose fathers have been Christians, will not be long in discovering, or rather rediscovering, the profound defect that destroyed Paganism and filled centuries with a horror of its final phase. The natural forces, when they are turned into gods, betray mankind by something that is in the very nature of nature-worship. We can already see men becoming unhealthy by the worship of health; becoming hateful by the worship of love; becoming paradoxically solemn and overstrained even by the idolatry of sport; and in some cases strangely morbid and infected with horrors by the perversion of a just sympathy with animals. Unless all these things are subject to a more centralised and well-balanced conception of the universe, the local god becomes too vivid, we might say too visible, and strikes his worshippers with madness. The pantheist is always too near to the polytheist and the polytheist to the idolator; the idolator to the man offering human sacrifice. There is nothing in Paganism to check its own exaggerations; and for that reason the world will probably find again, as it found before, the necessity of a universal moral philosophy supported by an authority that can define. In any case, that quarrel between Paganism and Catholicism will again be one raising issues very unfamiliar to many even now; and issues that would have very much mystified the men who debated a hundred years ago the issue of Catholic Emancipation.

In any case, this emergence of new issues will reveal more and more one of the advantages of an old religion. Whole aspects of Catholic doctrine and tradition, hidden by historical accident and the special quarrels of recent times, will be revealed to the world when it begins to address new questions to the Church. This is a point that has not been sufficiently stressed in the relations between Protestantism and Catholicism. Very often a Protestant was not only a man merely protesting, but a man merely protesting against a particular thing. He sometimes thought that thing was Rome ; but it was really only one of the thousand aspects of Rome. When new aspects appear under new searchlights, he will be not so much defeated as simply outside the affair. A Baptist disapproves of baptising babies ; a Presbyterian disapproves of bishops ; a Prohibitionist disapproves of beer, and so on. But a Presbyterian, as such, has nothing very special to say about the Subconscious Mind. A Baptist as such has nothing special to say to a Behaviorist as such. But a Catholic may have a great deal to say to these people. For the Catholic commentary on life has gone on so much longer, it has covered so many different social conditions, has dealt so carefully with countless fine shades of metaphysics or casuistry, that it really has a relation to almost any class of speculation that may arise. Thus, in the matter of psycho-analysis and the study of the subconscious, the Church will probably be found sooner or later defending certain

essentials about Will and Conscience against a welter of
wild impersonality. Catholics remembering Catholicism
will have a right and reason to do this. But Calvinists
who have half forgotten Calvinism have no particular
reason to do it.

There is, for instance, one influence that grows
stronger every day, never mentioned in the newspapers,
not even intelligible to people in the newspaper frame
of mind. It is the return of the Thomist Philosophy;
which is the philosophy of common sense, as compared
with the paradoxes of Kant and Hegel and the Pragma-
tists. The Roman religion will be, in the exact sense, the
only Rationalistic religion. The other religions will not
be Rationalist but Relativist; declaring that the reason
is itself relative and unreliable; declaring that Being is
only Becoming or that all time is only a time of transition; saying in mathematics that two and two make five
in the fixed stars, saying in metaphysics and in morals
that there is a good beyond good and evil. Instead of
the materialist who said that the soul did not exist, we
shall have the new mystic who says that the body does
not exist. Amid all these things the return of the
Scholastic will simply be the return of the sane man.
There will perhaps be belated and benighted modernists,
lingering from the nineteenth century, who will repeat
the jaded journalistic catchword that the Schoolman only
cared to ask how many angels could stand on the point
of a needle. But it will be difficult to make even that
fancy appear very fantastic, in a world where men deny
that it hurts a man to stick the point of the needle in his
leg. If there are angels, they have presumably some
intellectual relation to place and space; and if there are
no angels, there are still men and presumably sane men.
But to say that there is no pain, or no matter, or no evil,
or no difference between man and beast, or indeed

between anything and anything else—this is a desperate effort to destroy all experience and sense of reality ; and men will weary of it more and more, when it has ceased to be the latest fashion ; and will look once more for something that will give form to such a chaos and keep the proportions of the mind of man. Millions of men are already at least wondering whether this solution is not to be found in the Catholic order and philosophy. Above all, the Church has regained that unique position in the world in a fair field and under the very reverse of favour ; having had for a hundred years no more than the common right of speaking and publishing and voting in popular assemblies ; and as her Master affirmed his divinity by becoming a man among men, she has become for a season a sect among sects, to emerge at the end as something separate or supreme.